IN THE SCHOOL OF SCRIPTURE WITH KARL BARTH: A DISCUSSION OF *CHURCH DOGMATICS*
Volume II

Doctrine of Reconciliation, and Suggestions for Doctrine of Redemption

GEORGE M. PLASTERER

Copyright © 2021 Pinnacle Leadership Press

All rights reserved. No part of this publication may be reproduced, stored in a retrieval system or transmitted in any way by any means, electronic, mechanical, photocopy, recording or otherwise, without the prior permission of the author, except as provided by USA copyright law.

Cover Photo: Lachmann, Hans. *Wuppertal, Evangelische Gesellschaft, Jahrestagung.* Sammlung Hans Lachmann (Bild 194), Mar. 1956.

ISBN: **9798730881594**

ACKNOWLEDGMENTS

Dr. William R. Placher, of blessed memory, was the first with whom I read *Church Dogmatics*. His guidance in reading Barth the first time was immensely helpful to me. After reading this massive text again, I came across a set and gave it to a young pastor whom I was mentoring through the ordination process in the United Methodist Church. He suggested we read a volume together and discuss it over lunch. These were precious times with Rev. Glenn Knepp, of the Indiana Annual Conference of the United Methodist Church. We became part of a reading group that included Lynn Eastman. They graciously read an earlier form of what this book was to become. The debt I owe to many professors in college and seminary as they expanded by knowledge of scripture and theology is immense and lays in the background of this work. Dr. R. Duane Thompson, of blessed memory, at Indiana Wesleyan University was instrumental in stimulating an interest in philosophy and Dr. Larry Wood at Asbury Theological Seminary introduced me to Wolfhart Pannenberg. Rev. Todd Outcault, also a member of the Indiana Annual Conference, and the author of many books, has provided valuable encouragement in publication. The churches I served deserve commendation for tolerating, some better than others, a pastor who enjoyed his study of the Bible and Christian teaching. Helen H. Renew with Pinnacle Leadership Press was much help to me in fulfilling a decade-long dream of publishing this work

My wife, Suzanne, has helped by working with me so that I would have the private time necessary, even in retirement, which has made the accomplishment of publishing this book so much easier.

DEDICATION

Dedicated to
Dr. William Placher
Of blessed memory
Who generously shared lunch and discussion of
Church Dogmatics with me while in Crawfordsville, Indiana

TABLE OF CONTENTS

VOLUME IV: DOCRTINE OF RECONCILITATION	9
Chapter XIII: Subject–matter and Problems of the Doctrine of Reconciliation-Atonement	15
Chapter XIV: Jesus Christ, the Lord as Servant	37
Chapter XV: Jesus Christ, the Servant as Lord	57
Chapter XVI: Jesus Christ, the True Witness	85
Chapter XVII: The Command of God the Reconciler	119
VOLUME V: DOCTRINE OF REDEMPTION	181
Chapter XVIII: The Work of Redemption	189
Chapter XIX: The Life of Humanity and Hope	211
Chapter XX: The Promise and its Future Realization	217
Chapter XXI: The Command of God the Redeemer	235
A Brief Afterward	251
Bibliography	255
About the Author	259

VOLUME IV
DOCTRINE OF RECONCILIATION

Jesus Christ ... is the all-powerful direction of God to us to occupy this place, to live in this kingdom. ... Jesus Christ is God's mighty command to open our eyes and to realize that this place is all around us, that we are already in this kingdom, that we have no alternative but to adjust ourselves to it, that we have our being and continuance here and nowhere else. In Him we are already there, we already belong to it. IV.1, 99

That is why we use the word direction – we might almost say the advice or hint. It is not a loud and stern and foreign thing, but the quiet and gentle and intimate awakening of children the Father's house to life in that house. That is how God exercises authority. All divine authority has ultimately and basically this character. IV.1, 100

As distinct from justification, and as its necessary consequence, this subjection of man to the divine direction is usually called sanctification. It is nothing other than the basic presupposition of all Christian ethics. Sanctification is the claiming of all human life and being and activity by the will of God for the active fulfillment of that will. IV.1, 101

He (Christ) exists as the Mediator between God and man in the sense that in Him God's reconciling of man and man's reconciliation with are event. IV.1, 123

It is primarily and properly this human Subject, who, as the object of the free and liberating grace of God, cannot be only an object in the event of atonement, but also becomes an active Subject. In Him man is made the new man, reconciled with God. IV.2, 19

God humbles Himself to man ... not to deify man, but to exalt him to perfect fellowship with Himself. We have tried to see and understand the event of the incarnation in the special light of this scope and telos. This exaltation comes to human essence in the person of Jesus of Nazareth who is the Son of God. It does so once, but once and for all, in this One. It does so in Him in a way which is valid and effective for all who are also of human essence, for all is brothers. It is to be seen only in this One. But in Him it is revealed as the divine decision which has been made and is declared concerning all men. IV.2, 117

At bottom, all answers which are not absolutely simple are completely false answers. IV.2, 121

The sinner ... is also ... a lazy-bones, a sluggard, a good-for-nothing, a slow-coach and a loafer. IV.2, 404.

The goal in the direction of which the true Church proceeds and moves is the revelation of the sanctification of all humanity and human life as it has already taken place *de iure* in Jesus Christ. In the exaltation of the one Jesus, who is the Son of God became a servant in order as such to become the Lord of all men, there has been accomplished in powerful archetype, not only the cancellation of the sins and therefore the justification, but also the elevation and establishment of all humanity and human life and therefore its sanctification. IV.2, 620

Christian love ... is not a kind of prolongation of the divine love itself. ... It is not the work of the Holy Spirit to take from man his own proper activity, or to make it simply a function of His own overpowering control. Where He is present, there is no servitude but freedom. This false conception is contradicted by the great frailty of that which emerges as love in the life of even the best Christians. If it were merely identical with the flowing of the stream of divine love into human life, if our little love were a manifestation or particle of the love of God, it could not and would not be so weak and puny. But the work of the Holy Spirit consists in the liberation of man for his own act and therefore for the spontaneous human love whose littleness and frailty are his own responsibility and not that of the Holy Spirit. IV.2, 785

A mute and obscure God would be an idol. The true and living God is eloquent and radiant. IV.3, 79

The main concern of the ongoing of the history of the prophecy of Jesus Christ which fills our time is with non-Christians. Their existence is a reminder of the darkness which resists it. It is for their sake that it must go forward, that Jesus Christ as the living Word of God is still on the way to-day. Their conversion from ignorance to knowledge, from unbelief to faith, from bondage to freedom, for night to day, is the goal of His prophetic work so far as it has a temporal goal. He wills to seek and to save those who are lost, who without Him, without the light of life, without the Word of the covenant, will necessarily perish. He is for them specifically this light, this Word. He goes after them. He is their hope. The promise of the Spirit is for them. IV.3, 364

... the twofold truth that it is indeed a hard and oppressive and humiliating thing to be a Christian, and therefore with Jesus Christ and His Word in one's heart to have to be against the whole and oneself, but that it is also an incomparably glorious, comforting and proud thing to be a Christian and therefore to be at the side of Jesus Christ, ... a subject in His service, ... to be a great or little, skillful or unskillful witness of this Word. IV.3, 367

We are now going to ponder what Karl Barth thought of as the heart of Christian teaching. I invite you to pray.

Lord, there may be times when I cannot employ honestly and comfortably all the words about Christ that the church at various times and places have believed are fitting. Nevertheless, I want this and every day to be days when he uses me according to the faith I have.

I believe in the principles he taught and lived. If there are times today when what I ought to do is not clear or when I hesitate to do what I know I should, let me remember that he has given me guidance and he has provided a model.

I believe you put into him as much of your spirit as one life can contain, as if in him the vast ocean washes against the beach on which I am standing. Whenever the mystery seems overwhelming, whenever you seem utterly unreachable and unknowable let me remember that in him you are reaching out to us.

I believe that when he died and you raised him from the dead, you gave us your sign that the last word belongs to you, not to death, and your word will be a word of love and hope and joy. Let that trust be in my life today or some other day the fear of death gets in the way of living life.

Help me to relax in the knowledge that doubt and faith exist together in one person. I believe; help my unbelief (Mark 9:24). Amen.

Volume IV concerns the Doctrine of Reconciliation-Atonement, published in three part volumes and one fragment of the fourth part volume on the Christian Life dealing with baptism. We also have the portion of his lectures that began his exposition of the Christian Life. The completed first three part volumes, published 1953-1959, cover 2762 pages. Barth will age from 67-73 during this part of his project. Although unfinished, this volume is the largest of all in *Church Dogmatics*. Volume IV.4, his discussion of the ethics of the doctrine of reconciliation, did not reach completion, although a 213-page fragment on baptism reached publication in 1967. From the writings of Barth, I will suggest some directions he seemed heading in IV.4. Barth says in his little preface of 3.4 that he is considering in Volume 4 the main task of Church dogmatics. Should we see some irony and humor here? He began his task in 1932. It has taken him this long to get to the main task.

I will emphasize throughout this volume the event nature of the Christian view of truth as Barth meditates upon that event from various perspectives. We never hold this truth firmly and clearly in our minds. We do not arrive at this truth by our rational reflection upon experience. Rather, we turn toward this event, acknowledge its truth, and allow this event to grasp us through proclamation and through the awakening power of the Spirit in us who must live by faith. Barth is not ashamed of the particularity of this event in Jesus of Nazareth. He celebrates it. The event or act of the Father in Jesus of Nazareth reveals the being of God. If we do not appreciate with joy the nature of this event, we will deeply miss the point of this volume.

Although the translators chose to refer to this as the doctrine of reconciliation, context determines whether they translate the German *Versohnung* as atonement or reconciliation. Thus, one could refer to Volume IV as the doctrine of atonement. Barth reserves the word "redemption" for the work of the Holy Spirit and with the eschatological perspective of the saving work of God. Another term, *Stellvertretung*, enshrines the notion of both representation and substitution. Barth envisages atonement/reconciliation as a total displacement of sinful humanity by the incarnate, crucified, and risen Son. He also views it comprehensively, in that it relates to the whole life and work of Jesus Christ, including the heavenly intercession of the Son.

Barth says in the foreword that he is conscious of the responsibility laid upon the theologian at this center of all Christian knowledge. To fail here is to fail everywhere. To be on the right track here makes it impossible to be offer a mistaken presentation in the whole.

Barth is clear that the doctrine of reconciliation includes a statement about humanity. It does so because of God electing us in grace. Reconciliation means God with us, and therefore the restoration of the proper ordered mutuality between God the recipients of grace. God does not work and act without the people of God. The atonement is about the fulfillment of the covenant. Barth will set out an account of the place, meaning, and inner structure of the human sphere. Ethical reflection is a construal of the moral agent and of the field in which the moral agent acts. What he lays out as ontologically, noetically, and morally fundamental are fundamental to our moral projects. Our own act corresponds to the grace of God. The ethics of reconciliation is an exploration of the shape of existence in analogy to Jesus.[1]

---

[1] (Webster 1995), 88, 98.

CHAPTER XIII

Subject-matter and Problems of the Doctrine of Reconciliation-Atonement

Chapter XIII, Volume IV.1, sections 57-58, published in 1953, while he is 67 years old, deals with the subject-matter and problems of the Doctrine of Reconciliation-Atonement. The objective reality of the historical birth, life, death, and resurrection of Christ as well as the once-for-all work of reconciliation-atonement on our behalf and in our place is the focus of this volume.

Barth begins his theme with a discussion of the work of God the reconciler (57). He will say that the primary message of the Christian community is the free act of the faithfulness of God in which God takes the lost cause of humanity, who has turned from its Creator and therefore ruined itself and makes humanity the possession of God in Jesus Christ. God will carry humanity through to its goal of showing the glory of God in the world. He recognizes he is dealing with the heart of the Christian message. He wants to be clear, true, and helpful. The work of reconciliation is the heart of Christian faith, the origin of Christian love, and the content of Christian hope. For Barth, "God with us" is the theme of the center of this volume. Such a theme focuses upon the God is genuinely with humanity. Everything depends upon human recognizing that this theme of the message, while applying to them, has to do with God. Christians know it but are always learning it in fresh ways.

Here is the roughest outline of God the reconciler.

First, God with us is the heart of an act of God in Jesus Christ. The Christian message is the report of an event rather than a statement of fact. As report of an event, the message does not have its basis in general considerations or observations. The message is not speculation about the being nature of God. The message is the report of the life and act of God as the One who is. The message tells us of a history that God wills to share with us and therefore of an invasion of our history. "God with us" is the truth about human history. We know God because we are witnesses of this act of God. The special truth of the Christian message is that God and humanity share a common history. God does not will to be God without us. God does not allow divine history and human history to separate.

Second, the Christian message deals with Jesus Christ as the report of the unique event that unites God with humanity. This event or act of God discloses the being and life of God in eternity and in worldly time, within the life of the Trinity and in the Trinitarian relation to humanity and all creation. What God did within Trinitarian life and what God does as creator and offering providential care of creation aims at this act and event. This act is the goal or purpose of all the acts of God. Within the general history of humanity arises this act of God in Christ that becomes the true history of humanity. The point of the message is not that God and humanity unite everywhere, but that rather, they unite in an event.

Third, salvation is the fulfillment of creation. General history becomes redemptive history. Created being can only look forward to salvation. Salvation is fulfillment of being. Salvation can only come to humanity. Creation and the providential care of the Father is grace, but such general grace is hardly the heart of Christian proclamation. "God with us" as the theme of the Christian message means the redemptive grace of God that constitutes the particularity of the event of Jesus Christ. The togetherness of God and humanity arises out of the singularity of this event. The event of reconciliation-atonement in Christ highlights the history of the togetherness of God and humanity. "God with us" discloses the divine invasion of our history. We can think of the grace of God as having the outer circle of the general grace of God shown in creation and in providential care for creation and the inner and special circle of the redemptive act of God in Jesus Christ. The Christian message is one of redemption and the gift of eternal life. Christ is the power and witness of the end or goal of humanity in the human present, and thus is the eschatological event.

Fourth, salvation of humanity is the basic will of God and the basis of the doctrine of creation. The event of God with us in Jesus Christ is a redemptive happening God gives humanity as the goal or purpose of humanity. Thus, we can think of redemption as an eschatological gift. Yet, with this end, the event of Christ also reveals the beginning of all things in the glory of God and the dignity of humanity.

Fifth, the issue is that humanity turns from its source of fulfillment and to itself. The line from creation to redemption is a radically and hopelessly broken one. Humanity opposes the redemptive end God appointed and made itself its own end. Humanity wants self-fulfillment. It becomes its own end. Humanity becomes the lost son in a far country and fallen into a sorry plight. The redeeming event of Christ reveals the gulf that exists between God and humanity. The redeeming event reveals the inadequacy of humanity as a covenant partner with God. The event reveals a gulf across which we cannot build a bridge. We do not truly know the meaning of grace until we see it at work here. Humanity has nothing to bring to God except the confession that we have sinned. Christ is God with us, the twofold sign that speaks of both the judgment and grace of God.

Sixth, God with us means that God is the One who fulfills the divine will for redemption. The Incarnation means God takes up the lost cause of humanity. God becomes the partner of God that humanity could not be. God closes the breach, gulf, and abyss between God and us. God intervenes as human being. God becomes human in a unique event that discloses the being, attitude, and activity of God. It speaks to the peace God has made with humanity. We see here the seriousness and force of the redemptive will of God. God with us reveals the glory of the divine grace and the horror of the plight of humanity. Christ is the event in which God becomes the means of the redemptive will toward humanity. The divine will, and therefore humanity as well, will reach a saving end. This event is the coming of salvation and the presence of the eschatological gift in its fullness. This event closes the gap as Christ becomes our representative. God is the redeemer of our being and the gift of its fulfillment. God is the goal and Christ is the way of God.

Seventh, and finally, we can answer the question of who we are as human beings. We are also with God in that God summons us and awakens us to God. We become free for God. We with God means faith, love, and hope. Humanity is not a mere spectator in this divine action in the Son. God awakens us to our true being. Salvation is from God. The actualization of the redemptive will of God opens humanity to the true possibility of its being. It does not open us to the extinguishing of humanity, but to its fulfillment. The Christian message addresses humanity as an active subject in the event of redemption. We can live our lives in the form of the praise of God through faith in Christ, through love that comes from Christ, and through hope directed upon Christ. The divine work of God with us accomplishes our salvation, which is, to use ancient Patristic language, our participation in the divine being. Christ assembles a Christian community and is present in that community by the Holy Spirit. The message stands or falls with Christ.

In these seven points, we have the heart of the creed in its second article and therefore the heart of the Christian message and *Church Dogmatics*. "God with us" is the report of an event, the inner circle of the relationship between God and humanity. The Christian message dares to declare this event as a disclosure of reality. The challenge is to pass this message to others. The Christian message points to the truth and reality of the report. The Christian message is nothing other than the declaration of the name, Jesus Christ, in whom such salvation God has already completed. Apart from Christ, the Christian message is not truth. The message is truth as it derives from this name. Christians address their report and witness to humanity. If those who share this message live on a resource other than Christ, they weaken and obscure the message. The message strengthens as it relies upon the work of the Holy Spirit.

I need to note here the beginning of an important theological issue that we will face throughout this volume. In six of the seven points above, Barth has focused upon the action of God in Jesus Christ in a way that can make it look as if he has erased the multiplicity of humanity in favor of the one man, Jesus of Nazareth. We will consider this possibility throughout this volume. Yet, I invite you as a reader to consider if anything we have read would lead us down this path? My response is negative. Thus, Barth is careful to preserve the freedom and independence of humanity in his discussion of divine providence. God rules in way that preserves the independent character of creation. In point seven above, Barth is careful to say that human beings remain active subjects in responding to the summons from God. They respond with gratitude and make their lives an offering of praise. Barth will never lose his concern that human beings in their history need to respond to the act of atonement.

Barth has significantly directed our attention to the nature of the act of atonement-reconciliation in Jesus Christ. As a result, we need to pause and consider a fellow theologian to whom Barth does not refer here but against whom he is arguing. Barth offers his tacit but definitive answer to the demythologizing program of Bultmann, which involves reinterpreting the incarnation of and reconciling work of Christ in terms of existentialist decision and timeless re-enactment. The point of this answer depends on the bold and thoroughgoing teaching regarding representation-substitution.[2] Barth will keep pointing us away from ourselves and toward the act/event of reconciliation in Jesus Christ. Barth also makes it clear in his foreword that Rudolf Bultmann is present even where he did not quote

---

[2] Editor's Preface.

him. He has found himself in quiet debate with him. He respects the man, especially his mind, aim, and achievements. He respects the zeal of his following. He wishes he could do him greater justice.

On December 24, 1952, Barth famously wrote to Bultmann, using a powerful image of how different these two scholars had become.[3] Apparently, Bultmann used an image that demanded Barth repent. In his response, Barth refers to the "animal mythology" contained in Melville's Moby Dick, a clear bit of intellectual humor. How would Bultmann demythologize that? "It seems to me that we are like a whale ... and an elephant meeting with boundless astonishment on some oceanic shore." The whale spouts the water high in the air for nothing. The elephant moves its trunk in friendship and then in threat. "They do not have a common key to what each would obviously like to say to the other." The only solution may be the eschaton, as Christ restores all things. The rift between these two theologians had become great, even if originally, they were of the same "dialectical" and "neo-orthodox" family.

Barth will make a shift in his theology that starts in II.2, as he discussed the election of Jesus Christ from eternity, and works itself out in Volume IV. Barth and Bultmann began with a focus upon eschatology and dialectical theology in the 1920s. Bultmann remained faithful to that emphasis. Barth shifted his theology to an election of Jesus Christ from eternity. This election meant a new focus of his thinking upon the lived history of Jesus Christ as priest, king, and prophet. We will see that the exposition Barth offers of the life of Christ will almost become a form of Platonic idealism. In any case, Bultmann, through his continuing emphasis upon eschatology he learned from Johannes Weiss, as well as his work on the form history of the Synoptic Gospels, will lead him to maintain his emphasis upon Christ as the eschatological event. In fact, the re-focusing on eschatology we see in Pannenberg and Moltmann was one of the reasons Barth had disappointment in the direction these theologians of hope had taken.[4] The problem Barth has opened for himself in going to the protological event of divine election is that he becomes so thoroughly Christological that the role of the Spirit becomes an afterthought. The benefit of maintaining the original eschatological focus of Barth is that it opens the door for the work of the Spirit in bringing genuine transformation now that leads us toward the fulfillment of Christian hope

---

[3] Barth, Karl, and Rudolf Bultmann. Karl Barth - Rudolf Bultmann Letters, 1922-1966. Ed. Bernd Jaspert and G. W. Bromiley. Trans. G. W. Bromiley. Grand Rapids, MI: Eerdmans, 1981. 105. Print. Thanks to @postbarthian!

[4] (Congdon, The Mission of Demythologizing: Rudolf Bultmann's Dialectical Theology 2015).

in redemption.

Barth continues with the notion of the covenant as the presupposition of reconciliation-atonement. Christ is God in the work of reconciliation. Reconciliation is the fulfillment of the covenant between God and humanity. Reconciliation is the restitution, the resumption of a fellowship that once existed, but dissolution threatened it. It is the maintaining, restoring, and upholding of that fellowship in face of an element that disturbs, disrupts, and breaks it. Covenant denotes an element in a legal ritual in which two partners together accept a mutual obligation: I will be your God and you shall be my people. The history of the covenant in the Old Testament finds its fulfillment in Jesus Christ as the atonement-reconciliation that God executes. Christ fulfills the covenant that Israel could not. Thus, Christ stands before God as the representative of all the nations, bearing the judgments of God and testifying by the grace of God. He is the eschatological, sovereign act of God who renews humanity and summons them to obedience by forgiving their sins. The work of God in Christ is also the Word of God that makes the will of God known. Christ is the eschatological realization of the will of God for Israel and therefore for humanity. The source of this actualization of the will of God is the kindness of God toward humanity, as Titus 3:4 makes clear. Christ accomplishes the will of God in the face of human sin and its consequences. Christ meets and overcomes the antithesis between human sin and the will of God for reconciliation and peace. While the covenant with Israel was provisional, the covenant in Christ is final. In Christ, God enters in, and becomes a human being, a human being amongst humanity, in order that God in this human being may carry out the divine will. When this takes place, atonement takes place. The actualization of the will of God is the overcoming of the antithesis between the reconciling will of God on the one hand and human sin on the other. Thus, we must view human sin as an episode that Christ overcomes. Reconciliation is the affirmation and consummation of the covenant. The communion of God with humanity occurs despite the transgression of humanity.

God is not neutral regarding the cause of humanity. On the side of God, this is grace, while on the side of humanity the only response is one of gratitude. Thus, humanity cannot be neutral toward God. The promise that the Lord will be the God of Israel and Israel shall be the people of God becomes truth and actuality in Christ. God takes a true and actual interest in the existence of human beings that goes beyond God being the creator and extending providential care to humanity. With the work and word of God shown in Christ, God has opened the divine heart to us, and we must see it. All other gods are false gods. The only God Christians know is the God who has a heart like this. The covenant of grace concept implies three things. First, God establishes the covenant of grace in freedom, recognizing the undeserved quality of humanity. Second, the covenant of grace implies the beneficent character of this presupposition of the atonement. God becomes the companion of humanity. Third, the covenant of grace engages humanity as the partner of God only in gratitude. The human rightful response of humanity is thankfulness. The failure of humanity is its ingratitude. Sin is ingratitude. The truth in Christ concerning God is that is that the Lord becomes our God. The truth in Christ concerning humanity is that humanity shall be the people of God. Thanks is the only legitimate response from humanity. Thankfulness is a modest thing to ask. It has the force of an either-or. We see the heart of God in Christ. Our response is gratitude.

By deciding for us, God has decided concerning us. What took place in history in Christ reflects the will of God from the beginning. By the perception of grace at the end of the ways of God we have been led to the perception of grace at their beginning, as the presupposition of all the ways of God. We do not arrive at this truth from self-knowledge or self-estimate of human reason or observation of nature or human history. We do not arrive at this truth from a religious disposition. He reminds us, again, that we can draw such conclusions only by looking to Jesus Christ, which excludes looking to any form of natural theology.

Within Trinitarian life, the Father elected the Son, who would become a human being for our sake. First, in willing Jesus of Nazareth, God wills to be our God and that we should be the people of God. The Word is Jesus Christ. We have knowledge or recognition of this covenant. In this recognition, we make a proper acknowledgement. In this recognition, we commit ourselves to a genuine regard for this center of the Christian message. This event summons us. The sin of humanity takes place under the finally triumphant No of God, active only as deriving from the left hand of God. In contrast, the atonement-reconciliation accomplished in Christ is a work of the right hand of God, a work of the positive will of God. The historical event of the atonement stands at the heart of the Christian message and faith. Atonement occurs in this way as wrestling with human sin. Even more, atonement is the great act of the faithfulness of God to God and therefore to us. We have reverence for the heart of the Christian message, as well as joy, certainty, and freedom of faith. In this recognition, we have a right distinction, acknowledgment, and regard for the event of the atonement. In saying what Barth has said, Barth parts company with Schleiermacher. For Schleiermacher, the fulfilling of time in Jesus Christ meant at the end of the historical development of humanity. In humanity, finite being as such attained in Jesus Christ that form to which they had always been potentially inclined and endowed in the relationship of complete dependence on God as infinite being. The eternal will of God done in Jesus Christ is in such a way that in Him humanity attains to the perfection ordained and necessary to human beings. Barth finds in this a strange mixture of truth and error. Barth will stress that in Christ, we have to do with something new and special in relation to creation. He is not a product of the created world as such. Creation derives from Christ; we do not derive the notion of reconciliation from creation. He is the meaning and purpose of creation. Second, the first Word of God is Jesus Christ, the beginning of all things. Christ is the Incarnate Word, the baby of Bethlehem, the man who died at Golgotha and raised in the garden of Joseph of Arimathea. He is the promise and the command, the Word that has become the work of God. Christ is with a view to us. The event of the atonement-reconciliation demands our recognition, claims our regard, and invites us to have certainty, joy, and the freedom of faith. Such a response depends on our right recognition of what God has fulfilled and revealed in time. God has elected and determined the Son as the fellow and friend of humanity. This man, Jesus of Nazareth, existed because God united with him in this unique togetherness of the divine and human. Barth is working out his Chalcedonian theology here.

Finally, the work of God the reconciler brings fulfillment of the broken covenant. God makes the covenant, true, and actual within human history. The Old Testament proclaims it and the New Testament attests to it in the historical identity of the man, Jesus of Nazareth and coming of the rule of God on earth. The promise and command of the covenant, that the Lord will be our God and that we shall be the people of God, becomes historical event in Jesus Christ. God keeps faith in time with the divine self and with humanity. The fulfillment of the covenant has the character of atonement-reconciliation, a concept that speaks of the restoration of fellowship. The grace of God triumphs over humanity and sin. It triumphs in the atonement as the fulfillment of the covenant. Such grace is "dear" and not "cheap," as Bonhoeffer put it. Barth will refer to John 3:16 but offers an extended exposition of II Corinthians 5:19. Atonement is the work of God and not of humanity. God does not need reconciliation with humanity. Humanity needs reconciliation with God. Such reconciliation has already taken place. Reconciling means the conversion of the world to God took place in the form of an exchange or substitution that God has proposed between the world and God present and active in the person of Jesus Christ. On the one side of the exchange, it means that in being present and active in the world in Christ, God takes part in its history. On the other side of the exchange, to God making humanity the righteousness of God means to become covenant-partners with God who keeps the covenant just as faithfully as God does. To make us that, God made Christ sin. His point is that the conversion of the world to God has taken place in Christ with the making of this exchange.

Barth will offer a survey of the doctrine of reconciliation-atonement (58). The content of this teaching is knowledge of Jesus Christ. For Barth, such knowledge means we learn certain things about God and certain things about humanity. Concerning God, we learn that in Jesus Christ, we see the humbling of divinity and therefore we see the action of the reconciling God (59). In Jesus Christ, we also see humanity exalted and therefore reconciled by God (64). In Jesus Christ, we see the unity of the one who guarantees our atonement and the one who witnesses to our atonement (69). Concerning humanity, I would invite the reader to adopt the posture of viewing Barth as a counselor to the preacher and/or other leaders in the church. He wants to focus upon the condition of humanity (sinner), the response of God (salvation), and the present work of the Holy Spirit (in the community and in individuals). The preacher, spiritual guide, and at times devotional writer, comes out of Barth in these sections. Although he is still the theologian, he is much more a guide to other preachers, teachers, and leaders in the Christian community. Thus, the knowledge of Christ shows human sin as the pride (60), sloth (65), and falsehood (70) of humanity. We would not truly know sin without looking to Christ. Therefore, salvation of humanity will also involve three acts. Reconciliation-Atonement involves the justification (61), sanctification (66), and calling (71) of humanity. Such knowledge of Jesus Christ involves the work of the Holy Spirit in gathering (62), upbuilding (67), and the sending (72) of the community. The knowledge of Jesus will develop the being of Christians toward faith (63), love (68), and hope (73). He is summarizing the work of Volume IV.1, 2, and 3.

We see the grace of God in Jesus Christ. Barth will want us to look in the direction of God first to understand what this means. Reconciliation fulfills the covenant of grace as a free act of God. God makes a fresh start. God acts to defend the divine glory. God acts to fulfill human destiny, God acts as creator, and God acts with faithfulness to the covenant. God did not have to continue loving a sinful humanity, but we know that in Jesus Christ, God has done so. Knowledge of the event of reconciliation in Christ allows Christians to look backward to God as creator and forward to the event of redemption. This Word shows us the possibility of life and knowledge. God does a new thing in making enemies into children of God. The frontier between God and sinful humanity is real, but God chose to cross the divide in Christ. Humanity receives its judgment in Christ, but even more, God has received and reclaimed humanity as a divine possession. God chooses to treat humanity as friend and child of God. Humanity can have peace with God due to this event. The grace of God is nothing less than God coming to us in Christ. As rebels, God has converted us to God. The work of the Holy Spirit gives us this self-knowledge in our hearts and places its confession upon our lips. Christian obedience rests upon this knowledge, experiences joy, and becomes a witness to this knowledge. The atonement is the place from which Christian theology gains knowledge of God and humanity. Preaching, instruction, pastoral care, dogmatics, and ethics begin here. Natural theology perishes. For him, the recent Catholic dogma on Mary widens the gap between Protestant and Catholic.

Barth then wants to look in the other direction and thus toward humanity. God has posited a new beginning. God has taken humanity, embraced us, surrounded us, seized us, and turned us back toward God. God has fulfilled the covenant. God has healed the breach by the sovereign act of reconciliation. The holiness of God and the sinfulness of humanity create the abyss. This teaching of the church means that God has fulfilled the covenant. He stresses that humanity remains a subject in relation to God. God has newly created humanity from above in the act of atonement in Christ. God has introduced true humanity, a new human subject, in Christ. Humanity is new as belonging to God and one whom God has accepted. Humanity is genuinely free as a covenant partner with God. Humanity has peace with God because the alteration of the human situation has already happened in Christ. Any truth and power Christians have comes from this knowledge and experience. The power of the divine act is the alteration of the human situation before God. Barth is clear that his presentation is not nominalism, for reconciled humanity is the first and basic thing we can say about the being of humanity. By the grace of God, humanity belongs to God. Human beings can still rebel, lie, and fear, but only in impotent conflict with the proper being of humanity. To recall his doctrine of election, in the act of atonement-reconciliation, God has made true in time that which God elected from eternity. Christians know that this new being of humanity has met them in Christ.

Barth then considers the being of humanity in Jesus Christ. The reconciliation accomplished in Christ reflects itself in the existence of the Christian, which is something we cannot say of others. Others lack the Holy Spirit who can open them to the experience and knowledge of conversion that has taken place in Christ.

The conversion of humanity to God in Jesus Christ takes place first, with faith in the fulfillment and revelation of a verdict of God on humanity. As such, humanity has died and perished from the earth, that no one can deal with humanity as such, that as such humanity has no future. Jesus Christ has taken the place of humanity as a malefactor. God has carried out the sentence on humanity as a sinner. No one can reverse it. No one can repeat it. It has fallen on Jesus Christ. This event is the divine verdict, the Word in which Christian faith believes. He points to the resurrection of Jesus as the fulfillment and proclamation of the positive sentence of God. Humanity becomes a suitable human partner for the divine partner. God delights in humanity. Humanity becomes the faithful servant, friend, and dear child of God. This human being comes forth from the grave with Christ. In virtue of this Word, the existence of humanity as a sinner and all its transgressions are not behind it. The being of the new humanity is a being in the truth and force of this twofold pardon. To that extent, faith, the work of the Holy Spirit that makes one a Christian, is the only form of this new being. Before God, we are not unrighteous and rejected, but righteous and accepted only by faith, not by love and hope. In oneself, in the daily and hourly thoughts, words, and works of a human being, he or she does not experience liberation at all. The being of human beings contradicts the being of human beings in Jesus Christ. In Jesus Christ, humanity is not a rebel, but a servant, not an enemy, but a friend, not lost to God, but a child in the house of the Father. The direction offered by God gently directs humanity into the freedom of the children of God. This direction has taken place in Jesus Christ.

Second, Christian love is the form this direction takes, which is also another form of the work of the Holy Spirit. Jesus Christ is the all-powerful direction of God to us. We open our eyes to see the kingdom all around us and that we are already in it. As distinct from justification, and as its necessary consequence, this subjection of humanity to the divine direction is sanctification. Sanctification is the basic presupposition of all Christian ethics. Sanctification is the claiming of all human life, being, and activity by the will of God for the active fulfillment of that will. Barth thinks of this "divine direction" as the form of divine advice or hint. The direction does not come loudly or sternly. It does not come as if it were a foreign thing. Rather, the direction comes in the form of the quiet, gentle, and intimate awakening of children in the house of the Father. In fact, he thinks of all divine authority as having this character. One cannot separate sanctification from justification, as though it has to do with the human contribution to reconciliation with God. God has demonstrated love for the world in Christ. God wills to be God only in company with each human being. Christian love is the proof of the love of God. It recognizes this love of God by following it, imitating it, and modelling itself upon it. Human beings can reflect the divine attitude toward the world. Such love is sanctification, freedom, and being a faithful covenant partner. The source of such love is the work of the Holy Spirit. We see such love in the togetherness of God with humanity in Christ and in the coming together of human beings with each other. Thus, we need to understand Christian love as love toward God and toward neighbor.

The conversion of humanity to God that took place in Jesus Christ has another form, third, in the positing and equipping and of humanity as the bearer of the divine promise. We think of this as Christian hope. The Christian is ready to participate in such a hope and live in the light of such hope. Humanity has a vocation or calling to fulfill. This hope involves the teleological element of the being of humanity in Christ. The event of the atonement-reconciliation in Jesus Christ is the restoration, renewal, and fulfillment of the covenant between God and humanity. As such, like creation, this event is not the end but the beginning. Reconciliation-atonement does not create a final and stable relationship. Rather, in all its completeness, the being of humanity is only a beginning in which humanity looks eagerly forward to the activity of God ad fellowship with God. Faith looks back to this activity and love looks to the present experience of this activity. Hope is still open for God and thus to that which has not yet happened in the restoration of the covenant. Humanity is under the verdict and gentle direction of God, but also lives under the promise of God and therefore this future event with yet another form of the fellowship between God and humanity. Thus, justification and sanctification have a goal. Such hope is not self-evident from what we have said thus far. Such hope is further proof of the overflowing goodness of God. The being of humanity in Christ is possession and action, as justification and sanctification teach us, but also expectation, as hope and vocation teach us. Such a calling of humanity is separate from justification and sanctification. God wills to make something of humanity and has a purpose for humanity.

We have the being of humanity expressed in the obedience contained in faith, love, and hope. The promise means the being of humanity acquires direction, destiny, and perspective. The promise points humanity to the actualization and preservation of the fellowship between God and humanity. The goal is eternal life, as the New Testament will put it. We receive a promise of our own future in the unrevealed depth of fellowship with God. The content of the promise corresponds to the being of God. The fellowship of humanity with God becomes complete as it enters this depth. This complete fellowship is eternal life. The future of humanity in covenant with God is to be the partner of God and to live as such. What we hope for is a being in a co-operation of service with God, the participation of humanity in the being and life of God. That is the honor, dignity, and glory of eternal life that God has pledged. Christian community hears this promise given to humanity and lives from the perspective of the promise. Since Jesus Christ is the promise, we no longer live in a world without hope. Humanity stands under the verdict (justification, faith), the direction (sanctification, love), and the promise (vocation/calling/summons, hope) of God. Humanity may live from the perspective of this future with God. The future of humanity is not handed over to the rulers of this age, but to the servants of God as King. Humanity may thus believe, love, and hope. The promise comes in its kerygmatic and pneumatic force. The promise is event in Jesus Christ. He is the future of the world and of every human being and the hope of the Christian. He came to the disciples in the resurrection, coming to them as their hope and future. His coming is the end and consummation of the promise. He is the meaning and basis of creation. He is the bearer and substance of the redemption and consummation that closes human time. The calling is to move toward this end and new beginning, to move forward to the One who was, who is as the center of all time, but who also comes as the end of all time. In hope and calling, we have to do with Christ. Christians see things differently. The Holy Spirit awakens them to faith and love. They live by the promise, seize it, and apprehend it. They conform to it. They have joy in anticipation of the service of God that awaits humanity. The promise refers to the last and ultimate things, but also to the penultimate and provisional. The great hope is the promise of eternal life. Such a hope sets the world in the light of its future with God. Daily hope persists where its basis and essence are eternal hope. The "little hope" is that of temporal life, while the "great hope" is that of eternal life with God in the future. Christ is the pledge from God that such hope will be reality. The provisional promise has strength only light of the final promise.

The third aspect of the reconciling work of God above and reconciled humanity below is the atonement, in which God and humanity stand in mutual relationship. Jesus Christ is the mediator. To review, we have looked upwards to God who loves the world, and downwards to the world that God loves. We have looked to the act of reconciling grace and then at the being of humanity reconciled in this act. Barth now wants to direct our attention to the middle point between them, an event that differentiates and comprehends both movements. We find the movements actualized, revealed, and identified in Jesus Christ, the middle point of these two movements. He is the atonement as the fulfillment of the covenant. He is fully both movements in the event of reconciliation-atonement.

Again, he will distinguish his view from nominalism. The focus upon this event in Christ could lead to such an error, making the event a formal or symbolic sign of the event of atonement. He avoids this error by stressing that this event corresponds to being as enclosed in Christ. Christ embraces the whole of the movements upward and downward that he has described. In Christ, the reconciling God and the humanity that needs reconciliation are one. Christ is the truth in all answers that we have concerning who God is and who humanity is. Christ is not a third type of being, but the one who embraces both God and humanity. Christ exists as the Mediator between God and humanity in the sense that in Christ, the reconciling work of God toward humanity and the reconciliation of humanity with God are event. In this event, God encounters humanity.

In this event, humanity works out the consequences of this encounter and revelation. Humanity exists in this action of God. Barth will make a crucial decision regarding the form and method of the exposition of the doctrine of reconciliation-atonement. He suggests the New Testament knows nothing of Christology apart from what Christ does for others. He thinks it not helpful to separate Christology from soteriology and ecclesiology. Christ exists in the totality of his work as Mediator and fulfills his work, but he does not completely fulfill it. Thus, his task in the next three chapters is to present a Christology that makes it clear that the doctrine of reconciliation has to do with Jesus Christ as the active subject. Christ is beginning, middle, and end of the doctrine. His task is also to bring what he says about Christology into immediate connection with what Christ is for us. In this way, he hopes to make clear that the event of reconciliation has to do with both God and humanity. Christianity does not deal with any god, but the God who acts in this reconciling way. Christianity does not deal with just any human being, but humanity already in relation to this reconciling God. The only response from this humanity is thankfulness and obedience. The only relationship between God and humanity of which Christianity can speak is this encounter and mutual correspondence. Thus, he puts himself alongside the formula of Chalcedon, Christ is "very God, very human, and very God-human." Christ is the subject of the act of reconciliation. The Christian community knows Christ as its Lord, the Messiah of Israel, and the Savior of the world. It knows Christ as the object of its faith, the basis of its love, and the content of its hope. The being of Jesus Christ takes place in the event of this man and is thus a being in history. This history of Jesus Christ is atonement. His being is the completed act of the reconciliation of humanity with God.

Barth will decide not to treat the person and work of Christ in abstraction from each other. He looks at the creeds from Nicaea, Constantinople, Ephesus, and Chalcedon as guiding lines. He will not use them to abstract the person of Jesus Christ from his work. Therefore, Barth thinks that the unity of the living God and living humanity in Jesus of Nazareth is the gracious activity of God in atonement-reconciliation. Barth takes seriously the Incarnation when he says that the being of Jesus Christ as this history of Jesus must light up the truth of the Christian doctrine of reconciliation as Christology. He will not allow us to dispense with Christology. Receiving proper exposition, it will lead us naturally to the notion that Christology provides the basis for justification, sanctification, and the vocation of humanity. It will be a doctrine of thankfulness that gives proper place to faith, love, and hope. It will give proper place to a discussion of ecclesiology or the Christian community as rooted in Christology. In this way, binding Christology to soteriology and ecclesiology, we can make clear that one simply cannot dispense, in a Christian way, with Christology.

Fourth, Barth discusses the three forms of the doctrine of the reconciliation-atonement.

Barth begins with his Christology. If one wanted to focus upon a study of the Christology of Barth, one could study these three sections together.

One (IV.1, XIV.59), in Jesus Christ, we witness God acting for us as human beings. God takes up the cause of humanity. He is "very God." He will want to learn what deity is considering the Incarnation. Thus, the general or abstract idea of God is of no interest. We learn who God is by turning to Christ. We allow Christ to define God, rather than trying to make Christ fit into our notion of God. God is as God takes part in this event. The divine being is event. We know God in the condescension of God in Jesus Christ, as it demonstrates eternal and almighty love. The eternity of God allows God to be in time and temporal. The omnipotence of God is so great that God can be weak and impotent, even as humanity is weak and impotent. God accepts the penalty for the unfaithful, hostile, and antagonistic humanity whom God loves. God will accept the judgment that humanity deserves. He will discuss it in Chapter XIV.59, Jesus Christ, the Lord as Servant. It corresponds to the priestly office of Christ in the theological tradition. Christ fulfills the priestly office by being the one makes the perfect offering, which is his life.

Two (IV.2, XV.64), in Jesus Christ we encounter true humanity. He is "very human." Thus, we will learn who humanity is through the Incarnation. Christ is the event of the conversion of humanity to God. He is human, but in a unique way than is humanity. Humanity is a limitation and suffering. Christ is true humanity. God has exalted humanity in Christ. In Christ, humanity is free. Christ is at the side of God in our humanity. Christ is above us, opposed to us, and for us. Christ is the realization of true humanity, and as such anticipates our true humanity. God become like us so that we can become like God. God experienced our bondage so that we can be free. Christ is deity humbled and humanity exalted. The reconciliation of humanity has occurred in Christ. Jesus Christ is the Servant as Lord. It corresponds to the traditional discussion of Christ as king. Christ is king, not in the course of his earthly life, of course, but in the exaltation he received through resurrection.

Three (IV.3, XVI.69), Jesus Christ is the "God-human being." His life confirms him as the authentic witness. He confirms in word and deed the truth of the atonement accomplished in his death and resurrection. Through his witness, we hear this truth. We hear the summons to express and repeat this truth. The truth of grace is that in Christ God has turned to the world and the world has turned to God, that in Christ God holds heaven and earth together (creation), and that Christ binds humanity and God together. Christ is the truth. Christ attests to this truth and is a pledge of it. Humanity encounters the truth in Christ. Christ is the promise of the truth that avails for us as atonement. Humanity needs to hear this truth, and in hearing, can accept it appropriate it. Truth encounters us in Christ as the promise of our future. Christ expresses, discloses, and reveals both God and humanity. God calls us into this relationship. As the Word of God, Christ calls us to God and to ourselves. Our destiny is to hear this Word and live under it. The conclusion of this discussion will form a transition to his doctrine of redemption, consummation, or eschatology. We will see hints of the content of his incomplete Volume 5 of *Church Dogmatics*. He will discuss this as Jesus Christ, the true witness. It corresponds to the traditional discussion of the prophetic office of Christ. In this case, his public ministry from his baptism to his crucifixion place Jesus of Nazareth within the prophetic tradition, yet, to Christian eyes, much more than a prophet. The character of truth is that in Christ, it encounters us, testifies to us, addresses us, promises us, and pledges itself to us. He is the prophet of his own future as well as the prophet of our future.

He will want to deal with the three-fold doctrine of sin as it relates to his Christology. If one wanted to focus upon the teaching of Barth regarding sin, one could focus upon these three sections. His exposition of Christology will disclose the nature of sin. The reason for the doctrine of atonement-reconciliation is the problem of sin. Sin is the dark prelude to the covenant of grace. Yet, sin is not autonomous in having its own sphere of being. It does not belong to creation. Sin is active and present only as an alien force. It says No to grace and covenant where God says Yes. Sin is the negation of what God does in condescension to us and taking up our cause in Christ (pride in XIV.60), the negation of what God has done in exalting humanity in Jesus Christ (sloth in XV.65), and the negation of the witness to the truth of Christ (falsehood in XVI.70). Sin is the No to the divine Yes in Christ. He will discuss each in its proper place in his Christology.

Barth will then provide a three-fold examination of the event of atonement-reconciliation as the Yes of God to humanity. As such, he will expound upon the justifying sentence of God (XIV.61), the direction of sanctification we see in Christ (XV.66), and the call or summons to discipleship that provides the eschatological and teleological aspect of Christian salvation (XVI.71). One could study these important doctrines of the church and of Karl Barth as a unit.

As Barth presents his view of Christology and salvation, we need to remember that in the background is an argument with Schleiermacher (*Christian Faith* Section 99), who taught that salvation is the result of influence mediated from a historical past and the accompanying assertion that the resurrection and ascension have no determinative place in Christian dogmatics. His concern is with the living person of Jesus Christ, who is the one who reveals grace.

Among the issues raised by scholars is whether Barth will present Christ as a platonic form of humanity, so that salvation is already a reality, and its appropriation is only a matter of knowledge that God has saved us. For Barth, theology testifies to the unity of God and humanity in Christ. Let us think of this in terms of classical philosophy. It wrote of changeless Being. Barth replaces it with the existence of Jesus. This event is Being. In place of the changeless and definite "is," Barth places "becoming." In a sense, Being is Jesus Christ. The Ideas of Beauty, Truth, and Goodness become the life history of Jesus. In this way, Barth deals with the disappearance of the timeless, so significant in classical philosophy, but that had become so questionable in the modern period. Robert Jensen suggested this in 1963.[5] In a sense, however, salvation is the divine act prior to human action, and salvation is the acknowledgment of that divine action. At the same time, the accusation of Platonism may go too far. What he says about Christ is not the result of philosophical speculation, but in the personal activity of God in eternity.[6]

Classical Christology viewed Christ's divine and human work as for us. Barth will view the work as occurring within Christ, as humanity is already present in the very understanding of the two natures. The covenant finds fulfillment in Christ and thus fulfills the covenant with humanity. The movement of God toward that which is other than God, which we find in the history of Jesus Christ, is the basis for our lives. The salvation history of humanity occurs in Christ. Yet, he will leave room human lives as they lead them. He will do so as he points to the time between Easter and the Parousia as the time for us to decide.

George Hunsinger has written helpfully on the Christology of Barth.[7] He will stress the Chalcedonian nature of his Christology. It states that the Son is perfect in divinity and humanity, truly God and truly human. As the Lord Jesus Christ, he had a rational soul and body. He was "co-

---

[5] (Cambridge Companion to Karl Barth 2000), George Hunsinger, "Karl Barth's Christology: Its basic Chalcedonian Character," 127ff.

[6] (Cambridge Companion to Karl Barth 2000) Colin Gunton, "Salvation," 154.

[7] (Cambridge Companion to Karl Barth 2000), George Hunsinger, "Karl Barth's Christology: Its basic Chalcedonian Character," 127ff.

essential" with the divine and the human. It affirms that in Christ the two natures, divine and human, are such unconfusedly, unchangeably, indivisibly, and inseparably. Their difference remains, even while present in the union they find in Christ. The properties of divinity and humanity remain faithful to their nature. Yet, both occur in one person and one hypostasis, in one Son and in one Word, namely, in Jesus Christ.

The insight of Hunsinger at this point is that Barth is the first theologian to move between the two alternatives then present in Christology, that is, between the Alexandrian and the Antiochian. This ought not to surprise us by now, for he is approaching the traditional creed dialectically, and therefore, offers newness as he wrestles with the tradition. Barth will want to avoid the excess of the Alexandrian approach, which could lead to Docetism. This approach would emphasize the deity of Christ at the expense of his humanity. This approach would emphasize the gospel of John. In fact, volume IV.1, Chapter XIV will have an emphasis upon this aspect of Christology. He will emphasize here, as does Chalcedon, that Christ is complete in his deity and he will argue for the superiority of the divine nature over the human nature. In IV.2, Chapter XV, Barth stresses that Christ is also complete in his humanity. Part of what Barth wrestles with here is that one cannot comprehend the nature of the Incarnation in a single unified thought. The Incarnation is incomprehensible, and thus, one can only write and speak of it dialectically.

Interestingly, Barth will offer a lecture in 1956 on the theme of the humanity of God. He will draw a contrast between his early emphasis in his commentary on Romans on God as Wholly Other to his present focus of the togetherness of God with humanity. God cannot remain Wholly Other and still have humanity come to know God. Such a statement is Christological. Christ is where we deal with God and humanity where they really are, and not in abstraction.[8]

Barth will develop a theology of the cross in Volume II.2 (the doctrine of election and predestination) and in Volume IV (the doctrine of reconciliation). For him, the crucified Jesus is the image of the invisible God. Barth has received just recognition for his Christological concentration of theology. It leads him to combine the traditional doctrine of the two natures of Christ as divine and human and the two states of Christ as those of humiliation and exaltation. God reveals divinity in the humiliation of Jesus and his humanity in his exaltation. He rejected a one-sided theology of the cross from Lutheranism. This rejection led him to take up the theology of the cross and make it more profound, for only in

---

[8] Karl Barth, *The Humanity of God* (John Knox Press, 1960), "The Humanity of God," 1956.

connection with the resurrection of Jesus can the theology of the cross bring a radical recognition of the forsakenness of the crucified Christ. He thought consistently of God in Christ. He could write in almost patripassionist way about the suffering of God and the death of God. When he can say that God rejected the Son and that God wills to lose so that humanity may win, he gets close to the idea of the death of God. Yet, Barth may not think enough in Trinitarian terms. Thus, the Son suffers and dies on the cross, while the Father suffers with him, but in a unique way. Such an approach avoids the paradox that God is dead.[9]

No modern theologian has emphasized more vigorously than Barth that reconciliation is the act of God alone, taking place in the crucifixion of Jesus Christ. For him, however, the event was self-contained. It was not an ongoing process toward some distant goal. Hence, Barth sharply distinguished the apostolic ministry of reconciliation we find in II Corinthians 5:18-21 from reconciliation itself. The apostolic ministry of reconciliation begins with the self-contained and completed event. Thus, apostolic ministry is not an extension of reconciliation. Barth did not refer to an eschatological consummation that transcends reconciliation. He mentions Romans 11:15 but does not consider that the reconciling action of God does not have to do here with the event of crucifixion. The restriction by Barth of reconciliation to this event also contradicts his main exegetical authority, F. Buchsel, on II Corinthians 5:19-20. Of course, the event concludes matters for believers, but not for the world. For the world, reconciliation has not finished, having begun in the cross of Christ and is in the course of fulfillment. Here is the problem. The more one thinks of the reconciliation of the world as an act of God, the more urgently the question arises as to the role of the human recipients. Reconciliation cannot take place unless it applies to them. In our theological reflection, we need to consider that the human response to the act of God is a constitutive part of the event. We as recipients of the reconciling act of God have a part in it simply by the fact that the Son represents us. God accomplished the complete conversion of the world. God did it in the form of an exchange or substitution. Barth found the thought of representation in the basic meaning of the term reconciliation.[10]

Further, the thought of inclusive representation leads to violation of the independence as persons of those Christ represents. This notion can result in the idea that Jesus Christ alone is the human being before God, has taken our place, acted, and suffered in such a way that we can add nothing of our own. This means the replacement and suppression of those in whose

---

[9] (Moltmann, The Crucified God 1973, 1974), 202-4.
[10] (Pannenberg, Systematic Theology 1998, 1991), Volume 2, 413-5.

place the Son came. None of this troubles Barth. For example, Barth says that God removed the human being who commits the sins. The point we need to consider is that the concentration on the concept of reconciliation on the death of Jesus Christ as a closed event of the past has fateful consequences. Barth does not think of the event as open to a process of reception. The result is that he can view the judgment on sin in the death of Christ as comprehensive and definitive.[11]

Barth admits that throughout this exposition he will be expounding upon the objective relevance of the doctrine of atonement. He will want to expound upon its subjective apprehension by us in our time and place as he expounds upon the role of the Holy Spirit in reconciliation-atonement. If one has an interest in the view Barth had of the being and work of the Spirit, one could study these six sections as a unit.

Thus, he also wants to be clear that the being and work of Jesus Christ helps him reflect upon the three-fold nature of the being and work of the Holy Spirit. He will engage the theme of the subjective apprehension of the reconciliation of the world God has made in Christ. Christ is guarantor and witness to truth, having its ground in the being and work of the Holy Spirit. In the Holy Spirit, the hand of God touches humanity in way that one can see, hear, perceive, accept, and receive all that God has for humanity. The hand of God has touched and seized Christians in this way. The Holy Spirit assembles, preserves, and maintains a community of those who are in Christ. Therefore, he will discuss the work of the Holy Spirit in the community before he discusses the work of the Holy Spirit in individuals. The Holy Spirit awakens people to faith to be part of a new community (XIV.62), is the life-giving power that provides divine direction in sanctifying and upbuilding people in love (XV.67) and summons the community to witness to the truth in the world even as the community stands vicariously for the world with hope based upon the divine promise (XVI.72). He will conclude by reflections that follow the same pattern for the community, only now applied to individuals who have faith and justification (XIV.63), love and sanctification (XV.68), and hope and calling (XVI.73). The work of the Spirit continues in its unifying form. Faith, love, and hope are primarily the work of Christ, then the work of the community, and lastly the work of the individual. He will develop a notion of the Spirit that is something like the notion in physics of the potent force, the unifying force of God in the world. Christ as the guarantor of truth has its ground in the being and work of the Holy Spirit. He stresses that the work of the Holy Spirit is still lacking in the world at large. The being of the Christian indicated by these theological virtues is a being in relation, that is, in

---

[11] (Pannenberg, Systematic Theology 1998, 1991), Volume 2, 431-2.

community. Faith, love, and hope in this relation to Jesus Christ are primarily the work of the Spirit in community, and then in the individual Christian.

One of the issues raised by scholars is the role of the Holy Spirit in this volume. Barth clearly has a doctrine of the Spirit. In this volume, the role of the Spirit is unifying that which was separate through bringing people to faith, building them up in love, and sending them into the world with hope. The Holy Spirit brings people into fellowship with each other. Yet, as massive as is *Church Dogmatics,* it remains a finite product. The distribution of topics and the amount of space offered is important. Many students of Barth would suggest that he has placed little weight on the role of the Holy Spirit and pneumatology. Part of the problem is the structure of *Church Dogmatics*. The portion he did complete is so massive that it obscures what he does say regarding the Spirit. He admittedly apportions less space to the work of the Spirit than he does to Christology, sin, and salvation. Since he did not complete it, the final volume, with the intended focus on the redemptive and hope-filled work of the Spirit is not available to us. Although the work is structurally Trinitarian, it leaves one open to the notion that the Father creates, the Son reconciles, and the Spirit redeems. Yet, one can admit that the biblical material does not fit this strict demarcation. This will have an important implication in his understanding of salvation. The issue is the relation of the Holy Spirit to Jesus and therefore to those incorporated in Christ by the same Spirit. Let us suppose for a moment that Barth has underplayed the relation of Jesus to the Spirit. Suppose Barth has made the humanity of Jesus too much a function of his direct relation to the Father, as over against a relation mediated by the Spirit. If so, Barth is weakening the link between his humanity and us. The reason is that he emphasizes the miraculous transference of what happened then, in the cross and resurrection, and places less emphasis on that relation mediated in the present by the Spirit of Christ through the community called the Body of Christ. One does not need to deny the miracle of the past transference to see that the mediation from then to now is an important one that Barth might not have explored with enough attention.[12]

Before we move forward, let me stress again that Barth is laying out his notion of the event of revelation in Jesus Christ and the corresponding event of faith in us as the work of the Spirit. A Christian approach to truth acknowledges the significance of both events. An event that comes from beyond us as an act of the Father revealing the being of God in the Son through the life, death, and resurrection of a man, Jesus of

---

[12] (Cambridge Companion to Karl Barth 2000) Colin Gunton, "Salvation," p. 152.

Nazareth invites us to respond to it by the awakening act of faith in us through the work of the Spirit. He does not want the community or individuals to have shame in living in accord this event. In this chapter, I have sought to summarize the flow of Volume IV from differing perspectives. We now turn to the actual exposition of his notion of the central theme of dogmatics – the doctrine of reconciliation-atonement.

CHAPTER XIV

Jesus Christ, the Lord as Servant

Chapter XIV, Volume IV.1, section 59-63, is a discussion of Jesus Christ, the Lord as servant. Barth will say, using the parable of the prodigal son as an image, that Jesus Christ is the God who went into the far country. He is the Lord who became a servant. The Son became obedient to the Father in humbling himself to be the brother of humanity. Christ takes his place with the transgressor. Christ judges humanity by judging himself and dying in the place of humanity. Yet, the Father raised Christ from the dead. The Father recognized and made effective the suffering and death of Jesus as a satisfaction made for us. In doing so, God converts humanity to God and therefore Christ is our redemption from death to life.

Barth begins with a discussion of the obedience of the Son of God (59). It constitutes the first part of his Christology, which will continue in sections 64 and 69. One way to study this part of the theology of Barth is to study these three sections as a unit to gain a firm grasp of his Christology.

First, Jesus Christ is "very God" as he goes into the far country. Here, he discusses the first aspect of Christology. The emphasis is upon "representation." The doctrine of reconciliation becomes the doctrine of substitution. Atonement-reconciliation is a history centered in Jesus Christ. This history is truth actualized in a history and revealed as history. Yet, we must also refer to it as an incredibly special history of God with humanity. Humanity learns the truth of its own existence as it looks upon the truth of revelation in the history of Jesus. Thus, he will want to understand deity considering the Incarnation. God has an interest in humanity in Jesus Christ. God has gone into the "far country." God acknowledges humanity in Jesus Christ, rather than pass by on the other side. God becomes the neighbor of humanity. He is the Lord who became a servant. The majesty of God shows itself in the obedience of the Son in offering and humbling himself to become the brother of humanity. He fulfills the reconciling will of God in his death and becomes the reconciling will of God through the Holy Spirit in the resurrection. This act of God becomes the eschatological event of salvation. The various titles conferred upon Jesus reflect the fact that Jesus is their center. They aim to witness to the truth revealed and actualized in Jesus. They answer the question Jesus poses. They gave an account of the history of Jesus. Here is a mystery that offends. We can reject this message of course, and the community itself has rejected it at various times in history. Yet, the New Testament is clear in its witness in a way the history of the church could never have in showing Jesus as the suffering servant of the Lord. Barth will stress that the Word did not simply become any flesh. The Word became Jewish flesh. The whole doctrine of the church concerning incarnation and atonement becomes abstract, valueless, and meaningless to the extent that this comes one regards this as something accidental and incidental. The New Testament witness to Jesus as the Christ, the Son of God, stands on the soil of the Old Testament. One cannot separate the witness from this historically contingent fact. This fact prevents Barth from going the route of a form of Platonic realism. The Incarnation occurs in a Jewish history and therefore in the context of Old Testament history and promise. He can reject any form of Docetism. Yet, the same one who is the object of grace is also the object of the wrath of God, as he takes the place of the sinner. He stands under divine sentence and judgment. God conceals the divine Yes of grace under the divine No of judgment. He experiences the onslaught of nothingness. His history must be a history of suffering. It becomes as natural to be lowly as it is to be high. The Son chooses to go into the far country, to conceal the form of lordship in the form of this world. Yet, the Son is true to his divinity. We deal with God in the form of a servant. Such humility is proper to the divine nature. In fact, the Incarnation is the path through which we understand deity. Christian theology does not understand deity as an abstraction, but the in the reality of Incarnation. Consistent with Chalcedon, he stresses that in this humiliation and condescension, deity remains deity. Barth is particularly dealing with kenosis theology and Philippians 2:5-11. Divine emptying while remaining divine allows Christ to be the one who actualizes the reconciling will of God. We must willingly learn who deity is by turning to Jesus. He takes his place with the transgressor. The acting subject of the reconciliation of the world with God is Jesus, mediator between God and humanity and the one who makes peace between them. In this atonement, God chooses to be with the world rather than abandon the world. Thus, God is the acting subject in the act of atonement. God is both the one obeyed and the one who obeys, all occurring in Jesus. In his suffering and dying, he is quite different from other human beings because he always stands on the side of God. God chooses condescension, humiliation, lowliness, and obedience. God brings help where there was no other help. God accepts solidarity with human beings. We must not think that such movement on the part of God is unworthy of the divine. Christ is the new humanity. The struggle of Jesus in the garden reveals that the will of Satan and the will of the Father coincide.

Second, the judge receives judgment in our place. God did all the above because God takes up the cause of the world as its loyal creator. Christ judges humanity by judging himself and dying in the place of humanity. Therefore, humanity no longer has the right to judge itself, for its judgment will lead to innocence for ourselves and guilt when we judge others. We see the glory of God in the world as God, the loyal Creator, takes up the cause of humanity, seeing the radical neediness of the world. The way of humiliation means God draws close to us. The peril of humanity becomes a peril to divinity. God has taken the neediness of humanity within divinity. God "for us" means God has not abandoned humanity. Therefore, the grace of God is not a cheap grace. To look at Jesus Christ who is for us means to look at ourselves as those who are guilty of sin, but who are no longer pledged to it, who have no other ground to do evil now that Christ has cut the ground from under our feet. The Son reveals the full seriousness of the human situation by accepting the judgment of humanity. Humanity wants to be its own judge, thereby revealing its pride. He knew no sin (II Corinthians 5:21) but became sin, so that it ceases to be our sin. Theologians think of this as the "passive obedience" shown in Jesus, as he took our place, receiving our accusation and judgment. This occurred in history, in his suffering, crucifixion, and death. Many people have suffered grievously and innocently. The difference here is the deity of the Jewish man who suffered in that cross. We are dealing with deity in the cross. We are dealing with sin in the cross. Reconciliation and conversion took place in that cross. Yet, in Christ humanity is also the friend and covenant partner with God. He was what humanity will become in the redemptive act of God. Christ has made an end of us as sinners in the cross. Thus, the cross reveals the abyss of sin swallowed up by divine love in the suffering of the cross. Of course, in active obedience, Christ also lived before God and did right.

Barth explains that the New Testament contains imagery from

several spheres: forensic, financial, military, and cultic. One can criticize Barth at the point of his forensic focus on atonement, an emphasis he gets from Calvin, loses the logic of sacrifice. The priestly ministry of the risen and ascended Christ does not receive the attention it deserves. Such an emphasis would rely upon the insights of Hebrews and the continuing priestly ministry of Christ.[13] Yet, Barth admits he could have provided a priestly image of the atonement. In that case, he would re-state the four answers given in this chapter differently. First, Jesus Christ is the Priest who represented us. Second and third, Jesus Christ gave Himself up as a sacrifice to take away our sins. Fourth, in our place, Jesus Christ has made the perfect sacrifice. As the perfect Priest, He took the place of all human priests, by offering Himself. He has substituted a perfect sacrifice for the imperfect sacrifices offered by human beings. The fact that He has made a perfect sacrifice means that He has fulfilled the will of God, the doing of which the action of all human priests and all the sacrifices made by human beings could only proclaim. The perfect sacrifice that fulfills the will of God took place in our stead and for us. For what other reason was there? God did not need to act as a priest and to suffer as a sacrifice in the person of the Son. However, we need this Mediator and His mediation. The will of God towards us is the purpose of this sacrifice. The divine good pleasure towards us is its end. In Christ, there takes place that which we need but which we cannot do or bring about for us. This sacrifice is a matter of our reconciliation, or peace with God, our access to God, and our freedom for God. Therefore, the basic alteration of our human situation, the taking away of that which separates us from God and involves the divine separation from us, our death as sinful human beings and our living as obedient human beings. The perfection of the sacrifice of Jesus Christ, the entire divine height and depth of the turning made in Christ, is the perfection of the love with which God has loved us. In the making of this sacrifice, God loved us in perfect love.

We need to pause for a moment and think critically about what Barth is suggesting. I will raise three areas for us to consider.

One consideration is that Barth is focusing on the passion of God. The being of God in act manifests itself in the temporal history of Jesus Christ. The temporal history of Jesus Christ is the temporal fulfillment of the eternal resolve of God. The temporal fulfillment of the eternal resolve of God is the existence of God as a human being in Jesus Christ. The existence of God as a human being is not only the existence of God as creature, but at the same time the surrender of God to the opposition to God that characterizes human existence. The consequence of this self-

---

[13] (Hohne 2019), location 4110.

surrender of God is the suffering of God of the opposition to God that humanity experiences, a suffering even to death on the cross. In this sense, the being of God is in becoming. The being of God is a being-in-a-becoming threatened by perishing. Humanity in opposition to God experiences the condemnation of perishing. God suffers this judgment in the existence of Jesus Christ. Thus, Barth takes the passion of God seriously. This leads him to criticize the traditional metaphysical concept of God according to which God cannot suffer without falling into conflict within the being of God. He will say that we cannot speak profoundly of the contradiction and rift in the being of God. Rather, we need to learn to correct our notions of the being of God. We need to reconstitute our notions since God experiences this passion or suffering. The point Barth will make here is that the suffering of God corresponds to the being of God in act. The Son is obedient to the Father, an obedience that occurs within the inner life of God. The oneness of being in which God is both the one obeyed and the one who obeys, differentiated the being of God in act from understanding it as a divine death. God can suffer and die as a human being. God suffers in this obedience in that in Jesus Christ God exists as a human being. In this obedience, God exposes the divine self to death. God maintains deity and revealed deity in the passion of this man as the eternal Son. God as God has declared God identical with the crucified Jesus. Barth will refer to this fatherly fellow-suffering of God. Indeed, the fatherly fellow-suffering of God as the basis of the humiliation of the Son has its realization in the historical even of the crucifixion. Therefore, the Father participates in the passion along with the Son. In this divine self-surrender, God does not abandon the divine self, of course, but God does surrender the divine self because God will not abandon humanity. The being of God remains a being in act only in the constantly new acts of the self-affirmation of God. Therefore, the will of God is to remain by and in this divine historicality in the face of the death of Jesus Christ is a new act. In saying Yes to the dead Son of God, God said Yes to humanity with the same Yes.[14]

Two is that Barth is raising the notion of the kenosis of the Son of God. The concern is that it amounts to renouncing of deity itself. This would then destroy the whole concept of Incarnation. If God is not truly and totally in Christ, what sense does it make to talk of the reconciliation of the world with God in Christ? However, one must explain how we can

---

[14] (Jungel 1976, 2001), 83-88. Barth is rejecting the formulation of the essence of God we find in Athanasius, the Cappadocian Fathers, and John of Damascus, for whom the Trinitarian life of God does not suffer, but only the human nature of God suffers.

think of such self-emptying without renunciation of the possession or use of divine attributes. The reason is that what it signifies is a transition from the divine sphere to the limitation of a creaturely form of existence. This aspect is clear in this presentation when Barth describes it from the perspective of doctrine of election. In this section, the Son of God is not only the Elected, but also the Rejected who took the place of perishing humanity. Barth made it clear that it is part of the deity of God that in divine transcendence and majesty, God can be God and act as God in an exalted as well as a lowly way. However, being actively present in the creatures God has made, even in their lowliness, is different from accepting the limitations of creaturely existence that they are limitations of the divine being. How can that be, without God ceasing to be God? Thus, despite his fine discussion of the obedience of the Son and rooting it in the Trinitarian life of God, it is no answer to say that in the eternal decree of divine election, God resolved upon this, and that the Son then took this path in obedience to the Father. Such an answer is possible only if we understand the obedience of the Son as an expression of the free self-distinction of the Son from the Father. In this case, the Son lets the Father be the one God by which God became the origin of all that is distinct from God. Therefore, God the Son could make God manifest as the Son of the Father in the form of creaturely distinction, in the finite form of creaturely existence as distinct from that of God. The self-emptying and self-humbling of the Son is primarily an expression of the self-giving of the Son to the Father in an obedience that desires nothing for self. It serves the glorifying of God and the coming of the kingdom.[15]

Three, and most significantly, as powerful as the presentation of Barth can be, can Christian theology really say that in the event of the death of Christ, Christ has made an end of us sinners and therefore of sin itself? We need to raise the question of whether the result is not the disappearance of our independent humanity. It becomes "inevitably totalitarian" (D. Solle) and "theological liquidation" (G. Wagner).[16] Barth will stress the notion of representation in 59.1. In 59.2, in his exposition of what it means to say that Christ is "for us," he will say that Christ takes the place of sinners as his second point. In 59.1, Christ stands under wrath and judgment, experiencing brokenness and destruction. Also, in 59.2, Barth will famously say that Christ takes our place in receiving judgment in the sense that the judge allowed judgment to fall on him. In all of this, Barth seeks to argue for the notion that Christ represents humanity before God. However, if the Son experiences punishment in representing our being

---

[15] (Pannenberg, Systematic Theology 1998, 1991), Volume 2, 378-9.
[16] (Pannenberg, Systematic Theology 1998, 1991), Volume 2, 431.

enemies of God, can the Son also accept the offer of reconciliation on our behalf? Barth does not offer a satisfactory answer, which would require doing justice to the situation of the recipients who need reconciliation. In fact, the entire thought of representation raises the question of whether it leaves room for creaturely independence of those represented so that they no longer see the claim of God on their lives as hostile. Rather, they would reconcile themselves to the claim of God upon their lives. If we are the ones who need reconciliation with God, then someone must remove the reason for our hostility to God if there is to be reconciliation with God.[17]

Third, Barth deals with the verdict of the Father. This section is notable for its lack of reference to the role of the Holy Spirit, who is the giver of life, in the resurrection of Jesus. At the same time, many thinkers, usually from a fundamentalist perspective, doubt whether Barth believed in the resurrection of Jesus. I think it obvious that Barth does. He begins by wrestling with the historical difference between the cross and our lives. How does this death become something truly "for us"? With a touch of Platonic realism, Barth says again that in the death of Christ humanity died, whether individuals recognize it or not. Scholars question whether Barth has rightly understood II Corinthians 5:14 here. Yet, bridging the historical gap is his reflection on the resurrection of Jesus. He becomes a theologian of the resurrection. In the resurrection, the Father has revealed the reconciling nature of the cross and received the Son and the appointed representative of humanity. The resurrection was an event in time, with a beginning in the saga of the discovery of the empty tomb and end in the saga of the ascension. The empty tomb is a presupposition of the resurrection, but the account of its discovery as empty is in the intellectual sphere of saga or legend. We must not think of ascension as a literal ascending of the risen Lord into space. He readily admits the resurrection narratives do not provide a continuous history. We ought not to attempt harmonizing the accounts. For Barth, the Father raised Jesus from the dead, giving effect to the passion and death of Jesus as a satisfaction made for us, as our conversion to God, and our redemption from death to life. The resurrection is a new act of God that proclaims the cross as the obedience of the Son. Thus, he does not think of it as an historical event in the same way as the crucifixion, even though the New Testament considers Easter as a happening in space and time. Yet, he will speak of it as a definite moment in history that would give rise to the faith of the disciples. Barth will have an extensive discussion of how what happened then still has its effect now. We are in the same position as the first disciples, the women at the tomb, and the shepherds of Bethlehem. We face the problem of decision, of

---

[17] (Pannenberg, Systematic Theology 1998, 1991), Volume 2, 413-5.

turning toward the God who has turned toward us. In any case, the resurrection of Jesus bridges the gap in time between the crucifixion then and our today. We can speak of the real presence of Christ with us because of the resurrection.

After the first part of his discussion of Christology, Barth will discuss his doctrine of salvation in the next two sections. He will show how Christ reveals the malady and misery of humanity in its pride and the divine remedy in justification by faith. Barth brings his Christology and soteriology close together. Barth is always a teacher of the church. However, he has focused upon the first part of his Christology, and therefore the Barth the theologian is primary.

Barth will discuss the pride and fall of humanity (60). His fully developed understanding of human sinfulness includes sloth (XV.65) and falsehood (XVI. 70). We would not know sin apart from knowledge of Christ, the reason he has not discussed sin until now. The fact that humanity needs the Son to represent it discloses who human beings are. Human beings willed to be as God, to be its own lord, to judge good and evil, and help themselves. Therefore, they withstood the lordship of the grace of God. They make themselves guilty before God individually and corporately.

First, Barth discusses sinful humanity in the light of the obedience of the Son of God. This approach is consistent of Barth to ground his knowledge of the human condition in Christology. One can have true self-knowledge only as one looks to God, a view derived from John Calvin. Knowledge of Christ, which comes from the Bible, reveals the human condition. He does not want to look to any other source of such knowledge. One problem Barth has here is that his Christological grounding of the knowledge of sin does not recognize that uncovering sin in the light of the revelation in Christ relates to something that is universal and precedes revelation. The fact of sin in Barth becomes a mere postulate of the Christian faith. In contrast, theology seems to need to develop and an understanding of sin that displays the plight of humanity as a universal condition, and not simply the result of Christian knowledge. The gospel does reveal pride, of course, but pride arises out of the anxiety that precedes it.[18] However, Barth would argue that deriving knowledge of sin from another source would lead one down the path of the liberal Protestant of the 1800s. His approach, however, is not a "back to ..." approach, which he does not think is ever a good slogan, for the people to whom one wants to get "back to" had their faults as well. However, he wants to adhere, even with the knowledge of sin, to the scripture principle of the Reformation. If

---

[18] (Pannenberg, Systematic Theology 1998, 1991), Volume 2, 252.

we properly know Christ, we properly know humanity. He showed this in III.2, only now, he must do so considering the need humanity has for salvation from its dilemma.

Barth will argue that in the trial of Jesus, those who judge Jesus are our representatives. We need to see ourselves in them. Barth renounces any appeal to empirical data regarding human brokenness. In that case, the assertion of human sinfulness depends for its validity on the decision of faith. Therefore, those who do not believe will not realize the brokenness of their existence. Those who refuse to believe in Christ seem spared the confrontation with the distortion of their human destiny as seen in the structure of their behavior. In contrast, we might rightly puzzle over the message of reconciliation and deliverance from an evil whose oppressive power and catastrophic consequences one can only believe in before the rescue can come. Of course, only knowledge of God can reveal the depth of human brokenness as turning from God. That is the truth contained in Barth here. Further, if human corruption were as deep as the teaching of Barth suggests, it would prevent human beings from gaining insight into their condition.[19]

Markus Barth has a discussion of this theme in which he places this basic teaching into a narrative of Pauline theology on justification. Although I can agree with much of it, I must say that when I came to this part of the narrative, where we know human sin only in the trial of Jesus, my reaction was its unreality. I think Paul would have referred to the self-evident inhumanity of human beings to each other, as he did in Romans 1.[20]

Second, what we see of humanity is that its sin is always a form of pride. Sin is unbelief in what God has done in reconciling the world in Christ. In contrast, one could think of such unbelief as arising from anxiety we have about ourselves. Such anxiety refuses to accept our lives as a gift. We are unable to be thankful. We are unable to move confidently into the future. True, pride is implicit in our desire and anxiety about our lives. When such pride comes into the open, it can have destructive and even murderous effects. A life of anxiety, unbridled desire, and aggressiveness, are also the roots of sin, in addition to pride and unbelief, both of which show themselves only when confronted with the revelation of God in Jesus Christ.[21]

Third, Barth discusses the fall of humanity. He wants to consider who humanity is considering who Christ is. The pride of which he writes is

---

[19] (Pannenberg, Anthropology in Theological Perspective 1985), 91-93.

[20] (M. Barth, Justification:Pauline Texts Interpreted in the Light of the Old and New Testaments 1969, 1971), 40-1.

[21] (Pannenberg, Systematic Theology 1998, 1991), Volume 2, 251-2.

the pride that goes before the fall. Humanity has not completely fallen away from God in the sense that humanity has lost God. Humanity is at the edge of that gulf, but not ontologically godless. Humanity cannot really escape God. We might call this the Magna Charta of humanity grounded in Christian faith. No one is hopeless. Godlessness may be strong, but God is never without humanity. Even in the fall of humanity, humanity is still the creature and covenant-partner of God. God made the covenant, so humanity cannot dissolve it. Humanity has not fallen lower than God has gone in Jesus Christ. In this context, he discusses religion. For him, religion is the exaltation of the soul to God, the setting up and worshipping of images of the being and essence of God. Religion is the action of sinful humanity that will inevitably involve self-contradictions. The religious relationship of humanity to God becomes a degenerate form of the relationship between the Creator and the creature. Religion is empty and deeply problematical. Yet, religion is also confirmation that God has not destroyed the relationship. Barth is offering a theological criticism of religion that highlights its positive dimension, but also addresses the misuse of religion, including Christianity.[22]

Humanity is in debt to God, but God in mercy forgives the debt. The corruption of humanity is radical and total, but we cannot speak of the loss of divine likeness. He agrees with Kant that humanity has an evil principle and in the power of radical evil. Barth famously ponders the story of Adam. He also did so in the book, *Christ and Adam* (1957). Adam simply did in the insignificant form of the beginner that which all people have done after him that that which is in a serious and flagrant form of our own transgression. He was in a trivial form what we all are as people of sin. No one must be Adam. We are so freely and on our own responsibility. God knows us in Adam. Adam is the truth concerning us. Barth points to Romans 5:12-21, the Romans commentary being another source for his reflections on Adam. Paul knows Adam as the one by whom sin entered the world. Yes, Adam writes himself across all human existence, telling the truth of humanity. Barth refers briefly to the notion of original sin and hereditary sin, which he rightly rejects. He admits that it can refer helpfully to the comprehensive act of humanity and the imprisonment of human existence in the circle of evil being and. In this imprisonment, God speaks as liberator in Jesus Christ. Yet, his problem with hereditary sin is that the act of sin makes one a prisoner from which Christ can liberate. Barth refers to the concept of the life-act replacing that of inherited sin, which Barth sees as an extremely unfortunate and mistaken one.[23] The difficulty with

---

[22] (Pannenberg, Systematic Theology 1998, 1991), Volume 1, 178.
[23] (Pannenberg, Systematic Theology 1998, 1991), Volume 2, 255.

such statements is that ideas of a fall and a transgression are not a human act. In many other areas of his theology, Barth has re-worked Kierkegaard. Here, he did not do so. Yet, in the minds of some, Kierkegaard is superior to Barth here in disclosing the basic anxiety that underlies human sinful action.[24]

Barth now turns to the consideration of the justification of humanity (61). He will follow this Yes of God to humanity with sanctification (XV.66) and the summons to vocation (XVI.71). The just act of God in Jesus Christ is the basis a new and corresponding making right or justification of humanity. Its reality calls for faith as a suitable acknowledgement, appropriation, and application. Franz Overbeck said that no modern person could understand Paul, let alone agree with him, on the matter of justification.[25] Barth will try it.

John Wesley will also try. I see much common teaching between Wesley and Barth concerning its foundational importance and even in content. Wesley will stress that any blessing human beings experience is the result of the free grace of God. Humanity has no right to think of itself as deserving of this grace or that it has claim on such grace. Christian faith acknowledges what the death of Christ has meant in redeeming humanity from eternal death. It acknowledges the power of the resurrection as the restoration of humanity to life and immortality. Christian faith relies upon the blood of Christ and trusts the merits of his life, death, and resurrection. Christ is our atonement and our life. He gave his life for us and lives in us. He is our salvation for he is our wisdom, righteousness, sanctification, and redemption. Such salvation offered by faith is attainable in the present. Such salvation involves salvation from the guilt and power of sin. It involves salvation from the fear of eschatological judgment from God.[26] He makes it clear the question of human justification before God is of the highest importance for every human being. His concern is that so few have understood it. Many people have confused notions concerning it. His concern is with the question of truth as it relates to the Bible and the analogy of faith. So many have erred concerning the foundation, and thus, cannot build anything worthwhile on what they have laid. For Wesley, the ground of justification by faith is that God created humanity in the image of God, but that humanity responded by falling into sin and disobedience. Adam became the head or representative of humanity. Yet, in the fullness

---

[24] (Pannenberg, Anthropology in Theological Perspective 1985), 132-3, for which see *Concept of Anxiety* and *Fear and Trembling*.
[25] (M. Barth, Justification:Pauline Texts Interpreted in the Light of the Old and New Testaments 1969, 1971), 11.
[26] John Wesley, Sermon 1, Salvation by Faith.

of time, as the Son became a humanity being, humanity had a new representative. As the representative of humanity, the Son bore our griefs, the Lord laid upon him the iniquities of us all, wounded him for our transgressions, making of his life an offering for sin. By the offering of his life, he redeemed me, and therefore the rest of humanity as well. He has made a full, perfect, and sufficient sacrifice and satisfaction for the sins of world. Since the Son has tasted death for every human being, God has reconciled humanity to God by not imputing the sins of humanity to it. God remits the punishment due and reinstates us to favor with God, restoring our deadness to eternal life. We now live under the new covenant in which humanity receives justification by the free grace of God. Justification is pardon and forgiveness of sin. Thus, God justifies the ungodly. Such justification occurs through faith. Such faith is a divine conviction that God was in Christ, reconciling the world to God, but more, a sure trust and confidence that Christ died for my sins, that he loved me, and he gave himself for me. Such faith is the only thing humanity needs in order to receive pardon.[27]

First, Barth discusses the problem of the doctrine of justification. He says that we must cling to the basic Reformation insight that only faith fellowship with Jesus Christ is the object of the divine sentence of justification respecting believers. In the cross, we have the negative sense of judgment upon sin, but justification carries the positive sense of pardon and places us in a new life before and with God. He stresses that this means the complete alteration of the human situation, a conversion of sinful humanity to God. He wants to show how the righteousness of God over-rules in the reconciling grace of God, and the grace of God overrules in the righteousness of God. The task is to answer the question of what God is for sinful humanity and what is sinful humanity before the God who is for it? In an excellent historical survey of the notion of justification by faith, he notes that much of Christian history would not know this doctrine as the center of theology. He finds this lack in the early church theology as well as in the orthodox tradition.

Second, Barth discusses the judgment of God. Sinful humanity puts itself in the wrong before God. Human pride leads to striving for a dignity that does not belong to humanity. Yet, even as humanity falls into the abyss of independent existence, it does not find freedom and is still within the sphere of God. When the Bible speaks of the division of humanity, we are to think of ourselves in both places, the wrongdoer and the one elected by God. The strange thought today is that we are under the judgment that falls upon us by the righteousness and grace of God. The

---

[27] Sermon 5, Justification by Faith.

thought is strange because humanity lives in this history of God with humanity in a way that humanity cannot perceive by looking at its own experience. Such a history is a drama that only those who participate in it by faith in its truth can perceive it. Humanity has no independent experience of being part of this drama. We can contemplate the self or human phenomena in a way that lead us to see the truth of this drama. The drama is our true history, perceivable only by faith in its truth. The prodigal son was dead, and then came to life. While dead spiritually, we have no awareness of the drama in which we life. Our today is one of transition of transition from wrong to right, from death to life, and thus one we have no way of perceiving apart from faith. This righteousness, this judgment of God, this justification, has taken place in Jesus Christ. What happened in Christ is the substitution of the Son for the human being. What we deserved as enemies of God is something that only God could suffer. This act means humanity stands in righteousness before God. God has the right to do this as our creator, but even deeper, humanity is a covenant partner with God, called by God for salvation and therefore eternal life and fellowship with God. Yet, today, we stand in Jesus Christ, who is our future. Thus, we shall not find the moment in any event of our lives. We do not acquire this future in our life history. In Christ, I already am what I shall be. Jesus Christ lives in our place, for us, in our name. In Christ is our righteousness and life. Such justification is the right of God as creator.

As impressive as all of this is, we need to pause for a moment. Barth impressively revived this Christological focus of the concept of justification by presenting Jesus Christ as the one who was judged in our place and raised again for the sake of our righteousness, the one in whom we have the pardon of God.[28] The Pauline teaching of justification took on crucial importance for an understanding of salvation only in Western Christianity. Barth rightly stresses this fact, adding that the Christendom of the martyr centuries knew Christ without the doctrine of justification as taught in the Reformation.[29] Yet, as impressive as Barth is on the matter of justification as faith-fellowship with Jesus Christ, one must raise the question here of whether he leaves any place at all for the particularity of others alongside the one Jesus Christ.[30] When we raise this question, we continue the questioning of Barth regarding election in II.2 and the notion of representation and substitution in IV.

Third, Barth writes of the pardon of humanity. Pardon is human justification. Such a pardon is the pronouncement of a sentence and is

---

[28] (Pannenberg, Systematic Theology 1998, 1991), Volume 3, 231.
[29] (Pannenberg, Systematic Theology 1998, 1991), Volume 3, 214-5.
[30] (Pannenberg, Systematic Theology 1998, 1991), Volume 3, 231.

absolute. God separates us from the past. God comes to us as the doctor comes to the sick, as the shepherd seeks the lost sheep, as the loving father with outstretched arms to the lost son. One does not truly experience justification without recognizing oneself as sinner. We have this past and must come from it. Given whom humanity is now in Christ, it can move forward to what it will be, and yet already is in freedom. Justification begins in the past and completes in the future. While the past as sinner is still present, the future as the righteous human being is already present. One does not live simply as one is but leaps forward in anticipation of what will be as the righteous. One receives the presence of the promise. 1) The forward thrust of the divine sentence is toward forgiveness of sins and adoption into the family of God, even against the menace from which humanity comes. In the forgiveness of sin, God refuses to allow sin to define the relationship God has with humanity. 2) God places us in a specific right in which God ignored the wrong of humanity. 3) This completed justification means God places humanity in a state of hope that comes in the form of our right as children of God. Such hope implies looking and reaching out for a goal in forgiveness of sin and divine adoption as children of God. We live on the way to this goal. Barth impressively shows that no room remains here for an external imputation, since believers share in the pardon only in Christ.[31] Modern Protestant theology stressed the comprehensive significance of this thought of being children of God. The older 17th century Protestant theology viewed adoption as children as one of the effects of justification. Schleiermacher equated the two, adoption being the positive side of justification, forgiveness of sins the negative. Astonishingly, Barth agreed, though unlike Schleiermacher he did not base the verdict of justification on conversion but related it to the pardon of God in judgment.[32]

Fourth, Barth discusses justification by faith alone. Faith is still the act of sinful human beings who cannot self-justify. Faith is humility, and thus acknowledgement of the sin of pride. Such faith does not mean unhappiness or discouragement. Such humility is genuine but comforted despair. Faith is the humility of obedience. Faith excludes human cooperation, even though this must not lead to our indifference, quietism, or libertinism. Before God, humanity is something rather than nothing. God finds no pleasure in the nothingness of humanity. Faith comes where Jesus Christ prevails on an individual. Christ is the event of the reality of justified humanity. Justification is the act and word of God. Such faith must be empty hand, the empty vessel, and the vacuum. Faith is openness to its

---

[31] (Pannenberg, Systematic Theology 1998, 1991), Volume 3, 231.
[32] (Pannenberg, Systematic Theology 1998, 1991), Volume 3, 212.

object as faith in Christ. Such faith is humble obedience, comforted despair, and a human act and experience. Faith is the appropriate response to the faithfulness of God to humanity as shown in Christ. Such faith is the imitation of Christ in that as he emptied himself to become servant, so our response is to empty ourselves and become servants. Faith is a downward movement toward poverty. The believers look to Christ to find their righteousness, their yesterday as sinners and their tomorrow as righteous, their end as a child of God and their beginning as sinners, their pardon, their peace with God.

Barth has obviously brought the Trinity into prominence in a way that previous generations had lost. Looking back, however, one can see the problem with structuring this work in the way he did. He rarely discusses the specific relations within the Trinity. He gives much attention to the Father-Son relation, but the Spirit does not receive much attention in the context of a discussion of Trinitarian relations.

However, in what follows, Barth is ready to discuss the role of the Holy Spirit in applying the reconciling work of Christ in healing humanity of its sinful pride through justification by bidding people to gather as a community and strengthen their faith. In what follows, Barth will discuss the role of the Spirit in the community and in believers. Barth is giving direction to the work of church leaders and those focused upon spiritual formation of the people. Far from neglecting this dimension of church life and discipleship, Barth invites our reflection upon the communal and individual work of the Spirit.

Barth is now ready to discuss the Holy Spirit as the one who gathers the Christian community in faith (62). He will complete his thoughts on the Holy Spirit as the life-giving power in sanctification and upbuilding people in love (XV.67) and summoning people to witness to the truth with hope (XVI.72). The Holy Spirit is the one who awakens a community, the body of Jesus Christ. This community is the present historical form of existence of Christ, the one holy, catholic, and apostolic church. The Holy Spirit is gathering the community of humanity that is a provisional representation of justified humanity.

First, Barth discusses the work of the Holy Spirit. He specifically wrestles with the subjective realization of the atonement. He offers us a simple picture of the course he has followed. Christology is like a vertical line that intersects the horizontal line. He wants us to imagine the horizontal line as the sin of humanity. Along that horizontal line, however, is also the church and the faith of the individual as intersected by the vertical line of Christology. The vertical line is the reconciling work of God in Christ. The horizontal line is the object of the work of God. He will now consider the final aspect of the encounter represented by the intersection of

51

the two lines. The horizontal line is the subjective realization of the event of reconciliation. The vertical line represents the divine act and offer, while the horizontal line represents active human participation in the event of reconciliation. He will discuss what is involved in this active human participation in the event of reconciliation. In this section he will deal with the Christian community and in the following section he will deal with Christian faith. He follows the pattern of the creed, which moves from the Holy Spirit to the church. Christ attests himself through the Holy Spirit. The Spirit works through awakening people to what God has done in Christ. Christ creates the relationship of the community and the individual with Christ. The relationship can only be one of obedience and prayer. The Spirit spends itself in attesting to the event of reconciliation in Christ. Christ sends the Spirit and the Spirit comes to humanity. The Spirit is the power by which Christ attests himself in creating human response and obedience. In that way, the Spirit is the awakening power. We do not know how the Spirit awakens.

Second, Barth considers the being of the community. He begins with the discussion of the church as visible and invisible. The community is the result of the work of the Spirit. As such, the community is a work that takes place among human beings in the form of a human activity. This community has a specific history. It is a phenomenon of world history. The community is a gathering of those who are servants, friends, children, and witnesses of God and the event of reconciliation. As a gathering from the world, the community is a separation as well. It has an ecclesiastical organization, constitution, and order. The church is visible, one historical factor among others. Like individual Christians, the community is sinful. In his anthropology, Barth discussed humanity as soul and body. In a comparable way, the being of the community is the existence of Jesus Christ. The church is the body of Christ, awakened by the Spirit. Thus, the Christian faith awakened by the Spirit is a definite human activity and phenomenon as well. Theology has neglected the relation between the soteriological operations of the Spirit in believers and the activity of the Spirit as the creator of life and in the eschatological role of the Spirit in the new creation. Barth reflects growing awareness in New Testament exegesis of the connection between the Spirit and eschatology. Thus, materially, we find this in Barth's description of the Spirit as the "awakening power" by which the risen Lord created the church as a "provisional representation of the entire world of humanity" that finds their justification in Christ. However, Barth will also say that the Spirit is the power in which Jesus Christ attests Himself effectively, creating in individuals response and obedience. Barth does not do justice to the personal independence of the Spirit in the Trinitarian life of God and therefore in the economy of salvation.[33] The church will have the temptation to view itself as a religious society among the various human communities. Yet, such a view ignores the third spiritual dimension of the church as awakened by the Spirit. This third dimension is in the hand of God, invisible as a human phenomenon, in which one only believe. The creed affirms belief in the church in the sense that it must take itself seriously as visible human community and as invisible spiritual community. It will create the forms best adapted to its mission for the generation in which God has placed it. Its Lord is its secret, living by the awakening power of the Spirit. It is like a moving tent of the Old Testament tabernacle. The community is the earthly and historical form of the existence of Christ. The church is the body of Christ. Christ is the Head and therefore the invisible secret of the church, open only to those with faith. It exists eschatologically as believing already in the destiny of humanity as God had defined it in Christ. It belongs to Christ and can only follow the movement of his life. As the body of Christ, first, the church is one (plurality is sinful). Given the present reality, churches need to reach out to the reality of the one church. Yet, to sacrifice truth for the sake of peace and love will not lead to the one church of Jesus Christ. Nor can they waive aside their confessions of faith. We can reach out toward the one true church only with humility, loyalty, and repentance. Second, the church is holy (set apart from the world). Barth offers a powerful reminder. The body of Jesus Christ may well be sick or wounded. When has it not been? However, as the body of this Head, it cannot die. The faith of the community may waver, its love may grow cold, its hope may become dreadfully tenuous, but the foundations of its faith, love, and hope, and with it itself, are unaffected. Its authority, effects, influence, and successes may be small. They may threaten to disappear. However, the authority and power of God are behind it and it will never fail. It may become a beggar, it may act like a shopkeeper, it may make itself a harlot, as has happened and still does happen. Yet, the church is always the bride of Jesus Christ. Its existence may be a travesty of His, but as His earthly and historical form of existence, it can never perish. It can as little lose its being as He can lose His. What saves it and makes it indestructible is that Christ does not forsake the church, any more than Yahweh would forsake the people of Israel, even with all the divine judgments described in the Old Testament. As he continues, third, the church is catholic (general, comprehensive, and everywhere). Each of the churches have their unique histories but underlying them is the commonality of represented in the church as the Body of Christ. Fourth, the church is apostolic, that is, in agreement with them. The community is in the discipleship or school of the normative

---

[33] (Pannenberg, Systematic Theology 1998, 1991), Volume 3, 3.

instruction and direction of the apostles. It lives by listening to them and accepting their message.

Third, Barth discusses the time of the community. This community has its time between the first and second coming of Christ and is therefore the provisional representation of the entire world of humanity that receives justification in Christ. Its strength is that it comes from Easter. It also has its consummation ahead of it. God still has time for humanity, and therefore for the church. Humanity still has space, and thus can still develop. It still is a history. Granted, human thanks is always equivocal. Faith is smaller than a mustard seed. Obscurity wraps around its knowledge. Witness is often impotent stammering. The voice of this minority is only the voice of the sinful humanity justified only in Christ. True, the last hour has struck. However, the Holy Spirit has time to work. The community still has time for prayer, faith, and repentance. We have time for preaching and gathering of the community. We can think of this as the time of grace. It can be a shining light, even if often feeble and defective, until the dawning of the great light that will be the end of time, the coming of new Jerusalem in which no temple will exist because the Lord is its temple. This end-time is the time of service that it can render gladly, even if its service alternates from strength to weakness.

Barth is now ready to complete this chapter with a reflection on the Holy Spirit and Christian faith and justification (63). He will continue his reflections on the work of the Spirit as leading toward love and sanctification (XV.68) and hope and calling (XVI.73). As he sees it, the Holy Spirit is the awakening power in which Jesus Christ summons a sinful person into the community of Christ and therefore to faith. Such faith acknowledges, knows, and confesses Christ as the Lord.

First, Barth discusses faith and its object. Faith is following. The object is Jesus Christ. Faith is a human activity that is present future. In the place of unbelief are faith and the new humanity of obedience. The Holy Spirit awakens this faith. Such faith confirms an act that has already taken place in Christ.

Second, Barth discusses the act of faith. The Spirit summons sinful persons to be sorry individually and corporately. The Spirit summons people to be confident in face of the establishment of their justification and new life that has taken place in Christ. Barth meant the fact of Jesus in the Word of the kerygma. Christian faith is acknowledgement, recognition, and confession. We need to discuss this order for a moment. Assent came to the fore again as a term for the obedient acknowledgment that we owe to the Word of God. Barth developed a powerful concept of acknowledgment that knowledge of what one acknowledges does not come first. He expressly reversed the traditional sequence of the elements of faith. In the terminology of the older dogmatics, we should have to speak first of assensus and only then of notitia. Recognition of the object of faith is a result of acknowledgment. Any other kind of knowledge does not precede acknowledgment, either recognition or confession. The recognition and confession of faith are included in and follow from the fact that they are originally and properly an acknowledgment, the free act of obedience. However, can we acknowledge a thing without first having knowledge of it. Barth appealed to the definition of faith as obedience in Romans 1:5 and he rightly saw that in this regard he was close to Bultmann. However, Barth still thought he could agree with Bultmann only in the negative sense that the act of faith does not rest on holding the biblical texts or church propositions to be true. He did not view himself agreeing in the positive recognition that he whom the Bible attests and the church proclaims, the living Jesus Christ Himself, is the object of the obedience of faith. Faith is a free act in Barth. However, is the sacrifice of intellect of blind obedience preeminently an achievement, especially when offered as a free act? The point is that for Paul, the obedience of faith refers to the entire process of hearing and thus contains knowledge. Thus, we should not view faith as blind obedience the claim of proclamation to authority. Rather, faith is an understanding obedience to the truth. Yes, this will mean understanding of our possibilities of existence. More importantly, faith understands the reality we encounter in proclamation, an obedience to the truth that comes through knowledge of the content of proclamation and acceptance of it.[34]

---

[34] (Pannenberg, Systematic Theology 1998, 1991) Volume 3, 151-2.

CHAPTER XV

Jesus Christ, the Servant as Lord

Chapter XV, Volume 4.2, section 64-68, deals with Jesus Christ, the Servant as Lord, published in 1955, when Barth is 69 years old. Barth continues his exposition of the doctrine of reconciliation-atonement with this chapter.

The editors now note that criticism of Barth has shifted from his obscure writing to his verbosity. Barth himself says in his preface that he apologizes that the volume is so large that it will be too weighty for summer reading. He also says that people have started referring to him as the old man of Basel. He admits that he is not producing *Church Dogmatics* with the regularity he would like. However, while he has the best will in the world to press on, the responsibility of an unnamed task has burdened him in such a way that he did not finish earlier. In his preface, he also refers to a student who asked him what is going to happen if he is no longer there. The student was right to remind him of this possibility, for "fast fall the eventide" is true for him. However, he is still here, and he will address himself the next part-volume, hoping that this volume will be thick enough to spare him questions that involve whether he will complete the work. He says the wider issue does not rest in human hands and will declare itself in appropriate time.

Barth begins the second aspect of his Christology with a discussion of the notion that obedience of the Son that led the Son to humble himself to become human now becomes the exaltation of the Son of Man (64). Given the length of his exposition, the temptation would be to think of Barth as dividing the reconciling-atoning work of Christ into different or successive actions. However, Barth will stress the unity of the downward (4.1), upward (4.2) and outward (4.3) movements of this doctrine. The parallel with the previous chapter is obvious. The reconciling-atoning action of God is one movement. He is dealing with one mighty truth and he occupies himself with this truth. He wants to do justice to the grace of God and therefore to the truth of the atonement as it claims us. The movement of atonement begins from above to below, but now we consider the movement from below to above. He continues his Chalcedonian Christology with a focus on the "very human" part of the creed. In dialectical fashion, he will express himself primarily in the language of the Antiochian Christology, meaning he will emphasize the completeness of the humanity of Jesus. The Incarnation is incomprehensible within a systematic or unified thought, so the only way he can express it is a dialectical form. In classical terms, we must focus upon Christ in His kingly office, just as we did in the previous chapter focus on the priestly office of Christ. This exaltation occurs, as he is the servant of the Lord, the new, true, and royal human beings who participate in the being, life, lordship, and act of God. As such, the Son is the Head, Representative, and Savior of all other human beings.

In section one, Barth discusses the second problem in the doctrine of reconciliation-atonement. The Christian view of atonement-reconciliation comprehends not only the look to the divine work, but also to the human being to whom it applies. Theology must deal with God, of course, but God also has a covenant people. The truth that the event of atonement is a movement from above to below encloses the further truth that the event of atonement is a movement from below to above. We now see that the Incarnation exalts humanity to fellowship with God. We see the emergence of a new humanity in this exaltation and fellowship. He criticizes monasticism and the pietist movement for thinking that human action can accomplish this fellowship, especially the focus upon Christian perfection. Yet, the fact that the history of theology has committed this mistake does not mean we should make the mistake of not dealing with the subjective side of atonement. The risk is always present to glorify humanity as theology discusses the subjective side. However, to engage in theology is to take risks. If we do not venture in the risk, we will win nothing. Theology must always appreciate the focus of certain traditions on discipleship. Yet, it also needs to be careful that it does not lead us down a path that exalts human effort to the exclusion of what God has done. Humanity receives exaltation in reconciliation. Christ achieves our fellowship with God. The object of atonement is the human Subject. However, the active Subject of the atonement is also humanity. We see here the tension in Barth between the universality of divine action and the question of human appropriation of that action. He says that we would develop a strange Christology if we did not give the same attention to the true humanity of Christ as to His true deity, giving expression to the Chalcedonian character of his Christology. He offers a series of variations on the words of Ephesians 4:15, where the author encourages us to grow up into the head, Christ, which in turn forms and supplies the body in every part, making increase of the body through love.

In section two, Barth discusses the homecoming of the Son of man. To use the imagery of the parable of Jesus, God went into the far country in humiliation, but humanity comes back in exaltation. This action of atonement is a single or whole action. The theology of the cross has a secret theology of glory. The priestly office has the secret of the kingly office. The difference of Christ from us is that he is the human being in fellowship and peace with God. He lived in full reconciliation with God. He is true human being returned to fellowship with God, to relationship with fellow human beings, to the ordering of His inward and outward existence, to the fullness of His time for which the Father appointed Him, to the presence and enjoyment of the salvation for which the Father destined Him. The atonement as it took place in Jesus Christ is the one inclusive event of this going out of the Son of God and coming in of the Son of Man. In its literal and original sense, the word "to reconcile" means "to exchange." The reconstitution and renewal of the covenant between God and humanity consists in this exchange, the abasement of God and the exaltation of humanity. The Incarnation is the exaltation of our essence with all its possibilities and limits into the completely different sphere of that totality, freedom, correspondence, and service. He is the human being who keeps the covenant of God with the people of God in the action of divine life.

He will describe three aspects of reconciliation.

One aspect of reconciliation is its basis is in the divine election. He will summarize II.2, Chapter VII. The election of grace is the election of Jesus Christ. Jesus Christ is the historical event in which there took place in time that which was the purpose, resolve, and will of God from eternity. Election is the decision and action of God in the Son to be for humanity. In this election, God rejects sinful humanity and allows humanity to participate in divine glory. Thus, the election of Christ is the election of humanity. Again, this raises the question of a Platonic form of realism. In this election is the resolve of God to have fellowship with humanity. He reminds us of the depth of this secret and the strange mercy contained in the exchange.

Election is twofold predestination. Divine election reminds us that God was never alone. God was always with humanity in the Son. The look back to the discussion of election is a look back to the unity of this human history with the act of God in the Christ-event. The truth is that the Christ-event is worldly in dealing with this human history.

A second aspect of reconciliation is its historical fulfillment in the event of the Incarnation. He describes it as the event in which the Son became true human being, an act of divine majesty, the event of the fulfillment of the promise, the actualization of the promise in an absolutely new event, and a focus upon this event and this man. In this act, God becomes humanity and the Creator becomes the creature. God initiates a new series distinct from all others. He describes it as the new human being and the new secret of divine majesty. The ground of knowledge (ratio cognoscendi) knows that Jesus of Nazareth is like other human beings and part of human history. Yet, to know this without recognizing in Christ the ground of being and the new act of divine majesty is to miss the new event of God. The movement from knowing to recognizing requires a new act of cognition that shares the same quality of the new event. Although a new form of cognition, it remains human seeing and interpreting. Such cognition will not try to master the new event. Genuine knowledge will require participation of the knowing subject in the new event. Thus, Christ speaks for himself and allows others to know him. Such self-disclosure induces human seeing and interpreting that attaches itself to the new event of God. The Holy Spirit is this ground of knowledge, at work in both the new event of God and in the new cognition of the human subject. Participation in this self-exposition of Christ, the event of the testimony of the Holy Spirit, is not for everyone, but only for those who ask for it. The event itself has the character of a divine secret. God is still God in this new event, while also being true human being. The new event is an act of grace. Knowledge of this new event is the knowledge of faith in Jesus Christ. Such knowledge includes knowledge of the love we owe to God, who has proven divine love for us in the Son. God assumed the being of humanity and brought humanity into the being of God. The God who acts in the mode of being of the Son is also active in the mode of being of the Holy Spirit. Thus, Barth will focus his Christology in the notion of the participation of the divine and human in Christ. This will also mean that his notion of salvation will focus on participation. We see the Platonic realism of Barth in that God raised human essence to essence in God and was, at the same time, true humanity. He refers to this as the secret of Jesus Christ.

The first aspect of divine-human participation in Christ is that the Son became and is humanity. Human action could not have brought such exaltation of humanity. Christian knowledge and life derive joyfully in looking back to the event of the act of God that remains a form of becoming as well. Christian knowledge and life remain astonished at its participation in this event. What God willed from all eternity took place in the event in which the becoming and being of the Son occurs in human essence. John 1:14 is irreversible. The movement is from above to below. The question is whether Barth offers clarification of the question of whether God ceases to be God in his Christology even in this discussion of the event of the Incarnation.[35]

The second aspect of divine-human participation in Christ is the existence of the Son in a man, Jesus of Nazareth. He became the fellow human being of all human beings. God became this incomparable Thou. Barth will discuss the hypostatic union of divinity and humanity in Jesus Christ in the context of denying to baptism and the Lord's Supper the status of a sacrament. In that sense, Christ is the supreme sacrament due to the Incarnation. Protestant theology insisted that in the New Testament, Jesus Christ, not the church, is the sacrament of unity and the one sacrament in general. Some theologians would appeal to this argument of Barth for a total restriction of the term in its New Testament sense to Jesus Christ.[36] Barth took up the thought and argued for a use of sacrament only for Jesus Christ in view of New Testament usage. Behind this argument is the notion that baptism and the Lord's Supper are not sacraments.[37]

The third aspect of divine-human participation in Christ is that the event of Jesus Christ unites divine and human essence. Divine and human participate in each other in Jesus Christ. If true, it occurs in the encounter of this one Subject, in the acknowledgment, recognition, and confession of its unique truth. Jesus Christ exists as Son by participating in human essence. We have a two-sided participation. In the Son, human essence participates in divine essence and divine essence participates in human essence. We can see here that Christian knowledge and life involves this acknowledgment, recognition, and confession.

The fourth aspect of divine-human participation in Christ, and as a conclusion, given his previous three affirmations, is that God became the history of Jesus of Nazareth, who is also Son of Man. Christ is our Brother. As he became servant, he also became Lord. As Reconciler, the existence of the new and true human being has occurred in him.

The task of this part of his dogmatics is to understand this exaltation with precision. He will then offer an extensive exposition of mutual participation along these three lines.

---

[35] (Pannenberg, Systematic Theology 1998, 1991) Volume 2, 378.
[36] (Pannenberg, Systematic Theology 1998, 1991) Volume 3, 41.
[37] (Pannenberg, Systematic Theology 1998, 1991) Volume 3, 344-5.

First, he will write of the event of the mutual impartation of the divine and human essence in Jesus. The impartation is a hypostatic union that makes Jesus true salvation and saving truth. The actuality of the Incarnate Son, the union of the two natures in Christ, is the direct confrontation of the totality of the divine with the human in Jesus of Nazareth. The event of this impartation occurred in Bethlehem, the path to the cross, and the exaltation of resurrection. This hypostatic union does not obliterate or alter the human, but it does mean that it acquires the marks of divinity by participating directly in the majesty of God.

Second, he wants to reflect upon the address to the human essence that we find in Jesus Christ. Its twofold character is that we are dealing with the acting divine Subject of the Son and the human essence of Jesus of Nazareth. In the address, we are primarily dealing with a determination of the divine essence. He stresses the distinction of his teaching from false gods, especially the god of Mohammed, for the true God embraces height and depth, royalty and humility, and lordship and service. This means we must shake off the spell of the immutable nature of God and embrace a form of immutability that embraces the notion of divine humbling as we find in Jesus Christ. We find this in the electing grace of God. The participation of the two natures in Jesus Christ is mutual as the divine participating in the human and the human participating in the divine. The electing grace of God suggests that the divine nature is the determination of the human nature in their confrontation in Jesus Christ. Yet, the human essence of Jesus of Nazareth did not alter. However, the confrontation that occurs in Jesus of Nazareth of divine and human essence means the exaltation of human essence. If the Word became human flesh, the Word became sinful human flesh. The encounter of divine and human essence in Jesus of Nazareth means the divine exalted the human into sinlessness. The identity of Jesus as true God and true humanity means we must reckon with his history to perceive the divine rather than an abstract notion of divinity. In Christ, human essence receives glory, dignity, and majesty that the Son had in the fellowship of the Trinity. In Christ, Trinitarian life opens to include humanity. Christian knowledge of God means that we cannot deal with God without dealing at once with human essence. We have no knowledge, prayer, or worship apart from the Son, who is the mutual participation of human and divine essence. In all of this, we are revealing our point of departure for considering human sin and sanctification, the edification of the community, and love.

Third, he stresses that the existence of Jesus Christ is the common actualization of divine and human essence. The reality of Jesus Christ is the event of Jesus of Nazareth. This event defines Jesus Christ and therefore defines Christology. He has been describing the being of Jesus Christ in its truth and reality. Again, this means we must attend to actual history rather than an abstract notion of divine being. We also find the difference of the divine and human will in Christ, where, of course, the human will serves the divine will.

Barth then turns to the third aspect of reconciliation, showing that the basis of revelation is in the resurrection and ascension of the man, Jesus of Nazareth. While some people remain skeptical that Barth believed God raised Jesus from the dead, I invite you to read this section carefully. In Christ, the homecoming of humanity has already occurred. He wants to confirm the truth of this exaltation of human essence. The decisive fact of this part of the doctrine of reconciliation is the great divine direction to humanity that sanctifies them and edifies them in the community by the power of the Holy Spirit. Since God has made a way to humanity in Jesus, humanity has a way to God in Jesus as well. Since God went downward toward humanity, humanity may move upward to God. We know this is true because the actuality of this new being and occurrence creates the possibility of a special perception to meet it.

He asks himself an important question. Has he simply presupposed or freely invented a concept? Has he created a myth? Must we only refer to church symbols? Is it possible that his teaching rests upon an enormous fiction? Such questions represent his debate with both Bultmann and Tillich. He raises the question of whether he has intellectual justification in witnessing to the truthful nature of Christian revelation. His confessional approach to theology will not allow him to offer such intellectual justification. His gift to the church is to help it construct a beautiful witness to the truth and goodness of Christian teaching and life. Thus, Christian revelation simply establishes itself in the knowing human subject. It makes a place for itself in human cognition. It gives this possibility precisely because the event is so strange and new. The event summons us to see, think, and interpret it as a divine act of majesty. The event has the character of objective being and occurrence, but becomes an event within us as well, having a subjective character of revelation. Christian witness and theology occur in the confidence of this truth. We have no ability to demonstrate its truth. We do not define how we come to know and recognize it. We complicate matters when we do. All answers that are not absolutely simple are completely false answers. Jesus Christ is the basic text as expounded by the apostles. We take our stand on this truth. We have no other starting point than this self-revelation. Forms of contemplation, physics, metaphysics, or church authority cannot provide a basis for this knowledge. We can only witness to this knowledge. We cannot get behind it. We cannot put it in our pocket and carry it around with us. We can know it only in self-grounded certainty. His basic text is the same as that of the apostles, namely, Jesus Christ. We cannot get behind the text of the apostles. We cannot control this text. The divine and the human work together. Yet, even in their common working, they are not interchangeable. The divine is still above and the human below, which is the Christology of Chalcedon. The human nature of Jesus did precisely what human nature is always to do in serving the divine. Their relationship is one of genuine action. God humbles divinity to humanity so that God may exalt humanity to fellowship with God.

First, wherever there is knowledge of Jesus Christ, it takes place in the power of His witness, in the mystery and miracle, the outpouring and receiving, of the gift of the Holy Spirit. The Spirit is the lighting of the light and the finger of God. The witness of the Spirit assembles, edifies, and sends a living community. A living Christian is a Christian who receives the witness of the Holy Spirit, conforms, and is faithful to it. Living preaching is preaching awakened by the witness of the Holy Spirit. The daily life of the Christian is a life that listens constantly to this witness. The content of the witness of the Holy Spirit is the powerful and effective presence of Jesus Christ. People who recognize Jesus Christ as their neighbor, brother, and Lord, have received the Holy Spirit. What more could we want? The witness of the Spirit is the self-witness of Jesus Christ, risen from the dead and ascended to heaven. Now, in the resurrection and ascension, we see the being of Jesus Christ as true God and true human being. Barth is contemporizing the resurrection. One does not need to transcend it or augment it. The divine humiliation and human exaltation we find in Christ are the fulfillment of the covenant, the completed reconciliation of the world with God.

Barth attributes to the resurrection the validity of the reconciliation. However, conspicuous by its absence, according to some, is no reference to the Holy Spirit or the continuing priesthood of Christ. Yet, throughout this section, I have sought to highlight the role of the Spirit. If Barth did not get the role of the Spirit right, he is not wrong by much. The reader needs to consider whether the life of Jesus in these pages becomes a series of illuminating episodes.[38]

The cross fulfills the revelation and history of Christ. Barth is personalizing the significance of the cross when he says that the cross is the fulfillment of the Incarnation of the Word. It fulfills divine humiliation and human exaltation. Humiliation is the basis of exaltation. Exaltation is the goal of humiliation. In an affirmation where I am not sure how much clearer Barth could be, he stresses that the resurrection and ascension is an

---

[38] (Cambridge Companion to Karl Barth 2000), Colin Gunton, "Salvation," 152-3.

event, taking place as a temporal happening. It has the same character of what had gone on before the resurrection and is an event within the world of time and space. It takes place in the body, but not only in the body. His concern is to contemporize the resurrection. Jesus Christ, stressing his history, is the reconciliation of the world with God and therefore the new humanity. He is this in his resurrection, but he became such in his life and death. The resurrection reveals him as the one who is truly divine and truly human. The resurrection reveals this man, Jesus of Nazareth, is Lord and Savior. He admits that the singularity of the event of revelation in the resurrection conditions the singularity of the knowledge that it awakens. Here is a simple reminder that anyone who affirms the "historicity" of the resurrection would agree. Thus, the resurrection will have the character of a miracle. Knowledge of it relies upon the witness of the apostles. Barth will suggest, in his use of German words here, that *historie* reaches its limit, if we understand it as objectivity and likeness to other events, so he uses the term *Geshichte*. He wants to contemporize the resurrection here. The resurrection is the commencement of the history of revelation. The risen Lord came from the earthly world, the way of all flesh. He came from death. He had gone to the place where all human beings must go, but from which none can return. Jesus also went to the realm of God.

In the third section, Barth discusses Christ as the royal man. He wants to help us gain knowledge of Jesus of Nazareth that will lead to new knowledge of humanity. In all of this, just as Barth dealt with the priestly office of Christ in the previous chapter, Barth has been dealing with the kingly office of Christ in this chapter. Christ is the substance of the Christological foundation of this second part of the doctrine of reconciliation. Christ is true and new humanity, the second Adam, and the sanctification of humanity. The tradition of the church is not building in the air when it teaches the Incarnation as understood at Chalcedon. He wants to allow this fact to speak for itself as it arises in the New Testament witness.

First, he begins with the formal statement of Jesus as a man among the human beings of their time. He says that one could not fail to see and hear, he demanded a decision from them, he was present in a way that one could not forget because his presence was the rule of God, and present in a way that was so irrevocable death could not end it and continues living in the community. He continues with a discussion of how Jesus of Nazareth corresponds to the plan, purpose, work, and attitude of God. We should note the humanity of this section. He refers to the gospel material consistently.

Second, he begins his presentation of the material content of Jesus as royal man. Negatively, consistent with many human beings, others ignored, forgot, despised, and discounted him. Jesus showed his godlikeness in his concern for the weak, meek, and lowly over the high, mighty, and wealthy. He introduced a revolution in values while not tying it to a specific political program. He had no need to overthrow any of the political and economic order of his day. In this way, we know God as judge and humanity as in need of judgment. Finally, the man Jesus is for humanity.

Third, his life was his act in that it is a sign of the irruption of the rule of God. 1) His life-act was His Word in the specific and comprehensive sense. It was a human Word. 2) His life act includes specific activity that accompanies his specific speech. This material identifies his proclamation with the rule of God. These actions include miracles, which seem forced upon him, make no use of therapeutic technique, liberate others, they were specific rather than part of a general welfare program, they summon people to faith, and they actualize the transformation the rule of God will bring. They are all acts of the power of God. This means that what takes place in them is a new light on the human situation. The rule of God is near in Jesus. Things are going badly with the recipient of the miracle. The person is needy, frightened, and harassed. The individual is unfortunate. The human situation is one of suffering, whether in blindness, deafness, lameness, leprosy, and possessed by demons, and so on. We may turn away from this aspect of human life. We may close our eyes to it. In a beautiful image, we may argue that human life is not really like a great hospital. Yet, apart from this aspect, the miracles of Jesus do not receive their proper focus. Human life as it emerges in the miracles of Jesus is like a great hospital, whose many departments in some way enfold us all. The acts of Jesus show a concern with the evil existence of human life. Human beings are prisoners. He relieves the burden of life and release humanity. God is at the side of the human being who suffers. God does not will that which troubles, torments, disturbs, and destroys humanity. God does not will the entanglement, humiliation, distress, and shame that comes to suffering. God wills the salvation, life, and wholeness of humanity. God does not will destruction or death. God engages the nothingness that aims to destroy humanity. God opposes its onslaught on the creation God has made. The activity of Jesus is a defiance of the power of destruction that enslaves humanity. We should note the divine likeness of the humanity of Jesus in this process. We can sum up this activity of Jesus by saying that faith is a form of freedom.

Fourth, the cross is a description of the existence, divine likeness, and activity of the man Jesus. His life shows no signs of escaping its end in the cross. He fulfills the divine resolve toward the cross. He accepted this context of history between Jew and Gentile. The disciples follow Jesus under the sign of the cross.

In the fourth section, Barth discusses the gentle direction or guiding power of the Son. This section has its parallel in IV.1, 59.3 when he considered justification as the verdict of the Father. The basic point here is that what the Son "represents," which is the substance of the Christology Barth presents, the Son can make actual or real through gentle influence. He wrestles with whether we can think of the reconciliation accomplished in the cross is an isolated history of this one man. Power flows from Christ as our Lord in a way that reaches and affects us. We must not become overly optimistic as to what this directing influence of the Son has upon the life of the church or the individual. He warns us against arriving at a far too cheap Christian, church, and theology. This conversion and knowledge of ourselves may not truly be in order. We must not throw doubt on what the Son has given. We must also avoid any error as to the meaning, extent, and depth of the change. Our gaze must not stray from Christ. Our knowledge of Christ controls our knowledge of the anthropological sphere. The Christmas message of the Incarnation means that we share in the direction of the Son. Jesus lives, yes, and I with him. We truly know who we are, as we know ourselves in Christ. Such a statement is ontological concerning humanity. Jesus does not exist in isolated form. Christ in his true humanity reveals humanity. The participation of humanity in Christ is the exaltation of humanity. Humanity exists with this ontological connection. This ontological connection between Jesus and humanity is dynamic, and therefore eschatological. We know ourselves truly, then, not by gaining knowledge of ourselves, but of gaining knowledge of Christ. We look away from self and to Someone, not an empty beyond. The royal man stands under the sign of the cross. We remember the self-representation of the new and redemptive actuality of the rule of God. His life moved to this end. Christ becomes our contemporary in this sense. The royal man has taken our place and accomplished our justification, sanctification, and conversion. Thus, the cross is the completion of his condescension. He actualizes in a dynamic rather than a static way the rule of God drawing near. The cross is the crown of his life. The life of Jesus reveals the character of an act of God. Christ discloses himself to us in the gospel. The resurrection is the self-declaration of Christ. As he discloses himself to us, he discloses us to ourselves. He discloses to us our new being. Such knowledge is not just impartation of information. Such knowledge is the power to become free as followers of Christ. A Christian comes into being in Christ but is always in the process of becoming. Its character is light, liberation, resolution, knowledge, peace, humility, righteousness, fellowship, prayer, confession, faith, hope, love, and life. Resurrection brings people upward. The Christian, while like other people, participates in the elevation we find in the resurrection.

The power to affect the direction of which Barth writes here is that of the Holy Spirit. The common view, even among his friends, that Barth has a deficient pneumatology will have to deal with what he says here. We see again that the Spirit is the unifying force that brings separated persons together. While Barth has emphasized the reconciling-atoning act of the cross in the past, the Spirit mediates the presence of Christ to the believer. The power whose operation the New Testament presupposes is the outgoing, receiving, presence, and action of the Holy Spirit. The Spirit makes it possible that people are witnesses of Jesus Christ. The Spirit awakens others by this witness, so that they see themselves in Jesus Christ, and determine to think, speak, will, and act in a new and unique way. The Spirit creates the fellowship in which both the witness and those witnessed to become brothers and sisters in Jesus Christ. The Spirit opens the mouth to confess Christ. The Spirit directs the preaching of the church. The Spirit calls the church to action, gives it orders and commissions. The Spirit directs and controls their activities. The Spirit gives them the power to execute them. Living within the sphere of the truth of revelation we find in the New Testament, we need no uncertainty, disquietude, or anxiety concerning the existence and activity of the Spirit. The community is healthy in proportion as it gives free course to the Spirit. The Spirit is holy because He is no other than the presence and action of Jesus Christ, His stretched-out arm, the power of His resurrection, the power of His revelation as it begins there and continues its work from this point. We receive the Holy Spirit from the risen Christ, entering the presence, action, and lordship of the Spirit. In this part of Dogmatics, the concern is with the transition from Jesus Christ to other people, the fellowship between Christ and other people, and therefore the concern is with Christians. The holy power or Spirit is the holy because the Spirit is the Spirit of Jesus Christ. The Holy Spirit is the self-revelation of the man Jesus that occurs in the transition, communication, and union that occurs in the community that belongs to Christ. In the presence and action of the Holy Spirit we find the awakening, calling, and creation of the community and of Christians. Because of the outpouring of the Holy Spirit, the insignificant history of Christians is the central history, so much so that for its sake world history and time continue. The petty history of Christians is true world history. Of course, God is at work in this occurrence.

Barth has been discussing the history of the communication between Christ and Christians as the Holy Spirit being the power of this communication. Barth will offer a general and formal statement involving three decisive factors of this history. First, the man Jesus is the basic and controlling factor. Second is the factor of the goal of this history, which is the existence of the community and of Christians. Third is the factor of the transition that links the first two, the downward movement from Christ to Christendom. The focus now is the transition and therefore with God in the mode of being of the Holy Spirit. From this center, we will need to recognize the light of the Christian thought of God. We shall now see the light of the triune God shine in and over this history. The transition has a mysterious and miraculous character since it consists of the intervention of the Holy Spirit. The miracle and mystery of the Holy Spirit in our earthly history expresses what God is as mediator and as creator of fellowship with us. Thus, even as the Spirit mediates the fellowship between Father and Son, the Spirit mediates the fellowship between the Son and the community of Christians. Yet, this unifying work of the Spirit occurs in earthly history deals with the problem of distance and confrontation, of encounter and partnership. The solution to the problem of the relationship between God and humanity is the intervention, presence, and action of the Holy Spirit. Therefore, the problem itself is a spiritual one. Father and Son are with each other in love. God in triune mode of being reveals that God was always a Partner. The Father was the partner of the Son the Son was the Partner of the Father, with the Spirit animating this Partnership. The Spirit is transition in distance, mediation in confrontation, and communication in encounter. The Spirit bridges the gulf that opens before us between there and here, before and after, above and below. The Spirit is the pledge that God has already bridged the distance. The triune life of God is free life because it is Spirit. The basis of the will and action of this life is the living act that God directs toward us. This act is the basis of the decrees of God. This act is the basis of the election of humanity. This act is the basis of the Incarnation. This act is the basis of the final redemption of humanity to eternal life with God. This history occurs in the divine moment of the Spirit.

    Barth admits the riddle and paradox in which he writes of the Spirit. We can find the basis for answering the riddle and overcoming the paradox as we reflect upon the Holy Spirit.

    First, given that the Son has become lowly in Jesus Christ, and yet lives as the royal human being, we have the fulfillment of the covenant and therefore God as Reconciler, Mediator, Messiah of Israel, and Savior of the world. We have the revelation of God in this event. The Spirit of truth leads us as individuals and as the Christian community to this conversion, faith, and confession. The Spirit discloses the truth of divine revelation to us. The purpose of this revelation is to disclose the love in which God turned to the world and humanity in Christ. The Holy Spirit is the Spirit of Jesus Christ by virtue of the witness of the Son as Jesus of Nazareth declared in the resurrection of Jesus from the dead. The Spirit convinces of the truth of the love of God for the world in Jesus Christ.

Second, the exaltation of the lowly one is an answer to the riddle posed by the Holy Spirit. While the Son lived in solidarity with us to the point of the cross, he lived a superior life of a new humanity. The Lord became servant. The marvel of his words and acts were part of the path he walked as well. The community is the Easter community. As such, the community has a theology of the cross, to be sure. Yet, the resurrection is the divine yes under the no of crucifixion. Barth sees an element of truth in patripassianism of some in the history of the church in that the Father suffers in the humiliation of the Son with a depth humanity cannot fathom. The community is also a theology the resurrection and therefore a theology of glory. The glory of God shows itself as the resurrection lighting up the riddle of the existence of Jesus. Barth has been considering the power and lordship of the man Jesus in terms of the transition to our participation in the exaltation of Jesus. The Spirit is the power of this transition.

Barth concludes with considering the manner of the working of the Spirit in encountering us. How does the Spirit touch and move us? What do we mean when we say we receive, have, be in, and walk in the Spirit? The answer is that the Spirit is the given direction of the Son. Each of his three points comes with biblical discussion in the small print. First, the work of the Spirit is an indication in the fact that the Spirit fixes a definite place. The Spirit shows us where we always belong because we are already there. Second, the gentle, directing power of the Spirit involves warning and correction. Third, the positive element in the work of the Spirit is definite instruction.

The primary issue here has been the participation of humanity in its exaltation in Christ. He has been trying to explain the transition. This happens through the Holy Spirit. The Son becomes the origin, content, and norm of the divine direction given in the work of the Holy Spirit. I have suggested that many theologians think that Barth is deficient in his view of the work of the Spirit in this section. Thus, I have paid special attention to this aspect of his teaching. Of course, you as reader can be the judge. Some theologians may go too far in their criticism.

We now approach the part of this chapter that I think the reader would be wise to approach differently. Barth has discussed the second part of his Christology. The next two sections reveal how this part of Christology relates to this doctrine of salvation. He wants to apply this part of his Christology as it reveals to the malady and misery of humanity (here it is sloth) and the means this part of Christology that seeks to bring healing (sanctification). Again, we see the close link between Christology and soteriology.

Barth now discusses the way this part of the doctrine of reconciliation-atonement discloses yet another dimension of the human condition, that is, its sloth and misery (65). He has discussed the prideful condition of humanity (60) and will discuss the falsehood of humanity (70). The resurrection reveals that what God needs to overcome in humanity is the wrong use of freedom. Humanity became a self-enclosed being, subject to stupidity, inhumanity, dissipation, and anxiety. The result is death.

First, Barth discusses the sin of sloth in the light of the Lordship of the Son of Man. This section begins reflection on the alteration of humanity considering the doctrine he has just expounded. Sin determines the human situation. He refers us to his discussion in IV.1, 60.1 to say that we are so corrupt in our self-understanding that cannot know ourselves truly apart from the truth of revelation. We do not see our sin truly. Revelation of this truth and our response of faith are necessary for us to see the condemnation under which we live, and the pardon God extends to humanity in the cross. Humanity may well build up a view of its glory and goodness, but we only encounter our own shadow. We have engaged ourselves in a conversation. Left to ourselves, we will not see the destructive quality of sin, since sin destroys peace with God, neighbor, and self. Only our encounter with the grace of God in the Gospel will bring us to knowledge of our predicament before God and others. Genuine knowledge of sin rests on knowledge of God, revelation, and the human response of faith. The point in this volume has been to discuss the truth and significance of Jesus as King, as the royal human being, who reveals himself in his death and resurrection to live in full communion with God and living in conformity to the will of God. As our representative, Jesus Christ elevates humanity into covenant partnership with God. The directive of Ephesians 5:14, which is a call to humanity to awaken from sleep, arise from the dead, and Christ shall give light, is a call the Holy Spirit continues to give. God does not allow us to rest in our lowliness. Any security we feel below is a prison from which we need liberation. This liberation is the sanctification of humanity. Knowledge of Christ frees us to see our sin. We must see clearly in the predicament of humanity to appreciate this sanctification.

Barth thinks that the experience of shame confirms the shameful situation of humanity. In judging Jesus, humanity has failed to stand by his side. Humanity has failed in the sense that those around Jesus represent us all. The Son is the bearer of human mediocrity and triviality, the friend of publicans and sinners, the brother of the ordinary human being, to reconcile the world as it is to God. Humanity is like a prisoner, who, when someone opens the door, will not leave the cell, but wants to remain in it. As such, shame is an event in human life that reveals sloth. The Son has acted to lift humanity up as the beloved creature of God so that it can find itself. He will make the point that humanity cannot do this. It can only receive the gift. A Christian stands before the cross only in gratitude of the knowledge that Christ died for him or her, quite apart from personal merit. At this point, however, some thinkers would wonder whether Barth thinks believers participate in the battle with sloth (or any other sin) at all. His point will be that Christian knowledge of sin allows us to state four things regarding the human predicament. First, we oppose the work of the Son. Second, our opposition disqualifies us. Third, this disqualification applies to us. Fourth, the battle with nothingness is our shame. Yet, God battles nothingness even in our sin. His point is that we cannot engage in this battle apart from the Holy Spirit.

Second, Barth discusses the sloth of humanity. For those who think Barth does not deal with spiritual formation, I would invite a close reading of this passage. Sin shows itself to be sloth and misery as it resists the gentle influence of the Son working through the Spirit. We often think of sin in its Promethean pride. Here is sin in its triviality, evil inaction, loafing, and tardiness. It counters the direction of the Son in elevating humanity. Sloth is rejection of the outstretched hand of God, the refusal of divine grace, and rejection of individual calling. Its root is anxiety and mistrust. Humanity refuses to develop its relationship with God, with fellow human beings, the created order, and the proper use of the time one has. God has in mind this slothful person for exaltation, sanctification, and purification in Jesus Christ. This human being is the discontented person who, in the hopeless attempt to deny finitude, destroys peace with God, with fellow human beings, and does nothing but harm to oneself. God has in mind this human being who is slothful, refuses to act, and rejects the grace addressed to him or her, in the form of care. God knows this person, even though this person will not know himself or herself. God loves this person because of this fact.

Among the almost devotional reflections of Barth, he says that we fail to obey the call freedom. He will offer four areas in which we refuse the freedom God offers. 1) We refuse to be free in our relationship with God. We do so in our stupidity and folly. 2) We refuse freedom in relation to our fellow human beings. We remain in our isolation, seclusion, self-will, and unwillingness. We remain in our inhumanity. We want to be alone instead of being those we already are in this One. The terrible nature of inhumanity is this. Without ceasing to be human beings, human beings act as though they were animals or devils. Inhumanity is the denial of our humanity. Inhumanity can clothe itself in the necessary establishment and defense of institutions of law and order. It may equally take the form of their no less necessary criticism and overthrow. It can disguise itself as ceaseless activity, pure scholarship, pure art, promotion of common interests, family, and church. Our inhumanity endangers the bond that joins us to other human beings. Our inhumanity also endangers that which unites us with God. One cannot love God and hate other human beings. Inhumanity leads to a collapse of the structure and order of one's human nature as the soul of one's body, of the order in which one is oneself. Inhumanity extends to human life as characterized by its limited temporal duration. Our personal history is with others. What are we in our time? What is the meaning of our life? Why has God given us time to live and work? How shall we stand before the judgment of God? You were no help to me in my history, which interwove with mine. You ignored me. You had no time for me. You merely played with me. You appeared to help but harmed me instead. You led me astray. You confirmed me that from which you ought to have kept me. You kept me from that in which I needed confirmation. You would not yield to me. You pushed me to the wall. You humiliated and wounded me. You trampled over me. You blocked my path. You betrayed me. You took from me the dearest that I had. The encounter with you cost me my life. The answer is, yes, we shall have to render our accounts in relation to others. However, all of us have our own burden of accusation. Therefore, we are slothful sinners, not only in relation to God, but also in relation to our fellow humanity. 3) We refuse freedom with the created order. The vagabond in me causes me to refuse my responsibilities to others and to be a disruptive and harmful influence. Lack of discipline also works itself out in that our allotted duration of human life will become unendurable. We are not self-sufficient. We are anxious and fearful. We fight against the idea that everyone has an allotted time. When we affirm, "seize the day," we express the panic in which we live and the closed door we experience. Fourth, we refuse our freedom in the historical limitations of humanity.

Barth will then reflect upon death. As the Crucified, He lives at the very point where we reach our frontier, and our time runs out. He is the Victor there. He calls us to look and move forward confidentially and courageously. He gives us the freedom to rejoice as we arrive at our end and limit, for Christ is there. He lives there the life that as eternal life includes our own. He is our hope. He bids and makes us hope. We would rather things were different. We try to arrest the foot that brings us constantly nearer to this frontier. Because we know that we cannot change things, that we cannot cease to move remorselessly towards this place, we look frantically around for assurances on this side of the moment when they will all be stripped away, anxiously busying ourselves to snatch at life before we die. This is a form of our sloth. We must begin by asserting that this approach is also futile because our destiny is inexorable. We make no use of the freedom that God grants us. We see only nothingness awaiting us, so care fills us. We are prisoners of the ceaseless movements of care that we must make. The distinctive feature of this care is that it derives its power from its opponent. It has all the power of the end, of death without God and without hope. This illusionary opponent is the force that inexplicably rules in human care and affects the life of humanity. Of course, we conceal this form of care, in either excessive activity or excessive passivity. This form of care plays a special role in the formation of human ignorance of God, and the unwillingness to honor and love God as God. This form of care also destroys human fellowship. Such care leads to the disorder that we have called the disintegration of the disciplined unity of humanity as the soul of this body.

Third, Barth then discusses the misery of humanity. He will make three assertions that disclose the truth of the exilic nature of the human predicament. First, such sloth led to death. His concern is for the direction of the Son that sanctifies human beings. Misery is a mortal sickness. If we had to bear it alone, if Jesus had not carried it in our place, it could end only with our death and destruction. Human misery is an exile. If we take misery in the customary sense, the dreadful feature of this hurrying and plunging to death is that at every point humanity exists in a radical perversion. Even in this misery, human beings are whole people. Second, human action will always be the act of sloth and misery. Human misery consists in the corruption of this best. Third, we confront human misery as bondage of the will. The New Testament calls this misery human life in the flesh.

Barth is now ready to discuss how God deals with sin as it shows itself in the sloth and misery of humanity as he deals with the sanctification of humanity (66). He has dealt with justification (61) and will deal with vocation (71) in the same light. In the preface by the editors, they comment that this transitional discussion is the most complicated and elusive in the volume, wrestling as it does with the mystery and miracle of the Holy Spirit. God has already achieved the exaltation of human beings in the death and resurrection of Jesus Christ. The exaltation of human beings is the creation of their new form of existence as the faithful covenant-partner of God. Such action rests on their justification before God and their sanctification in Christ. Sanctification attests itself by the divine direction in the lives of people.

John Wesley will offer a quite different possibility in his account of sanctification. He will affirm that Christian perfection is love of God and neighbor that implies deliverance from all sin. One receives it by faith. God gives it in a moment. We are to expect it every moment. Christian perfection is loving God with all our heart, mind, soul, and strength. This implies that the disposition of the soul is toward love. Thus, pure love governs thought, word, and action. Yet, such perfection can exist with general human weakness, ignorance, and mistakes.[39] He will need to clarify his thinking along these lines often. Human life is such that our knowledge will always be imperfect. Thus, we will make mistakes. We will participate in the general bodily weakness of the human condition. We will exhibit weakness of understanding, slowness of mind, confusion, slowness to apprehend, incoherency of thought, and lack of imagination. We will vary in our ability to remember what we have experienced or read. Our facility with language may be slow. We may have improper language or impoliteness in behavior. Further, we are liable to temptation.[40] He could say that the sum of Christian perfection is that one word, love. The first branch of it is the love of God and the other is the love of others in a way that the two are inseparable. We find the whole of Christian perfection summed up in these statements. Further, when Paul writes of the fruit of the Spirit as being love, joy, peace, longsuffering, gentleness, goodness, fidelity, meekness, and temperance, when we see these graces knit together in a mature Christian we can think of Christian perfection.[41] In these views, Wesley is far closer to the Roman Catholic and Orthodox mystical traditions than he is to the Reformed tradition out of which Barth writes.

First, Barth discusses justification and sanctification. 1) We are dealing with the one act of salvation, which from the one side is justification and the other side is sanctification. 2) Justification is the transcendent pardon of humanity, while sanctification is the immanent participation of humanity in divine life. 3) These two doctrines belong together. 4) He rejects the notion of an order of salvation in the temporal sense. He bases his reflections on John Calvin, *Institutes,* Book III. The presupposition of our participation in Christ is that God has accomplished the sanctification of humanity in Jesus Christ in a way that is effective and authoritative for all. In their sanctification, Christ attests that He is the Lord of all.

Second, Barth discusses the holy One and the saints. Awakening to faith is the work of salvation. God begins fashioning people to represent God in the world. Therefore, they have the freedom to render obedience and establish themselves as the saints of God. Yet, we are not long on this way. Our sanctification is participation with the Holy One, and the Spirit mediates this participation. Saints have a direction. We approach here the weakness of Calvin's doctrine of the participation in Christ. He finds no place for a recognition of the universal relevance of the existence of the man, Jesus, of the sanctification of all people as God has achieved it in

---

[39] John Wesley, A Plain Account of Christian Perfection.
[40] John Wesley, Sermon 40, Christian Perfection.
[41] John Wesley, Sermon 76, On Perfection.

Him. Calvin referred only to those foreordained to salvation, reconciliation, justification, and sanctification in Jesus Christ. Therefore, His existence has no positive significance for those excluded from this election and are thus reprobate. The consequence is that when Calvin describes the work of the Holy Spirit, in which Christ illuminates and calls people to faith, he restricts it to the circle of the elect. This involves a serious distortion of the biblical message and involves Calvin in an inhuman teaching. It dissolves the strict correlation between the glory of God and the salvation of humanity. It grounds election in an inscrutable and immovable decision instead of seeking election in Jesus Christ. It makes the elect an end in themselves, and thus pointless and unprofitable, since the realization of their election serves no positive function in relation to the rest of creation. It makes the elect have limited confidence in the love of God, which becomes arbitrarily and limited and inscrutably set. How can we better understand this participation of the saints living under the gentle influence of the Son? Modestly stated, they are disturbed sinners, awakened to the opposition of the world to the grace of God. The Spirit has awakened them, but their course is slow, lame, and halting. They have begun a movement to the being of their Lord. Beyond this, we can say that God has called them. Of course, sanctification is not the redemption and glorification that shall come. Finally, we can say that God has liberated them. The capacity for the freedom of the children of God is sanctification. Such freedom is provisional. They are still captive and prisoner, but freedom is ahead of them through participation in the Holy One.

Third, Barth discusses the call to discipleship. Such people received the call of discipleship and awakened to conversion. "Follow me" is the substance of the call in the power of which Jesus makes people saints. Looking to Jesus is a vision that stimulates those who receive it to a definite action. The call issued by Jesus is a call to discipleship. The best work on this topic is *Cost of Discipleship,* by Dietrich Bonhoeffer. 1) The call to discipleship is a summons that discloses who Jesus is. 2) It binds the person to Jesus. 3) The first step is faith in the form of a new beginning and self-denial. 4) It makes a break with the sighs of the world that derive from its oppression to the powers of this world. In all of this, Christians must not think of themselves as warriors against the world, and especially as doing battle with non-Christians. The liberation of humanity has already taken place in Christ. The decisive conflict is within oneself. Christians may well have to accept suffering at the hands of others. Christians are not to add to the sufferings of others, but to fight against such suffering. The task of the church may well offend others. Yet, the task is a friendly and happy one. Our purpose as the church is to liberate these others as well.

Fourth, Barth discusses awakening to conversion. We should note the non-systematic character of this entire discussion. The exaltation of humanity can take place in people on earth, in their time and place. Conversion is awakening, which suggests that humanity is asleep. Sadly, Christianity can sleep as well. The awakening is a creaturely and a divine action. Yet, the initial shock comes from God. It remains a mystery and a miracle. The Christian community depends on this experience in that God gives it and actualizes it. This movement means renewal. 1) Since the movement involves the whole person, it affects relation to God and humanity. 2) It involves inward disposition and action as a totality. 3) Such conversion is personal but not selfish, leading to accepting public responsibility as well. 4) Such conversion extends over the course of each human life. Understanding conversion in this way leads Barth to summarize that conversion is an event, an act, and a history. Since conversion is the work of the Holy Spirit that leads us to Christ and away from self, we must not puzzle too much beyond this when we consider the basis and origin of conversion.

Fifth, he discusses the praise of works. Christians offer the praise or affirmation of God in their works. We are Christians for a purpose. One offers good works in a provisional offering of gratitude and thanks for which the act of the love of God ordains the destiny of humanity. The praise of works is the acts and fruits that derive from human activity. Without good works, reconciliation-atonement would be futile. Sanctification is participation in the excellent work of the gift of grace in Jesus Christ, and therefore, offers good works in the world.

Sixth, he discusses the dignity of the cross. They receive the mark of the cross. The bearing of the cross was and is for Jesus Christ His coronation as the one Son of Man, as the royal human being. In the same way, for the Christian, the cross that one must suffer is one's investiture with the distinction, glory, and dignity proper to one as a Christian. Sanctification is participation in the grace shown in Christ, and this means especially uniting with Christ in the cross. Their sanctification involves something greater themselves. Yet, this "something greater" is not empty or faceless, but rather, is the person of Christ. Without moralizing, Barth offers a few words concerning the bearing of the cross for our sanctification. The cross should lead us to humility. It should lead us to accept any punishment that may come from bearing the cross. The cross disciplines our faith, obedience, and love. In the New Testament, the cross is the result of persecution. We may suffer such persecution, but we should not seek it. The cross is provisional, for we await the joy of the time when God will wipe away our tears. Christian hope also participates in the joy that comes after the cross.

We now see the Trinitarian emphasis of Barth appear as the Holy

Spirit applies the healing work of sanctification to the community and to individual believers. He is offering his spiritual counsel to the church and to individuals. However, throughout this volume, I have pointed to the way Barth weaves the work of the Holy Spirit into his Christology and therefore into his view of the sanctification of humanity. He has anticipated the focus of the last sections on the work of the Spirit.

Barth is now ready to discuss the cooperation of the Holy Spirit in the work of the Son as one who brings reconciliation-atonement in the upbuilding of the Christian community in love (67), even as he has discussed the gathering of the community in faith (62) and will discuss the sending of the community in hope (72). The Holy Spirit is the power that quickens Christians in the world to be the body of Christ. The Spirit causes the community to grow, sustaining and ordering it as the communion of the saints of Christ. This reality makes it a provisional representation of the sanctification of humanity. Human life has taken place in the Son.

First, Barth discusses the true church. The Spirit actualizes the sanctification of humanity through building up the community in love. The church is an earthly and historical human construct, of course. However, the church arises out of the work of the work of the Holy Spirit. The Holy Spirit is the power by which Christ makes the community a provisional representation of the sanctification that has already taken place in Christ. God in Christ is the builder of the church. The goal toward which the true church proceeds is the revelation of the sanctification of all humanity as it has already taken place in Christ. Christ is the powerful archetype of the cancellation of the sins of humanity and therefore of the justification of humanity. Now, we see Christ is the powerful archetype of the elevation of all humanity in its sanctification. Its provisional quality means it is fragmentary, incomplete, insecure, and questionable, but also that the divine work within it is true, effective, genuine, and invincible. The meaning and content of this time God has given the church is the fulfillment of the task of the sanctification of humanity. The true church is necessary in a saving way for the elevation of humanity that has already taken place in Christ to become a reality. This elevation of humanity must not remain far behind or high above us. This elevation of humanity must be an actual redemptive happening that continues to take place. If we do not take the true church seriously, we do not take the saving work of God seriously. If we hold ourselves aloof from the church, we also distance ourselves from our Savior and Lord. The focus of this part of *Church Dogmatics* is the upbuilding of the community, reminding us that the focus needs to be away from self. Our concern is for the edification of the community rather than self. Upbuilding suggests ongoing construction. God is the builder. The upbuilding of the community is an aspect of human sanctification. This upbuilding occurs by

God as we know God through the man Jesus and in the power of the Spirit. If we speak of Christ, we also speak of the community, which is the Body of Christ. The community is active in the upbuilding involved in sanctification. It needs correction and improvement in accord with apostolic instruction. Building up means integration. The community is a fellowship that respects the freedom of its individual members. Integration and mutual adaptation are essential for the sanctifying work of the church to reach its goal. This integration is the work of the Spirit. At the center of this building up of the community is its worship. From this center, the community touches the daily lives of its members.

Second, Barth discusses the growth of the community. As the creed puts it, the church is the communion of saints. The community takes place as a confessional and theological fellowship. The community has a fellowship of thanksgiving, penitence, prayer, bearing the burdens of the world, service, hope, proclamation, and worship. The building up of the community takes place as growth, engaging in its expansion. It enlarges its numbers in the world. Barth offers a few helpful reflections on the church that I think have some relevance for the church today. Barth notes that in seeking addition, the church will not forget what a great and rare matter it is when people come to faith. The church will have to resist the temptation to win more members by diluting the wine with a little water. The church becomes disturbed and saddened, but not horrified, when it discovers that increasing the number of Christians is not easy, that it does not go forward indefinitely, and that a clearly defined limits seems set to it. The church is only a provisional representation of the new humanity at the heart of the old humanity. Thus, it will never give to its present historical form the totality of humanity. It will not equate its present form with the end, which comes to it afresh from God. Yet, its true growth is intensive in its height and depth, giving the basis for its growth. Growth is a mark of life. God is not a prisoner to height or to the distance between the event of revelation and our time. Rather, the work of the Spirit breaks these boundaries so that the Spirit awakens us. The content of the work of the Spirit is Jesus. The kingdom was present already in the work of Jesus and by him is at work in the church. Therefore, Barth could say that in virtue of the mighty work of the Holy Spirit, in the form of the community that prays for its coming, the kingdom is really on earth and in time and history, though the community as such is not the kingdom of God. Yet, neither in relation to the church nor in relation to Christ does Barth stress self-distinction from God as a condition of the presence of the kingdom.[42] Thus, in terms of Trinitarian relations, the Spirit mediates the presence of the risen Christ.

---

[42] Pannenberg, *Systematic Theology* Volume 3, 37.

Third, Barth discusses the upholding of the community. He sees this as the gracious preservation of the community. The communion of saints needs defense, protection, and preservation because it is in danger.

Barth will consider first the danger that threatens from without. We ought not to assume that the world accepts the existence of this little fragment of the world, for it claims both a different origin and a different goal. A living community will always have to reckon with the fact that it must be in some form a community under trial and even under the cross. The first form in which this may happen consists in the fact that it comes under pressure from the world around that seeks to either do away with it or at least reduce it to a more innocuous form. A second form is that the world does not allow itself to take seriously the disturbance caused by the existence of the community. It quietly accepts it. It uses the most terrible weapon of intolerance, which is toleration. It meets it with sheer indifference. The world may well regard it as the wiser course to leave Christianity alone, to go its own way as if the church did not exist, opposing to it the brute fact of its own secular spirit and methods, of its own sure and secular techniques and economics and politics and art and science and way of life.

Barth now wants to consider the danger that threatens from within, a matter of the effective action that corresponds to its nature. Here, too, we shall have to speak of two forms of the danger. In both forms, it arises out of the fact that the community in its human activity is a part of the world. The world is not just around it but also within it. The saints are wicked rascals. They are very ready to follow those outside. Indeed, they sometimes set those outside a bad example. The enticement that threatens the community is always the same. Stimulated from without and welcomed from within, it may feel suddenly or gradually that the requirement of following the will of God is too hard. It relaxes a little of its friendlessness in the world, the incongruity of its existence as compared with that of other human societies. It takes the tension out of the relationship of trying to find a suitable form in which to be a worldly community as well as a Christian.

One form of the danger from within, a form of decay, is that of alienation or secularization. Instead of, or side by side with, the voice of the Good Shepherd, it hears the voice of a stranger to whom it does not belong, but to whom it comes to belongs. This danger from within argues for mediation, of bridging the gap between those outside and those inside, of works of sincerity on the one side and serious and necessary attempts to win the world for Christ on the other. It might focus on the translation of the Christian into the secular at the command of love. It might speak of translation of the secular into the Christian, a baptism of non-Christian ideas, customs, and enterprises by new Christian interpretations and giving them new Christian content, amounting to minting of Christian gold on behalf of poor non-Christians. When the church has respect for the fashion, theme, and glory of the world, it starts down the road of secularization. When the church no longer fears that that it does not rely solely upon Jesus Christ and the free grace of God, it starts down the road of secularization. Secularization is the process by which the salt loses its savor. When the church becomes secular, both church and world have the greatest possible misfortune. This misfortune occurs when the church wants to be a church only for the world, the nation, the culture, or the state. It wants to be a world church, a national church, a cultural church, or a state church. It then loses its specific importance, meaning and the justification for its existence.

The second form of the danger from within, a form of the decay of the church is that of self-glorification or sacralization. The church asserts itself because it has a highly developed consciousness of itself. The terrible thing is that by trying to be right, it can set itself in the worst possible wrong. Although Christ is the community, one cannot reverse this important statement. The community is not Christ or the kingdom of God. Sacralization means the transmutation of the lordship of Jesus Christ into the vanity of a Christianity that vaunts itself in His name, but finds itself, its traditions, its confessions, and its institutions enamoring. Sacralization means the suppression of the Gospel by a false sacred law. Sacralization means the setting up of an idol that is dead like all other images of human fabrication. Such an idol cannot hear, speak, illuminate, help, or heal. Those who create the idol end up worshipping only themselves. Ephesians 6:10-20 reminds of this battle.

Fourth, Barth will discuss the order of the community. The upbuilding of the community needs order as well. Barth will value church law, first, as it has the character of service to the church. Second, it offers liturgy for worship. The promise is that those gathered will receive food and drink. They will eat and drink as brothers and sisters at the table at which Christ presides. We eat and drink from the one cup and one loaf. Christ nourishes us. We repeat the events of his life in the event of the Supper. We gather to pray for and with each other. Church law will guide our practice of confession, baptism, and the Lord's Supper. Third, church law is willing to adjust to new situations. Church law is willing and ready for new answers. Fourth, church must be exemplary law. It has responsibility to be such internally with its members and outwardly in the world. It has a concern for its witness in the world. However, one needs to hear the voice of Christ in that order.

Barth concludes his discussion of reconciliation-atonement with the cooperation of the Holy Spirit in building Christian love (68), even as he discussed the individual coming to faith and justification (63) and will discuss their hope and calling (73). The Holy Spirit quickens individuals to give them freedom to correspond to the love in which God has drawn them to Christ and raised them up to overcoming sloth and misery. John Wesley would say of Christian perfection that it is nothing more nor less than loving God with the whole heart and loving the neighbor as oneself. His concern was to define what he meant by "entire sanctification" and "Christian perfection." Regardless of our terminology, Barth and Wesley are one in defining the sanctifying work of the Holy Spirit as one of love.

First, Barth discusses the problem of Christian love. In this discussion, Barth values the work of Anders Nygren, *Eros and Agape.* Of course, the center of the Christian life is what God has done in Christ. He defines self-giving as the act of love, which contrasts with faith as reception. Christian love is a movement away from self and toward one genuinely different from oneself. Such love is a movement for the sake of the other. One acts with such love freely. A false form of love in our experience is that we love the object for how it can nourish and sustain us. The movement of this love forms a circle. It seeks the infinite in a transcendence of everything finite but must always return to its beginning. It may direct itself toward the true, good, and beautiful. It may direct itself toward the Trinity. Yet, such love is always possessive and betrays itself as such. In contrast, Christian or agape love has respect for the fellow-humanity and togetherness natural to us as individuals.

Second, he discusses the basis of love. God is love, of course. This love elects, purifies, and is creative. God is also Spirit, and the Spirit of the Father and the Son bears witness to our spirit that we are children of God. Thus, the Spirit brings about participation in the love that binds Father, Son, and Spirit. Our love reflects the love of the Trinity.

Third, he discusses the act of love. As the Christian has faith and hopes, the Christian loves. The presence of the Holy Spirit brings freedom. We can discuss the matter of equating love of God with love neighbor, based on Mark 12:29-31. Barth, in *Romans,* stated that the invisible divine Thou meets us concretely in the neighbor, so that the elation to the neighbor decides whether we love God or not (p. 259). Barth offered a self-critical review of this position, where he had too carelessly followed the view of Ritschl and Kant. Equating love of God and love of neighbor can easily lead to a moralistic interpretation of Christianity. The relation to God can fade out as a distinct theme and be lost in co-humanity. In opposition, Barth rightly recalled that the New Testament also speaks of the love of God of that of believers for God and Jesus. We might justly ponder whether Jesus would not come close to equating love of God and faith in the imminent rule of God. Barth gives good reasons for not making the equation, but he could be more convincing had he shown that love for God is more than the act of faith.[43] The one who loves God cannot be solitary. One loves God as a response to the witness of a community and the love for God one has will bring one back to the community. To love God is to place oneself in the service of love to others. Such love is an expression of the witness of the individual within the community and within the world. The Holy Spirit gives one the freedom to give such love.

Fourth, in a discussion of the manner of love, he offers his exposition of I Corinthians 13, in that love alone determines human life in the Christian community (verses 1-3), love alone allows the community to live victoriously (verses 4-7), and love alone is the promise of the community (verses 8-13).

---

[43] (Pannenberg, Systematic Theology 1998, 1991), Volume 3, 188-9.

CHAPTER XVI

Jesus Christ, the True Witness

Chapter XVI, Volume 4.3, section 69-73, discusses Jesus Christ, the true witness, published in 1959, when Barth is 73 years old. The editors of the volume note that the theme is Christ as the true witness. Therefore, the atonement is not merely true, but an active truth shining and revealing itself in the darkness of the world and overcoming it. Reconciliation-Atonement moves out and communicates itself, becoming the creative source of a reconciled community and a reconciled world. It becomes the light of life, engaged in triumphant self-demonstration in the enlightening and quickening power of the Holy Spirit. As the true witness, Jesus reveals the sin of humanity as falsehood and establishes the vocation of humanity. This will carry with it the sending of the Christian community and individuals in hope.

Barth begins the third aspect of his Christology with a consideration of the glory of the mediator (69). Barth has focused on Christ as fully deity in IV.1 (59) and in full humanity in IV.2 (64) and now he focuses on the God-Man. Christ mediates between a loving God and a lost humanity. One can get the idea in the previous volumes that the risen Christ simply brings home the past work of Christ in the cross, bringing actual "knowledge" of that work, and not just information about it. Although he will have a discussion of the Holy Spirit, some would note the relative lack of weight offered to that discussion. In some ways, Barth is doing little more than reinforcing his idea that salvation is a finished act in

Christ. In that sense, he adds little to his previous discussions.[44]

First, he considers the third problem of the doctrine of reconciliation. He will take up again the theme of religion that he explored in I.2, under Part III (17), the outpouring of the Holy Spirit. One needs to read both to get a full view of religion as Barth viewed it. He had enough intellectual openness that he could always reformulate a similar theme. The theme here is that Jesus Christ as attested in Scripture is the one Word of God whom we must hear, trust, and obey in life and in death. The third problem of the doctrine of reconciliation is that as reconciliation takes place, it also declares itself in witness. Reconciliation is the active and superior Yes to humanity. God does not permit humanity to offer a final No, for it would mean a final contradiction and opposition. God the Reconciler is at work. Reconciliation is the history in which God concludes and confirms the covenant with humanity. The act of reconciliation in the cross is the intrinsically perfect and unsurpassable divine action. When he says that revelation takes place in reconciliation, he is contemporizing the consequences of the resurrection. God carries the covenant to its final goal despite every threat. God takes the disobedience creature within the fellowship of the Trinity. He has shown this in the way Christ is fully deity in condescending to humanity and fully human in exalting humanity. Christ represents humanity in its fullest extent, ensuring that humanity will reach its divinely appointed goal. Reconciliation is Emmanuel, God with us. This means that salvation is reconciliation. He also raises the problem of the relation between the divine act of reconciliation and the human appropriation of that act. In this section, we shall deal with Jesus as the chief prophet and teacher of the church. One might describe the anticipation of the future of God in the work of the earthly and the exalted Christ as the prophecy of Jesus Christ, so long as we consider the distinctiveness of the eschatological proclamation of Jesus as compared with all preceding prophecy. The sole content of this prophecy is the imminence of God.[45] Barth will focus on the prophetic office of Christ as occurring in the context of the history of Israel. Christ is the Word of life and therefore the light of life.

Second, Jesus is the light of life. We take as our starting point the fact that in the life of Jesus Christ we deal with the presence and action of God. A mute and obscure God would be an idol. The true and living God is eloquent and radiant. To choose another aspect, we now take as our starting point the fact that the life of Jesus Christ is that of the covenant grace willed and determined by God, addressed and given by God to the

---

[44] (Cambridge Companion to Karl Barth 2000), Colin Gunton, 151.
[45] (Pannenberg, Systematic Theology 1998, 1991), Volume 2, 449.

person for whom and to whom it is active. As the life of grace, it is this eloquent and radiant life. Nature and grace unify in that Christ lives. Christ becomes a history of God with humanity. As the order of reconciliation, it is also the confirmation and restoration of creation. In the life of the Savior, we also have the life of the faithful Creator. Grace would not be grace if it were to remain mute and obscure or could try to be in and for itself alone. To select a third starting point, the life of Jesus Christ, even as the life of God and the life of divine grace, is the life of a human being who as one of us, has lived, lives, and will live this eternal life. He is the Stranger whom we cannot overlook or remove because He is at home among us, like us, and with us, belonging as we do to our human situation and history. The life of Jesus Christ shines in these specific contours. It is near us in these contours. One cannot confuse it with any other life. It encounters us, speaks with us, addresses us in terms of I and Thou, and all in such a way that one can have no doubt concerning either the fact that its speaks or the content of what it says, nor any suspicion that we might speak only to ourselves. For as the Bearer, Bringer, and Herald, of the life of God and divine grace, of eternal life, there comes to us Another to speak to us spontaneously and unexpectedly, without any request or requirement on our part. In all of this, Barth admits that Anselm informs his answer. The point of his argument is that he believes in order to understand. From a polemical perspective, only the fool says there is no God. The prophecy of the life of Jesus is valid because it is a declaration of the life of Jesus. He admits that he is begging the question and that he argues in a vicious circle.

    Barth is now going to explore the question of the presence of truth in other religions and the question of the salvation of non-Christians. Barth will have confidence in the victorious reconciliation achieved by Christ in such a way that that he also has confidence in the possibility of the salvation of persons who do not yet know or acknowledge Christ. In terms of truth, he will acknowledge that Christ is the truth. The Bible, the church, other religions, and words outside the church testify to the truth. One is not to dismiss them. One can thus conclude that interreligious dialogue for Christians is one of engaging people who will have truth, the testable reference being Christ and Scripture.[46] We need to have some care here. Barth is not admitting to a form of natural theology, for if anyone has any truth, it is materially consistent with the Word of God in all its forms. Given his affirmation of the precedence of the Word of God, we can appreciate the point Barth makes. However, Barth seems so fearful of natural theology that the notion of the prevenient grace of God operative

---

[46] (Cambridge Companion to Karl Barth 2000), *J. A. Di Noia,* "Religion and the religions," 254-5.

upon all persons, the summons the Spirit gives to all persons that invites them toward truth, goodness, and beauty, does not seem open to him.

Why should we follow only one Prophet? Why should we not give at least a little honor to our own prophecy alongside and in opposition to His? One might accept easily that He is a great prophet. The modern Synagogue could accept it. The Koran states it. Western Idealism could accept it. With this message, we need not expose or compromise ourselves, or provoke suspicion or unpopularity, or give offense to anyone, least of all ourselves. However, what will happen if we are not content with this? What will happen if the explicit or implicit meaning of Jesus Christ is that He has the words of eternal life? The objection will always be that such a statement involves an unjustifiable act of caprice. What right do we have to go before our fellows with a claim of this nature? What authority do we have to set ourselves above all others who think they know otherwise? From what exalted place do we think we can violate them with this kind of demand? Further, we feel uncomfortable, secretly making the same reproach against ourselves, feeling its force and effects, and wishing that we could evade the necessity of making the statement. The point of the reproach is obvious. Intellectually and aesthetically, we are obscurantist. Morally, we are arrogant. Politically, it shows intolerance and disrupts the co-existence of humanity with differing outlooks and confessions. However, we have no option in this matter. Christian freedom is the freedom of the confession of Jesus Christ as the one and only Prophet, light of life, and Word of God. It stands or falls by whether it is freedom for this confession. If we are going to represent and champion it, we must do so with a clear conscience. We do not want to make absolute our own Christian subjectivity, or that of the Church, and its tradition. In any case, this entire line of reproach rests upon a misunderstanding. The statement that Jesus Christ is the one Word of God has nothing whatever to do with the arbitrary exaltation and self-glorification of the Christian in relation to other people, of the Church in relation to other institutions, or of Christianity in relation to other conceptions. The statement is Christological. It looks away from non-Christian and Christian alike to the One who confronts and precedes both as *the* Prophet. It says first that in relationship to His own community and all its members Jesus Christ is the One to whom it must in no circumstances oppose with any degree of sovereignty its own Christian prophecy, teaching, and testimony to the truth. One cannot legitimately advance and state this except as the people who live in this sphere submit themselves first to the gelatinization and criticism that come through Jesus Christ as the one light of life. The church cannot cease attesting it to all. The point Barth makes is a simple one. Jesus Christ is the one and only Word of God. He alone is the light of God and the revelation of God. It delimits all other words, lights, revelations, prophecies, and apostolates, whether of the Bible, the church, or the world, by what we find declared in the existence of Jesus Christ. He is the total and complete declaration of God concerning who God is, as well as the people whom God addresses in the Word of God. The living Lord engages the world as the one Word of God in a continual completion of divinity. What we have here is the irresistible and relentless outworking of the second commandment, "Thou shalt have no other gods but me," as in Exodus 20:3. What this Word tells us is that we are those whom God justifies and sanctifies in this life. God has taken our place. God set us in His place. In this life, the kingdom of God has come to us, displacing our old life, our new and eternal life beginning. God has accomplished our deliverance, conversion and even glorification. We are already dead and risen again; we are already citizens of the future world. The future world is the new and true world God revealed as the dominion of God and Christ. We are those who God eternally loved and elected in Jesus Christ and called to the grateful realization of their election in time, each in his or her own time. If it were a matter of the word of Christianity among the world religions, or the word of the Christian Church in one or other form, or the words of the Bible in themselves and as such, a view of this kind might be possible. As such, one may arrange all these with many other words. However, we are speaking of the light or Word of the life of Jesus Christ. Barth agrees that true words are outside the church. He refers to them as secular parables and even parables of the kingdom. Christians do not hear truth simply from the lips of other Christians, from the Bible, or from the Christian tradition. In fact, Christians should be grateful in receiving such parables regardless of the source. Yet, we discern them due to their agreement with the witness of Scripture and to the fruits of that word in the world. Christianity must avoid pride and sloth when confronted with them. It must be ready to hear them. We must also be aware of the possibility of deceiving ourselves. A point the "modern church" needs to hear is that if we attempt to canonize a free communication of its Lord it would become a different church from that of yesterday that did not yet have it and therefore did not know this new canon. Reduced to its simplest formula, what we have said is that Jesus Christ was, is, and will be the light of life, and because the light of life, of His own reconciling life, therefore and to that extent the one light incomparable in its majesty and authority. Creation is such a light, even if a broken light. It speaks of the theater of the glory of God, and therefore of the creaturely world as the setting or background, the sphere or location, of the event and revelation of reconciliation as the triumph of divine glory. It draws attention to the lights, words, or truths that also and already shine in the creation of God as such, to the indications of the constant factors in cosmic being and occurrence as chosen, willed, established, and overruled by God. The critical distinction that one must make in the relationship between the self-declaration of God in the prophecy of Jesus Christ and the self-attestations of the creature does not result in the exclusion of the latter, seeing they derive their force from the same God.

Third, Barth will consider Jesus as Victor. Jesus Christ is priest and king, but also the prophet, herald, and proclaimer of this accomplishment, working and acting as such. The prophetic war against evil occurs by revelation of the salvation achieved through the atonement. This prophetic war occurs in a hostile environment. He has opposition. His prophetic service consists in the overcoming of this opposition and answering of this challenge. Death constantly confronts His life, unfaithfulness and apostasy confronts the covenant, and strife confronts reconciliation. This opposition also confronts the prophetic office and work, ministry and action. Contradiction confronts His Word; falsehood confronts His truth. His Word and truth expose, resists, and overcomes contradiction and falsehood. Jesus Christ is the prophet who knows and proclaims the will of God that He does in His existence. Barth is quite insightful here, as the Bible links the demonic with the lie quite often. He relates the telling of truth to the overcoming of evil! The statement of the Synoptic Gospels that the rule of God is at hand, materially identical with the "I am" statements in the Gospel of John, is the sum and substance of His prophetic message and therefore of the knowledge He mediates. Christian knowledge is history in the fact that the victorious outcome of this conflict, and therefore the fulfillment of Christian knowledge, God has decided from the outset in Jesus Christ as Victor. The real presence of reconciliation in the living Lord Jesus is the theme, basis, and content of Christian knowledge. Such knowledge is not just information but transforming. The transformation of Saul to the apostle Paul is an example of such transforming knowledge. Christ initiates and enacts history in Christian knowledge. Jesus Christ is warrior, and as such, He is victor. I must note again, however, that as powerful as all this is, while John often portrays the Spirit in the role of mediating this knowledge, Barth is silent about this.

We must now give a brief account of the course of the history of the prophecy of Jesus Christ. Its course is a history of conflict. As the hymn suggests, "Till Thy love conquers, there can be no peace." This love and its light are not lacking. In this love is peace, and in this light is grace. It shines in the darkness, and its history is one of conflict against darkness. Darkness is the sum of all discord. Hence, no peace can exist between it and the love of the Father and the Son. The light of this love can only fight, repel, and destroy it. In relation to it, Jesus and His Word bring a sword on earth, as in Matthew 10:34. We could not speak even of the beginning of His prophecy without incidentally considering its continuation in opposition and strife. To understand it, we must avoid an error to which we are in continual danger of falling victim in an anxious concern for the relationship of Christianity and the church to the world around. This conflict is a matter of the attack on darkness. Only secondarily, and under the law imposed by the attacker, is it a matter of the defense of darkness against light. Barth will consider the attack of grace on the world, for such light shines in the darkness. Humanity will keep trying to sanctify and free itself, but God has already done this in Christ. The attack tells us of a new humanity. The future has begun with the fact that God has fulfilled the covenant with humanity, that God has loved the world and reconciled it with God, that God has introduced the justified and sanctified human being as the second Adam, who was before the first. Humanity is now free to set out from the fact that this its relation to God, fellow human beings, and the individual, God has ordered for the best. Human beings are free to let themselves go, and thus to not take themselves in their own hands again. They are free no longer to be the servant they were, to be what they were not, namely, a child that has life before it. They are free to be themselves in the hand of God. In connection with the order in which humanity is not free to be humbled, humanity is also free to rejoice. Humanity is free to become serious, thankful, and obedient. It is free to think, speak, and act responsibly. It is free to believe, love, and hope, to serve God and humanity. It is free to rejoice. Humanity is now free to engage with others, to live in contact, solidarity, and fellowship not only with God, but also with the world reconciled to Christ, and therefore with fellow human beings as companions in the partnership of reconciliation, as brothers and sisters in the fulfilled covenant of God. This grace also attacks the "something" within humanity that resists and rebels against what God has done.

    Barth will focus, once again, on the danger of developing a worldview. The opposing element in humanity grasps at the possibility of a worldview. We might list many such worldviews, such as magical, naturalistic, idealistic, skeptical, historical, and political, aesthetic, and moral. We might think also of religious worldviews, and at decisive points all the others contain open or concealed religious elements. Establishing worldviews is a way for human beings to set themselves against the truth. It reaffirms the pride that is the essence of this resistance to grace. Common to all of them are the following characteristics. 1) Human beings grasp at the possibility of viewing the world from a certain distance. The Word of grace removes the distance. 2) Human beings grasp the intelligible world of nature and history, of multiplicity and unity of their phenomena, of the laws perceptible in them, and the direction and meaning of their processes.

Human beings will have a principal place. The Word of grace places the action of God in the world, something our worldviews deny. 3) Worldviews focus on the reality of general states, relationships, and consequences, of the truth of finitely perceptible sequences and their infinite extension both backward and forward. A worldview focuses on the truth of that which always and everywhere is the same. The Word of grace speaks of a unique and highly particular event. 4) Worldviews are doctrines with which human beings view the world from a standpoint that deduces from the many things that they think they have seen. The Word of grace is a declaration of a decision already taken, and the summons to orient one's life by it, since only obedience or disobedience is possible in relation to it. 5) Worldviews are the attempt of human beings to come to terms with themselves concerning themselves. The individual becomes observer, constructor, and manager. The Word of grace has the dangerous force of an offense that strikes human beings from outside, from a superior height, and in virtue of which they must try to understand themselves and can only understand themselves.

Barth equates worldview with ideology, whereas Barth has made clear that the only binding of the theologian is to the Word of God. In that sense, Barth is a theologian of freedom in that theology is always free of hegemony or domination of worldviews. For that reason, theology takes the form of a critique of all ideologies. His focus on revelation, which re-orients human thinking life toward Christ, gives theologian, pastor, and Christian freedom in relation to any ideology. The critique of ideology is also positive revelation. Such an approach could lead to an aloof approach to society. Of course, in the hands of Barth, it does not.[47] Suppose you are liberal-progressive in your political ideology. For you to speak truth to power would be to address the truth of revelation to your progressive friends. If you are a political conservative, we could reverse the situation. At one stage of his life, Barth could offer a critique of religion. At another stage, he offered a critique of Nazism.

I do not want to get into the interesting distinction between a worldview (Weltanschauung) and world-picture (Weltbild). I will mention it briefly. The former is systematic and intentionally developed. The world-picture is a term that refers to our given cultural context; it is something native and unreflective. We do not choose our world-picture, any more than we choose the location or language into which we are born. A worldview by contrast is an ideology that human beings devise, select, and

---

[47] Posted by J. Scott Jackson, http://derevth.blogspot.com/2015/02/gorringe-on-barth-freedom-of-theology.html He refers to Timothy Gorringe, *Karl Barth: Against Hegemony* (Oxford, 1999) and Clifford Green.

promote. It takes up the given world-picture into a system that makes sense of it. The focused attention the worldview receives can make it lose its provisional status in the hands of any thinker. Barth wants the theologian, pastor, and Christian free of any such bondage.

Fourth, Barth concludes his discussion of the glory of the Mediator by referring to the promise of the Spirit. This will be his second discussion of eschatology, the other sections being 47.5, 70.3, and 73.1. In his discussion of revelation in Chapter II (Prolegomena), Barth focused on revelation as the presence of God in the Easter event, but now he will focus his discussion of revelation under the theme of the anticipation of the universal redemption and consummation. This section is anticipation of the direction the revision of his eschatology of eternity must take. The appearances of the risen Lord were promise and anticipation of an outstanding future. The future of the risen Lord is present in promise and accepted in a hope prepared to suffer.[48] The impartation of the Holy Spirit is the coming of Jesus Christ in the last time that remains to this day. He thinks of the coming Christ in a distinctly new ways from his from his coming in Jesus of Nazareth. The coming of Christ in three distinctly new ways derives from their eschatological character. The first distinctly new form of his coming is the resurrection and the Easter event. The second or middle form is the promise of the Spirit, the Spirit of Jesus Christ. The third distinctly new form is yet to come in the return of Christ and the redemption and consummation of creation. I find some of the language here overlapping with Pannenberg, as he discusses in Chapter 15 of his *Systematic Theology* the presence of eternity in time, bringing history to its completion and fulfillment. The impartation of the Holy Spirit is the promise by which the community may live in this time that moves towards it end. The new coming of Jesus Christ has an eschatological character in this second form as well. If the *Parousia* is an eschatological event in its third and final stage as well, this means that in it we have to do with the manifestation and effective presence of Jesus Christ in their definitive form, with His revelation at the goal of the last time. The world is no longer a lost world. In the appearance of the one man Jesus in the glory of God, God made present as a new and real element in the existence of the world the goal given to the world in and with its reconciliation to God. God made known the future of salvation as redemption from the shadow of death and the antithesis that pursues it, its future of salvation as its completion by the creation of its new form of peace, its being in the glory of God. The work of Christ in its form as revelation has not ended. As the Revealer of His work, He has not yet reached His goal. He is still moving towards it. The

---

[48] (Moltmann, Theology of Hope 1965, 1967), 87.

eternal light has already gone out into the world. The new and future redeemed and perfected world is already present. In this commencement, we find the goal reached only in Him. It has not reached the goal in the world or in the individual. In this context, Barth will discuss the "already" and "not yet" feature of Christ as Victor.

The return of Jesus Christ in this middle form is His coming in the promise of the Spirit. This is His direct and immediate presence and action among, with, and in us. In this promise, He is the hope of us all. The promise of the Spirit is the decisive answer to the question of this subsection. In this reality takes place the transition and entrance of the prophecy of Jesus Christ to us and to our sphere. God draws people into the history of salvation and gives them a part in it. Based on this reality, God justifies us. We find the phrase "promise of the Spirit" in Galatians 3:14, Acts 2:33 and one might compare the phrase in Ephesians 1:13. The phrase can mean that the Spirit promises. The Holy Spirit is present and active among, with, and in certain people. The phrase can also mean that which God promises. As Christ comes in this form to humanity, His second coming, His prophetic work, proceeds without a break. 1) In this form as the promise of the Spirit, we have the direct and personal coming of Christ. 2) He is no other, but the Son of God and Humanity, the Mediator between God and the world, in the totality and not merely a part of His being and existence. 3) Christ in the form of the promise of the Spirit is qualitatively the same as the first form and will be in the last. The promise of the Spirit is no more or less than the power of the resurrection of Jesus Christ operating in the time between the times. The return of Jesus Christ in this third form is an extension of His prophecy as ongoing history. The reconciliation of the world to God has not reached its conclusion as revelation. It still moves forward to its goal and has its own specific glory.

The main concern of the ongoing history of the prophecy of Jesus Christ that fills our time is with non-Christians. Their existence is a reminder of the darkness that resists Jesus Christ as true witness. For their sake, the prophecy must go forward, that Jesus Christ as the living Word of God is still on the way today. Their conversion from ignorance to knowledge, from unbelief to faith, from bondage to freedom, from night to day, is the goal of His prophetic work as far as it has a temporal goal. He wills to seek and to save those who are lost, who without Him, without the light of life, without the Word of the covenant, will necessarily perish. He is for them specifically this light, this Word. He goes after them because he is their hope. The promise of the Spirit is for them.

Barth has throughout this section opened a discussion of the Trinity. One of the gifts of Barth is that he has taught us that the Trinity is a framework within which we can solve theological puzzles rather than simply being a puzzle itself. In fact, *Church Dogmatics* is a parade of Trinitarian solutions to questions that modern theology had answered in Unitarian fashion. Yet, when Barth uses the Trinity, it dissolves into a discussion of the Father and the Son. In this section, Barth has discussed the proclamation of the gospel in its objectivity. Yet, he is rightly not satisfied. The gospel needs to be an occurrence "for us." When Barth raises the question toward the beginning, one might expect that he would raise the matter of Pentecost and the life of the Spirit in the community of the church. Instead, through some tortuous dialectic, he locates the proclamation in the resurrection of the Son. It appears that, for Barth, an act of the Spirit would not transcend the subjectivity of our hearing. Barth will then locate the objectivity of proclamation in Jesus as prophet. Even this move could recoup the deficit of the Spirit if he described the prophecy as arising from the Spirit. Yet, even as he discusses "the promise of the Spirit," the Spirit is never a personal agent either of the prophesying of the risen Lord or of our hearing it.[49]

Barth moves from the third portion of his Christology to how it reveals another dimension of his doctrine of salvation. He begins with another dimension of the human malady or misery, as liars and deceivers, which this aspect of Christology reveals. He will then discuss the saving action of God that will bring healing of this malady, that of vocation or calling. One of the real gifts of Barth is the elevation of calling and vocation. He closely ties Christology with soteriology. He completes his teaching on salvation, showing the malady of humanity in sin, sloth, and falsehood, and the remedy provided by God in justification, sanctification, and vocation. The direction of salvation is in the downward movement of God in the humiliation of Christ going into the far country, the upward movement of humanity as Christ takes humanity with him in the resurrection, and the outward movement in the central vocation of becoming a Christian in the world to witness to what God has done in Christ.

Barth will now consider the sin addressed in this part of his Christology, which is the falsehood and condemnation of humanity (70), even as he discussed pride (60) and sloth (65). We would not know the depth of the problem here were it not for the knowledge we have of Jesus Christ. He is quite skillful here as he links the demonic impulse toward lying that the Bible regularly makes with the need for speaking the truth in Christ. In the face of the true witness Jesus offers, humanity shows itself to be liars. The free God has sought the liberation of humanity. The self-assertion of humanity transforms what God has sought into perversion of thought,

---

[49] (Jenson 1997), Volume 1, 154.

speech, and conduct. Such self-assertion can only lead humanity to destroy itself and perish. In this section, Barth rightly opposes the restriction of the gospel to the proclamation of the forgiveness of sins that we find in Luther. The New Testament has a broader conception of gospel than that theme suggests, as important as it is. Barth also righty stresses the new reality by the Spirit and thus writes in terms of the theme of the royal rule of God.[50]

Barth first discusses the true witness. The Christian conception of sin is the liberation of humanity from aberration and transgression. It derives from knowledge of the existence and work of Jesus Christ as the Mediator of the covenant of grace. We know sin as Christ opposes, vanquishes, and does away with it. In this way, we can then speak of the Christian relevance of sin. The Gospel has the form and character of the true Law of God in the sense that it exposes sin. Sin is perversion of the goodness and righteous mercy God addressed to humanity in Jesus Christ. Sin is denial, rejection, misunderstanding, and misuse. Sin is hatred toward the promise of God. He refers us to his discussion in IV.1, 60.1 and IV.2, 65.1. However, one might disagree with Barth in that the gospel is also the claim of God upon us so that one can call it the law of faith. The gospel becomes the origin of the law as well. He ignored the difference in salvation history, where the law belongs to the old covenant and the gospel to the new covenant. The law ends when someone proclaims the message of eschatological salvation. Thus, the law is hardly a form of the gospel.[51] What is truth? It is not an idea or principle. An encounter with truth will not be immediately illuminating, pleasing, acceptable, and welcome to humanity. The truth unmasks, discovers, accuses, and judges people of sin. However, the truth that does this is Jesus Christ as the true Witness of His true deity and humanity, as the authentic Witness of the saving grace of God that has appeared in Christ, justifying and sanctifying humanity. Throughout this section, the fine print will include an exposition of Job as a true witness who suffers. We find truth in the unexpected place of the cross, the man who suffers. In his pure form, Jesus Christ is true witness and the prophet of truth. The secret of his existence is that he is the true witness. His prophetic work has the form of passion or suffering. He is the core of kerygma or proclamation of the church. He encounters us in the form of suffering, or he does not encounter us at all. We can be sure that our time is not the theater of a decrease of darkness. Jesus Christ is the first Pilgrim and Warrior in this history. As Victor, the suffering Servant of God, the afflicted Prophet, accompanies and encounters us. He is the Hero of God. He is the mighty Warrior in his weakness. He remains a mystery to us

---

[50] (Pannenberg, Systematic Theology 1998, 1991), Volume 2, 461.
[51] (Pannenberg, Systematic Theology 1998, 1991), Volume 2, 461.

because his prophet work on earth and in time is in the form of suffering, which obscures for us his work as the pure form of the mediator between God and humanity.

As lying, too, sin is breaking out from the reality of the covenant, which God has founded already in creation, which God has fulfilled in the humiliation and exaltation of Jesus Christ, and which God has established and unshakably confirmed as the promise made to humanity, but also as the norm and criterion of all human conduct. The revelation of Jesus Christ is the promise of the Holy Spirit. This Word of God forces the human being of this intervening time to make an answer. The answer of humanity is sin in the form of falsehood. As humanity did not have to persist in pride and sloth, no more did humanity have to persist in human falsehood. Humanity only had to give place to the Word of God encountering it as the promise of the Spirit, to give to humanity the place that rightfully belongs to it in the human heart, conscience, and existence. Then, humanity would immediately have found itself in agreement with the revelation of Jesus Christ as the promise of the Holy Spirit. We must be clear what is the witness of the true Witness in relation and contradiction to which sin is falsehood, or false witness, and by which humanity stands accused, condemned, and judged. The true Witness is the living Jesus Christ present in the reconciled world in the promise of the Spirit and acting towards it in exercise of His prophetic office. What is there about the existence and life of this man that makes Him the true Witness, and therefore the light in which He reveals the darkness of falsehood? The relationship Christ had with His Father, His Yes to the Father, is what makes this human being the true Witness.

Barth makes the beautiful statement that one is merciful when one takes to heart the need of another. Jesus Christ has once and for all taken our need to heart. A prophet and witness speak. Yet, this prophet and witness did not open his mouth (Isaiah 53:7) nor cause his others to hear his voice in the streets (Isaiah 42:2). Humanity can be wordy and noisy in its tireless and attempts at self-communication and self-expression. The Word of the cross does speak. Christ does speak in the promise of Spirit as the Crucified. The Word of the crucified arises out of the silence and death of this man, in which all the words of others reach their end and limit. Only the Lord of life and death can break this silence. Those who hear the crucified, dead, and buried man, Jesus Christ, are hearing God. The work of God as the conclusion of peace between God and humanity, the work of atonement and deliverance, of justification and sanctification, falls with severity upon the one man who gave himself to accomplish it. His death is the will of God, in which he bore the sin of the world as the Representative of all human sin. In this context, the cry of his forsakenness from the cross is a true word. The dreadful question corresponds to the situation. Yet,

God is not a remote and aloof spectator of this event. The Father is in unity with the Son through the Spirit. We are at home with a form of truth, goodness, and beauty in the world. Yet, what are we to make Jesus Christ the Crucified, whom at his most painful point, we say is the truth. We will not find God where we think we should. We shall find God in the lonely man of Gethsemane and Golgotha. In that place, we shall find the lonely God. He is among the smitten and abased. Yet, God raised him to the throne of the glory of divine grace. God has raised the throne of the glory of divine grace in which, at a cost God paid, God has made peace between us human beings and God, justifying and sanctifying as a divine covenant partner fallen and wretched humanity, and saving humanity for eternal life with God. There God says Yes to humanity. Only in the height of human corruption of human desire and wish is God to humanity alien, remote, and hostile. There in the depths of human nakedness and true reality, God is the Neighbor and Brother suffering with humanity and for humanity. God is the Good Samaritan who shows mercy on humanity. This is what the crucified man Jesus Christ has to say to us as the Word of God, since only God can say it.

Barth will say that in the work of the Holy Spirit, Jesus Christ, as the true witness is present in our sphere of time and history as this speaking Witness, that He strides through it as such, that He acts and operates in it, that He encounters us people of this sphere with His promise and claim. Jesus Christ comes to us here and now, as the man who came once and then came again first in His resurrection from the dead as the Crucified. In this form, He is the truth. In this form, He speaks the Word of God. In this form, He is present to us and active among and in us as the Prophet, the true Witness. In the work of the Holy Spirit in this form, He is the speaking truth.

Second, in this context, the falsehood humanity interests us as an unspiritual phenomenon and problem, as the disguise that people of sin assume when Jesus Christ confronts them as the true Witness. The falsehood of humanity is the great enemy that resists the divine promised declared in the prophetic work of Jesus Christ. It consists in a movement of evasion. It presupposes humanity's distant or closer encounter with Jesus Christ and His truth. It takes form only in relation to Him. Evasion means trying to find another place wither the truth can no longer reach humanity, where it is secure from the invading hand of the knowledge and implications of the Word. However, humanity knows that it cannot really escape it. This is how falsehood speaks. This is the view of the people of sin. They do not question the truth. They do not oppose to it any antithesis. They do not persecute it. They do not ignore it. These are innocuous and irrelevant preparatory stages of the human enterprise. They kiss the Master, as Judas did in Gethsemane. They are not against the truth, but with it and for it, appealing to it with sincerity, profundity, and enthusiasm, making it their business to defend, propagate, and magnify it. We must prepare ourselves to see the falsehood of humanity appear in an earnest, respectable, devout, and Christian form. As untruth, it has taken, swallowed, and digested and assimilated the truth. It has it within itself. It perverts it. Since the truth necessarily resists its perversion, it has it to its own judgment and final destruction. It has it, and therefore it cannot fail to have the power of a certain faded luster. The true and succulent lie always has something of the scent of the truth. In some manifestations of falsehood, it is heavy with truth in the form of truisms, so that if we think we know and should describe it as falsehood we are bound to look like iconoclasts and must anxiously ask ourselves whether we are the liars, blaspheming holy things and holy people. The true and succulent lie has a radiant aspect of righteousness and holiness, of wisdom, excellence, and prudence, of zeal, austerity, and energy, yet also of patience and love for God and humanity. Falsehood is well able to domesticate the cross of Jesus Christ. Is it not plain that in all these reinterpretations humanity is trying to overcome the element of offense and to make it inoffensive? What is humanity? It considers itself as in the glorious position of being able to imagine and create a god under this or some other name, or even none at all. If it can do this, what can it not do? By way of a second conclusion, we may add a word concerning the phenomenon and problem of the common lie, of falsehood in the moral sense.

Third, Barth concludes his reflection by focusing on the condemnation of humanity. Here is his third discussion of eschatology, the others being 47.5, 69.4 and 73.1. To be condemned is to receive judgment from God. Falsehood is the condemnation of humanity because only in part it will not accept the truth of human deliverance from guilt and slavery. Humanity finds itself startled the true witness is in the form of one suffering and dying upon the cross. Humanity tries to turn the truth into its opposite, desiring to live by and in the untruth into which it attempts to change the truth. Humanity exists in a subjective reality alien to and contradicting its objective reality. Human beings are a bewitched people in a bewitched world. The false image in which human reality represents itself to human beings has no center. That it lives by the reality we can see by the fact that humanity cannot refrain from seeking a center or meaningful source of its being, from trying to give itself such a center. However, the perversion of the truth into untruth in which the reality represents itself in this image shows itself in restless probing in which it seems legitimate to set one thing after another in the center. Humanity will make one thing after another the necessary origin of its being, to see, to understand, to think, to act, and to behave now in the light of one thing, and now another. In short, humanity will try to live in a certain euphoria of assurance, yet always to experience disillusionment, always ready to change the zealously adopted standpoint, to burn tomorrow what it worships today. Having no center, the image is also without any periphery. Having no definite source, the being of humanity has no definite goal. It has no limit or law. It has no real co-existence. The image in which human reality represents itself seems to indicate such a co-existence to the extent that it has some truth. However, since it reflects only the truth changed into untruth, this co-existence dissolves at once into a mere proximity and finally hostility. Humanity lacks any unifying force. Thus, the relation of humanity to fellow human beings oscillates between commitment to various interests that makes them seem indispensable as instruments for various purposes, to open or secret enmity in which they become annoying, disruptive, and dangerous figures against whose existence and self-expression it can only adopt a defensive and offensive attitude. We always seem to be dealing with the truth and with human life before and in it. However, the truth always escapes humanity, and so does its life, like a butterfly slipping through the fingers of a child. Life involves an unceasing dialectic. The human situation is profoundly indeterminate. What is truth? When confronted by it, we would rather try to conceal it. We see the pain of the situation in human speech. The problematic nature of human speech concentrates the painfulness of the situation. If speech is "the house of being," (Heidegger) the occupier seems to have left without giving any definite address. Human speech is the arena of such ceaseless misconceptions and errors, as well as of so many intentional great or small concealments and distortions, and of so many tragic and comic misunderstandings for which both speakers and hearers share the responsibility.

To be damned is to be committed to an eternity in which God has rejected us and therefore we are lost. It is to have to be finally, what we wish to be when we change truth into untruth and live in and by this untruth. This sword has not yet fallen. This worst thing has not yet taken place. However, it is indeed bad enough to have to exist under the threat of damnation. Human life stands under the warning sign, the painfulness of which we have briefly indicated. We have always been careful to speak only of the attempt by humanity to change the truth into untruth. It can never reach its goal. The truth is identical with the living Jesus Christ, its true Witness. The truth is identical with the personal work of His self-declaration as the self-revelation and self-impartation of the reconciliation effected in Him. The truth is identical with His prophecy, with the promise of the Spirit, and therefore with the present reality of God and humanity in this time of ours. It goes into offensive action against this attempt in all its superiority to untruth. Thus, the human being who produces untruth is continually confused, unsettled, and attacked by it. Can we count upon it or not that this threat will not finally be executed, that the sword will not fall, that God will not pronounce the condemnation of humanity, that the sick person, and even the sick Christian, will not die and be lost rather than be raised and delivered from the dead and live?

We can be open to the possibility that in the reality of God and humanity in Jesus Christ we might find contained much more than we might expect and therefore we might find the supremely unexpected withdrawal of that final threat. This would mean that in the truth of this reality there might be contained the super-abundant promise of the final deliverance of all people. To be more explicit, we need to be open to this possibility. We must forbid ourselves from counting on this as though we had a claim to it, for humanity can have no claim to this possibility, since such a possibility is supremely the work of God. However, we can hope and pray for it as we may do already on this side of this final possibility. That is, we might hope and pray cautiously and yet distinctly that, despite everything that may seem quite conclusively to proclaim the opposite, divine compassion should not fail. We would then hope and pray in accordance with divine mercy that is "new every morning" where God "will not cast off forever," as stated in Lamentations 3:22-23, 31.

We now come to the second half of Volume 4.3, considering Jesus Christ as the true witness.

Barth begins with a consideration of the vocation of humanity (71) even as he discussed justification (61) and sanctification (66) as part of the reconciling work of God. The creative call of the living Jesus Christ awakens humanity to an active knowledge of the truth. Christ receives humanity into the new standing of the Christian and into fellowship with Christ. Afflicted and well-equipped humanity becomes witness in the service of the prophetic work of Christ.

First, Barth begins with a reflection on humanity as living in the light of life. In 69.2, Barth discussed Christ as the light of life. When he refers to the light of life in this subsection, he also means understanding humanity in the light of Jesus Christ. Thus, the "life" referred to in the title is the crucified, who comes again in his resurrection, in the promise of the Spirit, and in his conclusive and universal revelation. God is reconciling the world in Jesus Christ. Humanity can leave falsehood and deception behind as it embraces the outward movement of a calling or vocation in this world. Humanity stands in this light because God has surrounded the human sphere with this light. God has prepared the way for the light to shine on, in, and through humanity, and thus for the event of human vocation. He will point us to his doctrine of election again. Divine election is the source of vocation, even as it was justification in IV.1 and sanctification in IV.2. In pre-temporal, supra-temporal, and post-temporal eternity, God is the one who elects sinful humanity and therefore gives humanity a vocation that actualizes human justification and sanctification. Vocation is the event in which God has set humanity in fellowship with Jesus Christ in a way that serves the prophetic office of Christ, and therefore the prophetic Word of reconciliation. Vocation suggests that God sets human beings in the service of God and in service to fellow-humanity. In the promise of the Spirit, Christ comes to individuals from far or near as the Prophet of the grace of God to them. He will work out the basic theme of this section in terms that the vocation of humanity, in the light of the life we find in Jesus Christ, is to be a Christian. We are to understand all humanity in the life of Jesus Christ, but vocation or calling is the event that affirms it. Though fellow-humanity may be un-Christian in their ways, one must tolerate them as future fellow-Christians. This tolerance may have to be for a long time, even one's whole life. So long as God does not put an end to the non-Christian course of life, thereby putting a stop to his or her present nature, speech and impulse, the Christian cannot refuse tolerance. For all the sincerity of Christian patience with the non-Christian, Christians cannot leave them at peace. Absolute tolerance toward non-Christians would mean not taking them seriously. Thus, the Christian will only be to them a most disturbing fellow-human being, effectively reminding them by their existence as Christians where they also belong and what is their own true though not yet grasped being as their promised future.

Second, in this event of vocation, we begin with the action of Jesus Christ who lived and died in his time as the humble servant whom God exalted as Lord. Time finds its fulfillment when the event of vocation occurs. Without it, time is empty. All time becomes a time of grace and salvation. Since vocation occurs in time, it has a process. We can understand it only as a spiritual process. He distinguishes this process from scientific discovery, artistic intuition and creation, political revolution, or moral reorientation. The event of vocation is a spiritual process because it deals with Jesus Christ in the power of the Word and Spirit. The Spirit is the shining of the light of life. We are dealing with Jesus Christ in the form of his coming again in the power of the Spirit.

Barth then wants to consider what happens to humanity in the process of vocation. He affirms that the vocation of a human being is a single occurrence that is also a temporal process. From a human perspective, then, we might think of successive events supplemented and transcended by the next. We might think of ladder or psychological genetics of the Christian life. In certain traditions, including pietism, one refers to this as the order of salvation. He thinks it ill advised to think down this road. He wants to respect the temporal character of vocation and respect its spiritual character rather than attempt a psychological description of the evolution of the Christian. The whole discussion of the order of salvation focuses our attention upon Christian experiences and states rather than on Christ. Vocation is the act of Jesus Christ in humanity. We rightly refer to the event as illumination. The event means God acting upon the entire human being, refashioning the person to be a theater, witness, and instrument of divine action. We can legitimately think of this event as awakening. Such a term means something previously hidden becomes visible. One was asleep and in a world of dreams. While sleeping, one cannot know what one now knows when awakened. One awakens to true life, the life that is reconciling, justifying, and sanctifying. Awakening turns us from the false situation we had to the true situation we have in the light of Jesus Christ.

Here is a place where Barth and John Wesley part company. Wesley clearly thought of the Christian life as open to stages on the analogy of our natural lives. Thus, in a spiritual sense, we may be more like babies in our spiritual lives. Of course, some persons may persist in this stage far too long! Instead, Wesley held out the possibility of perfection in the love of God and neighbor, which for him was crossing the boundary into spiritual maturity.[52] Contrary to Barth, it may well be beneficial to open the door to a discussion of the dynamics of conversion, focusing on the role of the Spirit in conviction, call, illumination, and enablement that will lead into a discussion of the process of salvation in individual life, such as regeneration, justification, healing, and liberation. Such a discussion will need to include the vital role of the community in its preaching, teaching, worship, baptism, the Lord's Supper, and leading a Christian life. It would focus on the importance of the transmission of the faith from one generation to the next while recognizing the hope for the world to come. Such a transformation of life will occur in a process guided by forming believers into the image of the Son through the work of the Spirit.[53] One could have this unbarthian discussion in a very Barthian way.

Barth will consider what he calls the perverted ecclesiastical practice of administering a baptism in which the baptized becomes a Christian unwittingly and unwillingly that has obscured the consciousness of the one and for all this beginning. Infant baptism replaces vocation by the comfortable notion that one needs no such beginning of Christian existence. Rather, we can become and be Christians in our sleep, as though

---

[52] John Wesley, Sermon 40, Christian Perfection.
[53] (Karkkainen, Spirit and Salvation: A Constructive Christian Theology for the Pluralistic World, Volume 4 2016), 266-72.

we had no longer to awaken out of sleep. We must not allow infant baptism to induce in us this comfortable notion, nor conceal from either others or ourselves the fact that to go further in the Christian life as daily penitence this life must first begin as vocation. Even baptism properly administered in responsible consciousness is only the exponent of the turning in the life of the baptized that means his or her first fruitful encounter with Jesus Christ. That is, baptism cannot be the turning itself, or even the commencement of it. This human process is so ambiguous, feeble, and even perverted, having so much in common with other human processes, especially of a religious character. The effect is that we are continually tempted to understand baptism only as one such process, to regard its particularity as only relative, and thus to reject the idea that in the process in which an individual becomes a Christian we have a radically distinct occurrence.

Third, vocation deals with the creation of the Christian, as well as the preservation and nurture of the Christian. Whatever we may say about vocation will only elucidate this simple answer. Christians are those who determine their existence among humanity with faith in Christ. They live with the knowledge that humanity belongs to Christ. They anticipate the form of existence that one day will belong to every human being. The Christian belongs to Christ, and Christ belongs to the Christians. Jesus Christ is the Lord of the Christian. We must now ask how people place themselves within the sphere of life in which Jesus Christ is their Lord. Christ sets people in attachment to Himself through the liberating power of the Word. The simplest description of the fellowship with Christ that is the goal of vocation is that the Christian becomes a disciple or follower of Jesus Christ. In this, Barth is quite consistent with Kierkegaard. He uses the metaphor that this earthly existence is a real test or examination. To be human is to engage the various tests of life. However, the greatest test is to become and to be a Christian. Our word and deed testify to whether we are up for the examination.[54]

Jesus goes, and the disciple accompanies Him on the say way. Jesus chooses the way first. As said in I Peter 2:21, the Christian follows Him on the way that He has chosen, treading in His steps. Such discipleship is a history of fellowship between the Christian and Christ, embracing the entire life of the Christian. Christians do not have their lives in their own hands, having useless concern of providing for and governing their own lives, for they recognize themselves as the possession of the One whom, from eternity, came forth to restore what human beings had ruined. The fellowship Barth has described as the goal of vocation has in Christian tradition a connection with mysticism. However, mysticism suggests the

---

[54] *Practice in Christianity* (1850, No. III).

disappearance of the true confrontation of God and humanity, of the One who addresses and the one who receives the call and answers it. Yet, the fellowship of Christians with Christ does mean their union with Christ. This union is that for which creation longs. Christians know themselves as members of the world reconciled to God in Christ, as human beings justified and sanctified in Christ in spite of their sin, as a legitimate partner of the covenant fulfilled in Christ. This decision means that Christians take themselves seriously as being in Christ. The Christian cannot part from Christ. Christ is present where Christians are, and Christians are present Christ is. When we say that Christ is in the Christian, we mean that Christ speaks, acts, and rules as the Lord of individual thinking, speech, and action. When we say that Christians are in Christ, we mean that their thinking, speech, and action have their ruling principle in the speech, action, and rule of Christ. The free human heart, reason, and action have their orientation on Him.

Since the basic vocation of a Christian is to become a Christian, Barth will now conclude with a discussion of three areas in which one needs to become a Christian.

Fourth, Barth discusses the importance of witness. He spends much of his time addressing the dangers he finds in the history of the church. Christians receive the kerygma of the eschatological divine act accomplished in the cross. He wonders if all we can say about this witness is holding this eschatological tension, this dialectic of worldliness and unworldliness. In the process, he wants to deal with the "classical view" view of vocation. He will address his concern that we identify vocation with those portions of the New Testament (Sermon on the Mount or the moral exhortations of the letters). He admits the importance of this answer. His concern is that lifted from its context, the classic approach becomes little more than self-glorifying Christian moralism. Christian ethos is not an end in itself. The ethos is not the common denomination of Christians as we consider the importance of witness in Christian life. He wonders how the classic view can keep a focus on the Christian life as a recipient of grace, how it can maintain its distinction between Christian and non-Christian, and how it can rest so much upon my strong or feeble practice of the witness it envisions. Further, among the dangers is pietism. Included in the danger of pious eccentricity would be the quietistic mystical type and the 17th and 18th century Pietists. Of course, the English-inspired social and evangelistic movement of the latter 19th and 20th centuries focused upon a personally committed Christianity and the preaching of the Gospel to those who had not heard it. At the left wing of this movement were the Salvation Army and Methodists. What he says of these specific movements is that they concentrate on the personal experience of salvation in a way that influences the whole church. Even theological Liberalism paid attention to the individual life of faith. The historical actuality of Christianity shows that no movement ever existed that made an exclusive concentration upon the personal experience of grace and salvation that makes one a Christian. Such movements have always opposed their inward tendency with the urge for expansion. Yet, it runs the risk of a retreat into a purely private Christianity. He hopes we can see that the exaltation of the personal experience of salvation into the principle of the structure of Christian existence is as inviolable as might appear at first glance. He does not think the classic view has enough theological or biblical support. Vocation in the Bible is calling to a task, as suggested by the biblical accounts. Yet, one notices that the classic view is not a constitutive element of the fulfillment of that task. Vocation means existence in the execution of this task. God does not issue this calling in vain. God becomes involved by commissioning them. God makes the divine cause theirs, and therefore God makes their cause the cause of God. God legitimates, authorizes, instructs, and nourishes them. Another theological argument against the classic view is that Christians are to live by the Holy Spirit, that the self-giving of Christ to the Christian and the giving of the Christian to Christ is the goal of vocation. Here is the true being of the Christian. What determines Christian life is the relation to Christ. The Christian participates in the great history of God with the world and therefore of salvation history. He reminds us that the focus of this witness is service or ministry. Christ lives as the Mediator, Head, and Representative of all. The Christian is the one who cooperates with this. Christ will not be alone, so Christ calls and gives a vocation to humanity. The meaning of Christian service and ministry is the divine Word. Christian vocation is the accompanying and confirming sign of the living Word. One becomes a hearer of the Word to become a doer of the Word. He intends this idea to be the controlling principle of the IV.4.

Fifth, Barth discusses the Christian in affliction. "Affliction" in the New Testament signifies the experience of pressure that circumstances place upon people from without by relationships or by a hostile and menacing environment, over the development, power, and duration of which one has no control. It simply comes upon one as tribulation, and one must endure it as long as it lasts. Our concern is with Christians in their specific affliction. In solidarity with human beings, they come under all kinds of external and internal pressures. Our present reference is to the additional, specific pressure to which circumstances place upon a Christian because they are Christian. How does there arise this specific affliction of the Christian? Precisely because the Christian is a witness of Jesus Christ, and to the extent that the Christian is active as such, that affliction comes upon the Christian from without, from the world in face of which the

Christian stands. Affliction is a secondary determination of Christian existence. Yet, like the personal experience and assurance of salvation, affliction as a Christian is necessary.

If the ministry of witness is the primary determination of Christian existence, and if the ministry of witness unavoidably brings the Christian into affliction, then we have to say that none can be a Christian without falling into affliction. Since the vocation to be a Christian is the vocation to be a witness, a person cannot become and be a Christian without having to experience and endure affliction as the work of the surrounding world.

How does the Christian come into the specific affliction that falls on him or her particularly as a Christian? 1) The world as it is must cause Christians this affliction as the witness of Christ. God created the world good and God seriously loves it. The world turns away from God. As the One who loves the world faithfully and sincerely, God has turned to its salvation, confirming the covenant made with it in and with its creation God has reconciled with the world in Jesus Christ. Yet, the world has not yet grasped and appropriated this reconciliation, and therefore its salvation. It cannot do so of itself. The world hears of this reconciliation through the Christian. Its understanding, appraisal, and evaluation of its own reality do not correspond to the truth. 2) They must bring it upon themselves with their witness. Christian witness exposes the Christian to affliction. For one thing, Christians cannot evade affliction by ceasing to be a witness, since this would be denial of their vocation and forfeit their personal knowledge, experience, and assurance of salvation that distinguish them from other people. 3) Their fellowship with Christ unavoidably plunges the Christian into this affliction. The affliction of Jesus Christ Himself is something in which all Christians participate. Christ has already shaken the world to its foundation in His death and resurrection. When the world opposes and oppresses Christians, it deals with Jesus Christ in the same way it did in His earthly life. In His Word and work, the world experiences a shaking of its foundations, but now, it does so through Christian witness. In trying to break free from Christ, the world can now only hurt Him indirectly, through its treatment of Christians. The passion of Christ moves forward in the afflictions of Christians.

We must now bring out with no less clarity the positive, bright, and joyful background that gives meaning and justification to the serious, stern, and dark picture that we have just drawn. 1) In spite of the difficulties, it is good to be and become a Christian in affliction. The Christian stands at the side of God, even in affliction. 2) Jesus Christ brings the Christian into affliction. He does so in a way analogous to the Easter revelation. They can expect no other than their existence in fellowship with the One who rose from the dead and lives as the crucified. Those who fight as witnesses of

Jesus Christ and in fellowship with His suffering fight under the promise of His resurrection, and therefore in glorious hope. 3) Christians acquire from the very first the character of what we might call an ecstatic forward movement beyond self to that horizon and goal. The witness of the Christian anticipates the penetration of the light of the fulfilled covenant of grace into the darkness that still surrounds it. 4) The future already determines the present of Christians in their affliction. Christians do not expect certain fruits or results. However, when they arrive, Christians receive them as signs of the free grace of God and anticipations of the future. 5) The Christian in affliction is one secured by the goal appointed for him or her in Christ. 6) Christians demonstrate their being in Christ in their action in the world.

Sixth, Barth will conclude with a discussion of the goal of vocation as the liberation of the Christian. Vocation as witness will lack authenticity if we do not also discuss the personal aspect of that witness. The liberation which we discuss is commencing and in no way complete. Vocation means God gives us the personal endowment and equipment to fulfill vocation. All that Barth has discussed in what God has accomplished in Jesus Christ becomes something known and understood as part of the experience and life of the Christian. Some critics of Barth will say that experience is not a significant factor for him. This section, properly read, will dispute that criticism. In vocation, the Word of God that goes to all persons becomes in such a way that one enjoys a special liberation. Such liberated persons receive the content of the Word through the Word opening itself to them. The gracious act of justification and sanctification becomes in vocation something known and properly understood as part of their experience and life. The reality disclosed and imparted to them in the Word becomes a factor in their experience. Such persons know the Word in a personal way, they experience it, they see, hear, and walk, and thus experience liberation as those who participate in it. They now serve as those freed and qualified in this way. They are people who live by the Word that has opened itself up to them and for which they have become open, by their experience of its content. Thus, vocation implies the distinction and alteration of the being of the one called. Vocation is union with Christ. We must acknowledge the radical change that occurs in Christian life, while at the same time being modest in what we express concerning such change. Vocation as witness points the neighbor to Christ. Such a liberated one remains in solidarity with the sinners who encircle him or her. The concern of God is with the rule of God. He has a concern here that orthodoxy as having Christ without living Christians. Yet, combining the mystical, liberal, or existential picture, the danger is Christians without Christ. He refers to the truth of the love of God for humanity, even if it had no witnesses. Yet, God has chosen to have human beings engaged in that witness. God has decided not to tread the path of time alone. The success of this witness is in the hands of God. He points to three characteristics of this witness as being the revelation of God in Christ as relevant for humanity, the coming judgment, and the gospel as good news. Gloomy Christians lead to a gloomy gospel, which would be a contradiction. He will then clarify what he means by liberation to point us to specific instances of it. As the witness of Jesus Christ, one stands in a place illumined, full of promise, and blessed, but in a way in which, in the power of Holy Spirit, Christ strides through the ages until he comes in his final form. Liberation comes in moving us from solitary life to fellowship, from unlimited possibility to the rock of the one necessity, from the dominion of things to the territory of humanity, from desire and demand to reception, from indecision to action, from the dialectic of the moral and immoral to the life in forgiveness and gratitude, and from anxiety to prayer. The life of the Christian is a life in transition. The Christian is a pilgrim. The Christian is a pilgrim between two worlds. The alteration is clear, definite, and unequivocal, but not accomplished. Christians are both companions with Jesus Christ and children of God and children of Adam and Eve. What takes place in personal life is only an analogy to that which it anticipates. The Christian is only the preliminary of the end. Christian existence is prophetic existence in this sense. What is at issue in the coming of Jesus Christ to the last judgment is the consummation and universality of the renewal that has come to Christians here and now. Christian existence is proleptic and pre-figurative. The liberation of Christians is a phenomenon that accompanies vocation and is a presupposition of their ministry of witness. Its purpose consists in giving to their voice that ring of veracity without which their witness could not gain credence. It consists in giving to their witness an orientation to the person, to the transition for which the life of the Christian and the lives of others who receive their witness are ordained. The personal liberation of Christians should fit them for this ministry of witness. Has this liberation really come to us? Are we engaged in this transition, in all these transitions? Does God in fact regenerate, convert, and renew. Are we Christians? The ageing Tholuck use to say, "Brother, how does it stand with thy heart?" Has the living Lord Jesus so encountered me, and is He so present to me, that I must recognize in Him the merciful and omnipotent decision of God in relation to creation? Do I acknowledge that God has claimed me for the Word of God, and that I cannot keep to myself that which I have received, burying it in my own little corner in creation? Do I believe in such a way that I have no option but to speak? Yes or no? This is the question in relation to my Christian status.

The Trinitarian perspective of Barth arises here, as he concludes his discussion in Chapter XVI with the role of the Spirit in sending of the community and in enlivening the hope of the individual Christian. He concluded Chapters XIV (gathering the community through faith) and XV (building up the community through love) in a comparable way.

Barth will next discuss the Holy Spirit as the one who sends the Christian community (72). As the Spirit gathers a community in faith and builds it up with love, the Spirit sends the community in hope. Christ entrusts to the community the ministry of the prophetic Word. The community is the provisional representation of the calling of humanity and all creatures as they take their place in Christ. These people belong to Christ. Christ ordains the community to confess Christ before all people and to call them to Christ. Christ ordains the community to make Christ known to the world that God has concluded the covenant between God and humanity in Christ. The future manifestation of this covenant is already here. It lives in this great, effective, and living hope.

First, Barth discusses the people of God in world-occurrence. With the emphasis in Volume IV.3 on the prophecy of Jesus, we must also deal with the reality of the church. Vocation to be a Christian means vocation or calling into the church, the living community of the living Lord Jesus Christ. Jesus Christ is the one who calls these individuals in their plurality and unites them with each other. Vocation leads directly into the communion of saints. Vocation considers the doctrine of reconciliation from the standpoint of its mission or sending. He will direct us to the apostolic church. He will consider this matter under three topics.

The first topic he considers is the historical environment of the community of the people of God. This means that world-occurrence is important to the royal lordship of Christ and the fatherly providence of God. Yet, world-occurrence also experiences the reality of the absurd and nothingness. It opposes the goodness God intends. Human confusion elevates nothingness as master. The community does not accept this confusion as the final word. Humanity has fallen away from God, the neighbor, and the self, bringing about the history of confusion we find in human history. He does not want to leave the community in this dialectical tension between its faith in God and in anxiety toward the actuality of human history. He also does not go the direction of holding to a superior view of the tension, a Hegelian synthesis that arises out of the tension between the thesis and antithesis he has just described. The alternative is the childishly simple view that the reality of the grace of God addressed to the world in Jesus Christ is the third word to which the community attests. This third Word is beyond any view of integration of the tension. This view simply acknowledges that beyond the two-fold view of world-occurrence one needs to say more considering the revelation of God in Christ. The community of the people of God has a charge to witness to this world. The open secret is that in Christ God loves, elects, and liberates the world. In Christ, we do not see so much the clash of two kingdoms as the one kingdom of God. We have a new reality introduced into world-occurrence. He does not view this as Christomonism in the bad sense of that unlovely term. The coming of the rule of God for which we pray in the Lord's Prayer is the final and universal revelation of Jesus Christ. Here we find the basis of faith and anticipation, rather than idle speculation. The community exists in this hope for world-occurrence. The community looks forward to the revelation of the new reality of history that at present remains concealed. In its hope in Christ, it also has hope for the world. It waits for Christ. The coming again of Christ is the goal and end of world history.

The second topic he deals with is how the community needs to consider itself in this environment. The church exists as a phenomenon in the world, and thus it exists in the flesh and participates in world-occurrence. Yet, it must also be the people of God. One cannot grasp this truth simply as a phenomenon in the world. In this sense, the community remains visible and invisible. This invisible reality arises out of the election of Jesus Crist, who appoints it to witness and serve. Barth offers ways in which he sees the people of God in world-occurrence in its visibility and likeness to other historical institutions, but also its invisibility and distinction from then. It exists in dependence on its environment and in freedom in relation to it. It is strong in Jesus Christ only as it chooses his path of weakness in that it does not have a secure place in the world. Yet, the new thing the church perceives, and the world does not see, is the unique person of Jesus Christ. We have a new reality in world history. The church exists in the light of a goal that is the open secret of God. The world does not see this goal, of course, but the Church does. Significantly, I am thinking of the book by William Willimon and Stanley Hauerwas, *Resident Aliens* (1999), where they refer to the community as an alien colony (p.743). The community will have an alien character, as it is a stranger in the world. In its freedom in world-occurrence, it will not hear the voice of a stranger (John 10:5). Is the community strange enough to the world? Its weakness is that it relies upon a ministering word. Christ is the first and supreme Guest and Stranger who found no room in the inn and still cannot find any. As such, the community faithful in following in Christ must also be such a stranger in world-occurrence. The community is weak in is reliance on the ministering word it declares and in the simplicity of the Sunday service. It does not produce measurable results in the way other institutions measure them.

His third topic considers the way the community must live in this environment. The community exists in world-occurrence by virtue of its adherence to the open secret it has in its calling from Christ and in the power of its word in the Holy Spirit. The community belongs to Christ, the source of its life, and thus exists by its faith in Christ, love for Christ, and hope in Christ. The Holy Spirit co-ordinates the being of Christ with that of the community. The Spirit unites the transcendence of Christ with his immanence in the community. As I have suggested before, the Spirit for Barth brings and holds together disparate elements. In this case, the Spirit brings Christ and the community of the people of God together. Although Barth explicitly wants to avoid the Hegelian notion of synthesis, he reflects that idea here.

Second, the community is for the world, for it exists because God is for the world. I want to stress that the Spirit establishes the fellowship and then equips the community for solidarity with the world. The community knows the world as it is, for the world does not know itself. The community acts in solidarity with the world. Christ calls the church into existence, and the Holy Spirit is the immediate power that enlivens and creates the church. The community takes some responsibility for the world and its future. The world has need for Christ, even though it does not know it has this need. The Macedonian said, "Come over ... and help us" in Acts 16:3 and Jesus told the disciples to give them something to eat in Mark 6:37. A community interested primarily in itself will always be a source of disillusionment. The world is profoundly hungry, and the church must be like the Good Samaritan and stop to offer its assistance. The church lives as a provisional representation of the divine and human reality. Barth aptly called the church a likeness of the future of the kingdom of God. Barth can aptly call the church a provisional representation of the whole of humanity justified in Jesus Christ. Barth makes the critical point that the community is not an end in itself. Rather, the community has a relationship to the future of all humanity and indeed all creatures. Barth links the church to the missionary function. Yet, in 67.2, Barth could say that the community is not going toward the kingdom, but also coming from it. This Christological constriction does not accord with the biblical witnesses. In his function as the Messiah of the people of God, Jesus relates to the future of the kingdom whose proclamation is the theme of his mission.[55]

Third, for Barth, the community has a task to fulfill. Christ gives the community its task. The community is to be a witness. God sets value on humanity, and God in all divine power has an interest on behalf of human beings. The task applies to humanity. Humanity is the epitome and representative of the world to which God sense the community, as the creature affirmed by God, as the true object of divine goodness. The community must seek understanding humanity in its context. Yet, he does

---

[55] (Pannenberg, Systematic Theology 1998, 1991), Volume 3, 46.

not think this should lead to a general anthropology, for its product is that of human self-understanding. My disagreement here is that such considerations as we find in philosophical anthropology can assist us in doing what Barth wants the community to do, that is, understand our neighbors better. In any case, Barth stresses that humanity is always a stranger to the Gospel. The task of the community is to bring humanity out of this fatal self-misunderstanding and self-contradiction. Humanity is profoundly confused, assaulted, tortured, helpless, and troubled. Humanity may assume arrogant postures, which are symptoms of the lack, need, and misery of humanity. They are expressions of pain and complaint. In this state of anxiety, humanity may become religious, an atheist, a sceptic, philosophical, or even indifferent. In all of this, Barth is making a theological criticism of religion that highlights the misuse of religion, including that of Christianity.[56] He also admits that this task comes from the pure hands of the Lord but to the impure hands of humanity. Humanity will distort the light of Christ. The community consists of people doing their all too human work. The danger is slothful neutrality and thus failure to follow Christ. The danger is that it will offer its confession relevant to the time of world-occurrence but turn its back on being an obedient movement. Both dangers separate the community from the immediate direction of its Lord. The human being whom Christ addresses with the task becomes lazy, sleep, or independent of its Lord. Either the community holds itself too aloof from world-occurrence or it holds itself too closely. It must leave results of this ministry in the hands of its Lord.

Fourth, Barth will say the community has a ministry. It attests to the Word of God in the world. It serves God and therefore serves the world. As feeble as the people of this community are, it carries a promise. No matter how dark the world is, it finds itself in the good fellowship of angels and people who make it plain that its mission to the world is not the absurdity that it might often seem. The world needs to hear of the grace of God addressed to humanity as shown in Jesus Christ, yesterday, today, and tomorrow. The community sets up that banner. The community can explain and declare the gospel only as it turns to the people now around it. It must speak with the people around in view, in mind, and in heart. The community cannot speak past them or over them. It must know them. God makes them, loves them, and knows them. The community must share in that relationship God has with the world. The world needs this appeal and needs to be in the direction of the Son. Its speech has a special ministry in offering praise to God, preaches, instruction, evangelization, missionary work in the world, and theology (*Church Dogmatics* being an example).

---

[56] (Pannenberg, Systematic Theology 1998, 1991), Volume 1, 178.

The work of theology consists of biblical theology, dogmatic and church history, systematic theology, and practical theology. He will call church history a supporting science. Such a systematic and theological assertion seems like a misguided one, for even research into the Bible contains a non-theological element. As important as biblical studies are to theology, the theologian has no justification to exclude other disciplines form a full theological understanding. One reason is that the disciplines are interdependent.[57] Barth will provide an example of a spiritual and existential exposition of Romans, for example, which stands in sharp contrast the scientific study of Sanday and Headlam.[58] As Barth continues, he says theology is a dangerous and threatened undertaking, primarily because of pride. One can only hope that every age will produce a theology that future ages can take up, continue, and improve. One must willingly engage in serious questioning, analysis, argumentation, construction, discussion, and therefore with polemics. However, theology is supremely positive and peaceable. It fosters peace. One needs to pursue it soberly, good-humoredly, without nervous excitement, and without petty, self-opinionated bickering. Theology is a modest undertaking that can only aim to serve rather than dominate by rendering limited and transitory assistance to the cause of the community, to Christians, and to the world. Theology is a beautiful and joyful science. Only when we experience it as such can we be theologians. Theology must have in view the surrounding world, its thought and aspiration, its action and inaction, so as to maintain constant awareness of whom and what it speaks when theology speaks of humanity. Theology needs to present itself to the community of Jesus Christ in a way that others will notice it.

As Barth continues with the special ministry of the church, he reflects on the action of church as it prays, engages in the cure of souls, forms personal examples of Christian life and action, service, prophetic action, and fellowship. He will make the point that a community that views itself as a national church is a sick church, since it would resist the witness to the fellowship of all nations. Baptism and the Lord's Supper are the common meeting place in the community for people of differing cultures and economic classes.

Barth has provided a way for looking upon the Trinity to resolve theological puzzles rather than simply be a puzzle itself. However, Barth often uses the Trinity in a way that focuses on the Father and the Son. Thus, even though this section provides an explicit theory of the ecclesial reality of the Spirit, something seems to be missing. For Barth, the identity

---

[57] (Tillich 1951), Volume 1, 29.
[58] (Tillich 1951), Volume 1, 35-6.

of the being of the church with the being of Jesus Christ is central, and this happens in the work of the Spirit. Yet, the Spirit does not receive credit with actively uniting Christ and the church. Christ is the agent and the Spirit denoted by impersonal terms. Barth seems devoted the general trend of theology in the West that the Spirit is the bond of love between the Father and the Son. The point here is that the inner-divine community of the Father and the Son becomes two-sided. The Spirit is the fellowship itself and is not a partner. The two-sided community is the eternal ground of fellowship between God and humanity. He has an I-Thou relation within the Trinity that allows no third party.[59]

Barth concludes this chapter, even as he concluded Chapter XIV with faith and Chapter XV with love, but now considering the Holy Spirit and hope (73). The Spirit is the enlightening power in which Christ causes individuals of the community to become those who move towards their final and immediate future in hope in Christ. I want to spend some time on this section. Barth says he is discussing his view of eschatology here, which would have been a major theme in his fifth volume. Pausing here will help us see the direction he intended to travel in that volume. This will be his fourth and concluding section in which he discusses eschatology, the other sections being 47.5, 69.4, and 70.3. He will do this in the first sub-section. In the next sub-section, he will give us a taste of his direction for IV.4 of an ethics based on his doctrine of reconciliation-atonement.

First, Barth discusses the subject of hope. One can become a witness of Jesus Christ with the community because Christians can move toward the future in confident, patient, and cheerful expectation of the return of Christ to consummate the revelation of the will of God in Christ. Jesus Christ causes the Christian to become a human being who may stride towards his or her future hope in Christ. The prophetic action of Jesus Christ, while complete, is moving towards its fulfillment. Christ speaks in his resurrection and in the enlightening power of the Holy Spirit. However, Christ has not yet uttered the final word. The Christian is still on the way into a future that is an open and unwritten page, an impenetrable sea of mist. To what extent can God address the grace of God to Christians tomorrow, as it was yesterday and today? What the Christian expects is light, good, and salvation. Christian hope is a positive expectation of the future. Yet, the Already is a form of the one coming of Jesus Christ in his prophetic action, as is the Not Yet of redemption. The Christian hopes in the One in whom he or she believes and loves. Jesus Christ is the subject of Christian hope.

Barth offers yet another reflection that involves time and death. I

---

[59] (Jenson 1997), Volume 1, 154-5.

would point to the value for spiritual formation of this section. Christ came in his earthly existence, he came in his resurrection, he continues to come in the power of the Holy Spirit, but he will come in his final form. That which is before the Christian contains his or her end as a human being. At some future hour, there awaits the one event upon which all people can count. Death is not the end for all human beings, for those alive at the final coming of Christ will find transformation into life with God. They can count upon the conclusion of their temporal existence and therefore of their function as witnesses of Jesus Christ. Paul thought the final coming of Christ could be during his lifetime, but this thought was not central to his apostleship or the core of his message. Rather, a picture of the day of the Lord remained at the heart of his message. The end of human existence as determined by temporality is sure, even as its end in God means a true beginning. Given the amount of time since the resurrection, the Christian world has normalized death. The New Testament rejects this normalization. The end that will come in one form or the other might well seriously compromise, threaten, or darken the Christian's expectation of the future. The end means thus far, and no further. You have had your time. No more time remains. You have had your changes, possibilities, and powers of varying degree and nature. They are no more. This was your life as a witness of Jesus Christ. This was what you made of it, according to the measure of your faith and love, in acceptance of the task laid upon you. You cannot alter, improve, or rectify anything. You must now encounter your Lord, come before divine judgment, and pass through the fire. We have reached the most painful of all the limits of Christian existence. Our Christian ministry of witness will be only the fragment of the Gospel to which God has commissioned us to attest. What is the significance of the few years we have and the puny efforts we have made? Our work is little more than a small beginning. Our work is over. We are too late to do more about it. Yet, the hope of the Christian does not end with the personal end that humanity faces, but with the revelation of Jesus Christ. Christ is the One in whom the Christian trusts and loves, and who will pronounce a good, right, and saving halt, telling the Christian that he or she has done enough, God expects no more, the measure of this individual life is full, and the time of service is finished. Coming from Christ, such an end can only be a welcome and gracious event. In the end, the fragment that the individual sees will become a ripe fruit of His atoning work, as a perfect manifestation of the will of God fulfilled in Him, bearing witness to God and conforming to the image of the Son of God. God will judge will strict justice, but the justice of divine grace. This judgment is the future of his or her end. Christians move toward this end in hope. Whatever it brings me can only be the fulfillment of the promise in the preceding light of which, even though I am a pilgrim on the earliest stages of the path, I may already believe, and witness, and cry, and live either well or badly in His service so long as God has given me time.

Second, Barth concludes on the theme of life in hope. The future to which the Christian looks and moves is not obscure, neutral, or ambivalent future. It tells us positively that the future to which only the Christian can look is the *parousia* of Jesus Christ in its final form, His coming in completion of His prophetic work, and to His consummating manifestation. 1) In hope, Christians are not acting for private ends or the private affair of the Christian. Being Christian, the primary vocation of the Christian, points us in a hope beyond ourselves. The content of this hope is Jesus Christ coming in glory. This means pardon, translation out of the darkness and coming into the light, transformation, and eternal life. The Christian has this hope in the context of the final redeeming act of God, the manifestation of the reconciliation of the world that Christ has accomplished. This redemption brings peace between Creator and creature. It establishes the rule of God over humanity. Obviously, this hope is not just for the individual. Every Christian has a public ministry of witness. The Christian who hopes is a representative. Such a person looks forward, eventually, to the rising of the Sun of righteousness, the end and goal of all things, and therefore to their new beginning. Such a person also represents slumbering humanity that needs awakening. The Christian life in hope is a seed of eternity sown in the world. 2) The life of Christians in hope is their existence in expectation of the coming of Jesus Christ to judgment, and therefore of the end and the dawn of eternal light. Yet, the Christian living in this hope will see clearly the Not Yet of this time. One lives in this hope despite appearances, seeing the goal or horizon toward which one looks and moves. The tension is that a person living with this hope may so focus upon the goal or end that the person sees hopelessness for the world in the Not Yet stage. Such a focused attention to the goal is a pious illusion. Such an approach is to have a warm love for the eternal and a cool contempt for the temporal. The time before the end is hardly empty or hopeless. The demons would dance at such a perspective. The point of Christian life is to serve the Lord here and now in the context of a genuine hope for the individual, the church, and the world. The world of the Not Yet moves toward its goal in Christ and therefore has hope and meaning. Such a Christian lives with the provisional nature of this time as it moves toward its redemption. Such a Christian hopes with joy for the dawn of the great light but hopes with provisional joy for the little lights of today. Such a Christian sees the ultimate hope in the penultimate. 3) Life in hope is life that derives from God. God awakens such a person to this hope and grants freedom in it. The Holy Spirit awakens the Christian to this hope for the ultimate in the penultimate. In this life in hope, awakened by the power of the Holy Spirit, one comes to oneself and may be oneself. One born of the Spirit receives the call to service and lives in hope, and is therefore real humanity, rather than alienated humanity.

Christian hope is too high a thing for Christians not to have to seek afresh each new day and hour the freedom that they have and use. Only the breath of the living God makes individuals living human beings. The prayer of Psalm 51:11-12, that God would grant them a new and right spirit, is the continual prayer of Christians. How else can they do that to which God has called them? Christians will stride out of the present and into the future if they are "instant in prayer," as Paul concluded a list of activities in Romans 12:11-12. In this spirit, they will serve the Lord rejoicing in hope.

CHAPTER XVII

The Command of God the Reconciler

Barth completed Volume IV.3 at the age of 73. Before we explore the direction he might have taken in this chapter, I would like to explore a few biographical exchanges he had in the years following.

Karl Barth was at Rockefeller Chapel (really a Gothic cathedral!) on the campus of the University of Chicago during his lecture tour of the U.S. in 1962. In the same year, *Time* magazine featured Barth, indicating that his influence reached beyond theology. After his lecture, during the Q & A time, a student asked Barth if he could summarize his whole life's work in theology in a sentence. Barth allegedly said something like "Yes, I can. In the words of a song I learned at my mother's knee: 'Jesus loves me, this I know, for the Bible tells me so." That is the simple, unadorned story. Noel Vose of Australia, a Baptist theologian and founder of a Baptist seminary (which now bears his name), verifies the truthfulness of this story.[60]

He would meet Dr. Martin Luther King Jr. during this time. Dr. King had criticized Barth for the obscurity of his thought and for his rejection of natural theology. They united in their opposition to the Vietnam War.

---

[60] For the truthfulness of this story, see
http://www.patheos.com/blogs/rogereolson/2013/01/did-karl-barth-really-say-jesus-loves-me-this-i-know/

Barth in April 1962: "If I myself were an American citizen & Christian & theologian, I would try to elaborate a theology of freedom." He had already expressed an interest in developing the notion of the gift of freedom as the foundation of Protestant ethics. The freedom of God is the grace in which God chooses to commit divinity to humanity. God become the Lord of humanity. Further, humanity has freedom as a gift of God. Humanity is the creature, partner, and child of God. Such freedom is being joyful in this great gift as we embrace our election in Christ. Finally, protestant ethics is the reflection upon the divine call to human action that the gift of freedom implies. Ethics is a reflection upon what God requires humanity to do in and with the gift of freedom. If God is creator, then the focus of human action is on acting as a creature of God. If God is reconciler, then the focus of human action is partnership in that reconciliation. If God is redeemer, then the focus of human action is being a child of God.[61]

Carl F. H. Henry interacted with Karl Barth in a way that has gained some popularity. George Washington University made a late effort to include Washington DC in his American journey that had already included lectures at the University of Chicago Divinity School and Princeton Theological Seminary. Barth was weary. However, he made himself available for an hour of discussion. The university invited 200 religious leaders to a luncheon honoring Barth at which guests were invited to stand, identify themselves and pose a question. Henry identified himself as editor of *Christianity Today*. 'The question, Dr. Barth, concerns the historical factuality of the resurrection of Jesus.' I pointed to the press table and noted the presence of leading reporters representing United Press, Religious News Service, Washington Post, Washington Star, and other media. If these journalists had their present duties at the times of Christ, I asked, was the resurrection of such a nature that covering some aspect of it would have fallen under their area of responsibility? 'Was it news,' I asked, 'in the sense that the man on the street understands news?' According to Henry, Barth became angry. He pointed to Henry, and then famously said, 'Did you say Christianity Today, or Christianity Yesterday?' Henry says the audience of largely non-evangelical professors and clergy roared with delight. Henry says this was an unexpected response from Barth. All he could think was a loosely connected Scripture: 'Yesterday, Today, and Forever.' Barth continued by wondering if photographers could take pictures of the virgin birth. Barth then said that Jesus appeared only to believers. Barth correlated the reality of the resurrection only with personal

---

[61] Karl Barth, *The Humanity of God* (John Knox Press, 1960), "The Gift of Freedom: Foundation of Evangelical Ethics," 1953.

faith. We have discussed the way in which Barth thought of the resurrection of Jesus as history. He has a nuanced discussion in *Dogmatics,* but this exchange with Henry appeared to put him on the side of a "No" to the notion of the historicity of the resurrection. However, by the end of hour, Barth offered a gracious apology. He said he was not fully happy with the way he responded to some questions.[62]

While in America, Cornelius van Til, fundamentalist theologian, attempted to have an audience with Karl Barth. He had already written that Barth was the worst heretic of all time. His concern was the view Barth had of the resurrection of Jesus, especially as he used the German terms *Historie* and *Geschichte*. Some of the fundamentalists surrounding *Christianity Today* magazine at the time had hoped Bath would respond to their questions. They wrote to the friend of Barth, Geoffrey W. Bromiley. The portion of the letter that interests me here is that Barth declines to answer the questions. He does not think they have read honestly and fairly *Church Dogmatics,* and therefore he could not have a fruitful conversation with them. His further concern is that for two parties to have a fruitful discussion they must stand on some common ground. However, these persons have had their "so-called orthodoxy for a long time." They will cling to their views. They will approach him as prosecuting attorneys in establishing where Barth agrees or disagrees with their views. He has no interest in such a discussion. His main concern is that both parties must seek a truth greater than we are. They already possess such truth. Any conversation between them would result in these fundamentalists using his statements to confirm their judgment that he is the worst heretic of all time.[63]

Paul Tillich would publish the third volume of his *Systematic Theology* in 1963. He would die two years later. Barth wrote to him in this period that they understood each so well and cordially at the human level, but that materially they oppose each other from the foundation. He approved of a recent study of a pupil of his who had made the necessary attack on the abominable theology Tillich. For Barth, such a foundational difference made the relationship difficult.

He refers to a slight stroke in 1964 that robbed him of speech for a half day. He had some good humor about this, saying that the first words to pass his lips referred to Zacharias in Luke 1:22.

In 1964, Carl F. H. Henry would visit briefly with Barth again. He

---

[62] Carl F. H. Henry, *Confessions of a Theologian: An Autobiography* (Word, 1986), 210-211.
[63] http://postbarthian.com/2014/04/29/karl-barths-letter-in-response-to-cornelius-van-tils-questions/#comment-107171

would write that regardless of the flaws he saw in the dialectical theology of Barth, he realized that he "was in the presence of a believer in the gospel."[64]

He also refers to a visit to America in 1965 that took some time and energy as well. His faithful assistant Charolotte von Kirschbaum, who had been part of this work since 1930, had a serious illness that put her out of action from the end of 1965 to the beginning of 1967. He also travelled to Rome for the Second Vatican Council.

Chapter XVII, the projected Volume 4.4, section 74-83, would have dealt with the command of God the Reconciler. As sources for filling out what Barth might have said here, we have lectures on the *Christian Life* to give us some of the themes of this volume, as well as the published fragment on Baptism. As an anecdote, the Faith and Order commission of the World Council of Churches sent a delegation to Barth, asking that he not publish CD IV.4 because it undermined the emerging consensus on the sacraments that we find expressed in their document, *Baptism, Eucharist, and Ministry*.[65] Markus Barth will argue directly against the document in his *Rediscovering the Lord's Supper*.

I want to mildly defend Barth from the friendly criticism offered by Stanley Hauerwas in his Gifford lectures. He criticizes Barth for lacking a full account of Christian formation. My temptation is to say something like, "Well of course, but had he completed his *Church Dogmatics* you would be more satisfied." At the close of each part volume in Volume IV, I have suggested that Barth becomes a certain kind of pastor and spiritual guide for the church. My suggestion is that had he completed IV.4, we would see this dimension of Barth even more clearly. Christian life is to flow out of the commitment made in baptism, become an embodiment of the Lord's Prayer, and have its goal in offering one's life in thanksgiving to God as expressed the Lord's Supper.

This chapter would have been an exposition of what God does in the people of God. Barth would have begun with introduction that defined the task of ethics within the doctrine reconciliation (74).[66] Special ethics in this context must demonstrate how far the command of the one God is the

---

[64] Ibid., 243.

[65] I learned of this in the Karl Barth Discussion group on Facebook through Donald W. Dayton and Chris McMullen.. Chris referred to a student of Barth, David Demson, who suggested the same thing. Both refer to conversations they had in the mid 1980s.

[66] (K. Barth, The Christian Life: Church Dogmatics Lecture Fragments 1981) This book will form the basis of what follows in IV.4, even though the only portion officially part of *Church Dogmatics* is IV.4 fragment on baptism, which in this discussion is Section 75.

command of the Lord of the covenant, in which the free grace of the faithful God in Jesus Christ determines, orders, and limits the action of sinful humanity.

In *Christian Life,* Barth makes it clear that his exposition of reconciliation-atonement has revealed a new dimension of his ethical reflections. The ethical reflections on creation are prologue to his intended major reflection on the Christian life in this volume. This exposition would have showed the teleological end of creation. God is the gracious Father who has created what exists and offered the Son to reconcile sinners in a way that includes them in the fellowship of the Trinity.[67]

Barth has described what God has done in Christ and through the work of the Holy Spirit in us to bring reconciliation/atonement. In Christ, God has acted as priest, king, and prophet to deal with the human malady of sin as pride, sloth, and deception. He has shown the subjective application through the Holy Spirit in the life of the church and in the lives of individuals as the growth of faith, love, and hope. The command of God is the human response to such reconciling action from God in the reconciling actions of the Son and the Spirit. The response begins with baptism. It continues with a Christian life summarized in obedience of the command from Jesus to pray the Lord's Prayer. This prayer summarizes the Christian life. He will conclude his reflections by the human response of obeying the command to "Do this, in remembrance of me," that is, a reflection on the Lord's Supper as the appropriate human response of thanksgiving. He suggests that the Christian life has at its center worship and everyday life as the outer circle, with worship enlivening and empowering the outer circle of life in the world. Baptism and the Lord's Supper are the heart of worship, along with confession of faith, preaching, and prayer.

In IV.4 preface, Barth said Christian ethics is the free and active answer of humanity to the divine work he has described in parts 1-3 of Volume 4. Christian life begins with recollection of the divine gift that demands this answer and makes it possible, continuing with the task this gift gives to humanity. This part of Volume 4 would deal with the Christian and therefore human work as this corresponds to the divine work Barth has described in the first three parts. Thus, the divine work of justification through the priestly work of Christ will lead to the Holy Spirit awakening individuals to faith. He makes clear that he wants to do justice to the truth of the atonement as it claims us. The atonement applies to the way human beings live. The focus of theology is God. However, theology must also

---

[67] (Cambridge Companion to Karl Barth 2000), Nigel Biggar, "Barth's Trinitarian Ethic," 218-9.

consider the people of God as a covenant people. The event of the Incarnation and atonement exalts humanity into fellowship with God. Theology needs to ground itself in the objective character of revelation. However, it must not neglect the subjective side of the application to the people of God. Where we find transforming knowledge of Jesus Christ we also find the outpouring and receiving of the Holy Spirit. The Spirit assembles, edifies, and sends a living community. One who lives as a Christian has received the witness of the Spirit and conform one's life to the Spirit. The daily life of the Christian listens to this witness. Yet, the content of that witness is the presence of Christ. The point is that Barth wants his readers aware of the power of the Son that flows to humanity. This power comes from the Spirit, who mediates the presence of Christ to believers. The Spirit empowers the witness of Christians and the Spirit awakens others through their witness. The Spirit creates fellowship with Christ and fellowship within the community. This power is holy because of its connection with Christ. The Spirit calls, awakens, and creates the community of Christians. We need this power because we are slothful. The danger is that we will remain in the prison we have built. As sloth, sin is trivial, evil inaction, loafing, and tardiness. It rejects the exaltation of humanity into fellowship with God. We need the liberation that the Spirit will bring. The sanctifying work of the Spirit in us begins the fashioning of a people to represent God in the world. They will do so through their freedom and obedience as children of God. We experience this through the call to discipleship. Such conversion is personal event, of course, but leads away from self and toward witness in the world. We offer the praise of our good works as a provisional offering of gratitude to God, who has determined human destiny in Christ. Further, he grounds his notion of the Christian life in the prophetic work of Christ as the light of life. Christ is victor, and therefore the one who does not just impart information but one who brings transformation. Christ is victor because we are to imagine the Christian in the world as one of conflict with darkness. Christian life occurs in the context of the promise of the Spirit that directs us to the eschatological work of God in redemption. It directs us toward the glory of God. Thus, Christian life occurs in hope. As the light of life, Christ moves against our sin of deception and lying. This will lead him to emphasize the importance of the witness of the Christian for truth. Truth is encounter with Christ as the true witness of God. Such truth unmasks, discovers, accuses, and judges us. Barth wants us to consider that the vocation of the Christian is to become a Christian. The vocation occurs in time and is a process. The goal of the process is fellowship with Christ, where the Christian becomes a disciple or follower of Christ. As encounter, we must not imagine that this fellowship becomes free of confrontation. One becomes hearer and doer of the Word, which is the theme of IV.4. The ethics of the doctrine of reconciliation will display the life of the pilgrim, living in the reality of this world and on the way to redemption. They will witness in a world in which they will experience affliction and in which they will testify to their liberation. The Spirit sends the community into the world for this witness. The community is like an alien colony. It will always be strange in the eyes of the world. Christian life has its witness in the context of its final and immediate future in hope in Christ. Christian life is on the way to the utterance of the final word from Christ. Witness is the form Christian life takes before death. Yet, Christian life anticipates the hope humanity has in light of Jesus Christ.

First, in *Christian Life,* Barth begins with a discussion of the central problem of special ethics. Since Barth refers to his previous discussions of ethics, I will explore them with an eye toward how they help us understand what Barth wanted to do here.

In I.2, 24.2, Barth says that theological ethics turns to the command of God as reconciler. God now claims humanity in the command that arises from the event of reconciliation. His reflections upon the subjective response to the event of reconciliation as seen through the Son and the Spirit remind us that the truth of revelation is never abstract in Barth. Embracing the truth of reconciliation through the event of the subjective event of the Spirit in the community and in individuals with faith, love, and hope will mean transformed human lives. The command encounters us as those placed under the judgment of God, but also accepted by the grace of God. The command comes to us as the law of God, exposing and punishing our sin. It also comes as the means of healing and restoring us. The reason is that now in the church our fellow human being becomes our neighbor. The neighbor has a need that is significant to us and becomes the command of God to us.

Another hint is the sketch Barth offered in *Church Dogmatics* II, 2. The concept of the command of God denotes a dynamic reality. The command is that of the living God. The command is a specific Word directed to humanity. The command is a specific command of God in each specific form of the divine dealings with humanity. The command of God is not a principle of action revealed to and imposed on humanity. The question of what I shall do concerns the choice God has for the good today. The question is never outdated. Ethics cannot anticipate an event or series of events. Ethics indicates that a series of events exist between God and humanity. It cannot decide what God wills from humanity. Ethics can only instruct, teaching us how to put the question relevantly, look forward openly, and attentively, and willingly, to the answer that God alone can give. One can recognize the command of God because it always encounters humanity in the form of grace, as the direction of the God who loved humanity from the beginning, who intends better for humanity that it does for itself, and who acts for salvation. The command of God will show itself as the law of the Gospel. No eye has seen, nor ear heard, nor has it entered any human heart, what God has prepared for those who love God. The God who has reconciled the world to God in Jesus Christ is the true God. The human being reconciled to God in Christ is true human being. The meaning of this context is that the command of God is prepared for those who because God has first loved them, as in I John 4:19, may love God in return. Ethics must adopt this criterion and apply it here and now to that event.

Barth refuses to enter endless debates with various forms of non-Christian ethics. The difference is that Christian ethics arises out of the imperatives of the love that God freely addressed to humanity, and thus wills salvation for humanity. Alienation from a commanding authority and legalism are the places at which one ought to engage such a debate, but it often does not happen.

In 4.3, 71.4, Barth is careful to reject the moralism of all Christian epochs. Moralism (558-61) sees the goal of Christian vocation as a distinctive ethos. Such a view grasps rightly that that the Christ is to embrace the twofold command to love God and our neighbors. It will focus upon the normative descriptions of the Sermon on the Mount or the admonitions one finds the epistles, especially in its vice and virtue lists and the household rules. Christian vocation involves accepting such words as a binding Word of the Lord. One is a doer of the Word, which will be the theme of IV.4, if one accepts the call to such an orientation of one's life. Barth will agree that Christ is the Commander of the Christian. Christians stand at the side of God and in face of the world. Christians owe to Christ such obedience. However, as Barth is going to chart a different course, he wants to be sure that we hear this voice of moralism. In contrast, he cannot view Christian existence in this way. He warns that divorced from its context and viewed in abstraction, it becomes an ethos common to the rest of the world. The Christian ethos relies upon a principle that precedes it and which controls and determines it. If moralism seeks to be such a principle, it will always result in blurring the difference between Christian and non-Christian. Moralism runs the risk of not considering why we must love God and neighbor or obey the various prescriptions in the New Testament. He wants to avoid turning the Christian ethos into an end. Moralism turns into the formality of a demand. He views the uniting of the ethical norm of Kant to Christian moralism as particularly dangerous since it can speak of unconditional commanding and unconditional obedience. He wants to ask the question of the meaning basis of Christian ethos in a way that moralism will not allow. Christian ethos follows from the mutual relationship prior to the command and obedience that governs the ethics proposed by Barth. The commanding has its origin, meaning, and basis in the being of Jesus Christ in Christians and of Christians in Jesus Christ. Christian ethos itself is not the meaning and goal of Christian vocation. Barth then turns attention to the classic view of vocation (561ff), which turns away from moralism and embraces a view that seems self-evident. It commands itself as the simplest and most obvious answer to the question before us. He agrees that all ancient and modern dogmatics of all confessions and schools travel this path if they avoid moralism. He also agrees that the Gospel as the Word of God calls humanity is an invitation and demand addressed to humanity. It faces us with the freedom that Christians need to express in the world and in confrontation with the world. We have concern for such things only connection with the offer and impartation of a divine act of grace. Thus, what distinguishes the Christian from others is this address, reception, possession, use and enjoyment of the salvation of God and revealed to the world by God in Jesus Christ. Christians are those who have received this grace. The Spirit has illumined and awakened them. They experience new birth and conversion. They have peace with God. The justification, sanctification, and vocation of humanity in Christ have not been in vain, for these persons stand with Christ. They have received forgiveness and experience liberation. They have the freedom of the children of God. They enjoy the prospect of their resurrection. They enjoy new obedience in the power of the Holy Spirit. They do so, knowing they will experience temptation, assault, conflict, and tribulation common to humanity. Christians are in the world and confront the world, standing at the side of the God who acts and reveals who God is in Jesus Christ. This classic view becomes the comprehensive and exhaustive answer of what we can say about Christian existence and vocation. He admits that this view is satisfying in practical and theoretical ways, especially for its value in preaching and instruction. He sees it has value in its translation into many different languages and fine hymns. It provides a solid bond of Christian fellowship. It provides the only genuine and effective motive for Christian apologetics. In saying this, I imagine Barth has a smile. If we have followed him closely, we know this is a hint that something is wrong with the classic view. The purpose is to save souls, to show humanity the way of redemption, to cause them to become Christians for the sake of their personal salvation and to confirm and strength their faith. He agrees that something true and important finds expression in the classic view of vocation. The concern Barth has is that such a view can lend itself easily to the conclusion that Christian vocation is nothing more than a happy and satisfying personal experience. My soul becomes what is essential and important in the goal of vocation. It becomes a matter of possession. The worst of people have drawn this conclusion from the classic answer.

Regardless, Barth cannot accept the classic answer. He points to three difficulties he sees in the classic answer. First, the Christian way of life is not the basis and meaning of vocation. The Christian way of life arises out of its origin in the union of being between the Christ who commands the Christian who obeys. The classic view leads to the dangerous juxtaposition of divine gift and divine task, between Gospel and Law, between justification and sanctification, between salvation and service to the glory of God. Second, the classic answer has difficulty distinguishing between Christian and non-Christian. The Christian way of life is often not one that Christians practice very well. In fact, non-Christians may display some of its characteristics in a better way. Third, the classic view depends upon my personal awareness of the assurance of salvation. This assurance becomes the basis of standing on the side of God and in face of the world. If the ground of such assurance is in ourselves, we fail to see that assurance is not the direct consequence of faith, grace, and salvation. Rather, assurance must flow from something prior to our own experience. Further, (p. 566-71) a material difficulty of the classic answer is that while it legitimately focuses attention upon its personal relevance, such a human insight might be only too human. Is the personal benefit of salvation the content and heart of vocation? Can such personal application be the inner end, meaning, and basis of my Christian existence? Such thinking could lead to cultivating egocentricity that is too human, even for all its sanctity. The fact that such personal concerns are legitimate does mean that the individual has the last word on what it means to be a Christian. All that Barth has discussed in his doctrine of reconciliation in its Christological basis did not occur for us to rejoice in our little faith love and hope or secure for us our private good fortune. We are not to think that the fulfillment of the prophetic task of Christ, the priestly offering of his life, and the meaning of his election, is not simply for such private benefit. Such a notion seems like it makes egocentricity a sacred way of life. Yet, humanity is not the measure of all things. Barth admits, however, that quietistic mysticism, pietism, evangelicalism, and theological liberalism do not exhibit pure concentration on the personal experience of grace and salvation that is supposed to make a Christian a Christian. The tendency inward has its balancing outward tendency toward service. It seems that movements that exalt the personal experience of salvation in the principle of the structure of Christian existence carry within them the seeds of the countervailing outward dimension.

Modern ethical systems conceive of morality as determining through some criterion what an agent ought to do. They bind people together by codes. Ethics will be one of rules, of do and do not. The attraction of such an ethic in a modern experience of the world is that the agent is free, unconstrained by authority. Such an ethic of freedom has viewed the ethical rules as the deliverance of reason. They reflect what human beings desire. Such an ethic is hostile the classical Christian view of an ethics of virtue or the good. Such an ethic has overlapping concerns with those of Aristotle. Virtue ethics occurs in the context of communion, of the coming of God through Christ into a personal relation, most immediately with those who have turned in faith to the revelation of God, but through them, a relation God has with humanity. God establishes this relation through love and generating a network of relations into an ever-expanding network of love. The highest mode of being for humanity, in which humanity will find its freedom, arises out of that relation. Of course, the divine-human relation is hardly one of equals, which was also an affront to ethics arising out of modernity.[68] The point here is that Barth may have collapsed the modern ethical project and the classical Christian moral tradition into one when they had quite different basis.

Barth now shifts his attention to two theological arguments for questioning the tenability of the classic answer.

First (p. 571-94), Barth wants us to consider what scripture means when it addresses the notion of the event of calling or vocation. He wants us to consider the meaning and purpose of the event. His examination leads him to say that the personal benefit to the one called is not the primary concern. The goal of the calling of Abraham, Moses, the prophets, the disciples, or Paul had only an incidental place for the benefit to them as individuals. Calling gave priority to standing at the side of God and in face of the world. They are in a new position at the side of God and in face of the world in a way that leads to obedience and faithfulness. If all this is so, then the classic answer is contrary to scripture. Vocation is a task God gives individuals. God consecrates them for the task. Christian existence involves the execution of the task. The task involves confrontation with others, but not in isolation. They no longer belong to themselves or to human society. They do not seek the task. God has sought them for the task. Called to the side of God, God also commissions them for this task. The divine cause becomes their cause. The task is the center of their lives. Rather than arising out of their inner life, God lays it upon them. God makes them witnesses. The event of vocation means they know God is with them and they are aware God has opened their eyes to the acts of God in past and present, while embracing future activity in history. Others will not see this vocation. While the one called carries out vocation in the presence of others, others

---

[68] (Taylor 2007), 282-3.

will not see or hear. God makes Christians witnesses rather than spectators. Vocation means knowledge of God and the will of God. Vocation means God equips the one called as well. The point is that alteration of the situation of the individual is not the principle that controls the existence of the individual. Rather, commission and sending by God controls the existence of the individual. One has more concern for the task than one has for oneself. One receives the gifts of justification, sanctification, and liberation to serve the task God lays before the individual.

Second, (p. 594-614) the goal of vocation is that Christ live in the Christian by the Holy Spirit. The classical view would have us believe that what makes one a Christian is that which accrues to the individual in the form of present or future consequences for personal life. Yet, the true being of the Christian consists in the community of action determined by the relationship between Christ and the Christian. The action of Christ is prior to that of the Christian, connecting with the gracious and merciful creator and reconciler. Christ does not act to his own advantage. Vocation starts with the will and work of God and the goal is the world. The rule of God is the principle that controls the structure of the existence of the Christian. Yes, obedience will lead salvation, but the one called seeks first the rule of God. The cause of Christ takes precedence over personal concerns of blessedness or damnation. Thus, Christian existence participates in the great context of the history of God with the world and in salvation history. Each Christian has a role to play in this larger history of salvation. The Christian is a cooperating subject within that history. The fulfillment of vocation in a service or ministry allows the Christian to be a cooperating subject in the history of salvation. One renders service to one's Lord. Finally, the service or ministry of the Christian arises out of the life of Christ in the individual and the life of the individual in Christ. We have here the basis of vocation. Yet, Christ lives in the Christian in the same way in which Christ is the head and representative of humanity. Christ reconciles the world with God in his person. No one exists entirely without Christ. The Christian joyfully recognizes this true position of humanity before God and joyfully cooperates in witnessing to this reality. The cooperation of the Christian is vital to the ongoing work of God in the world. The work of God in Christ does not exhaust the work of God. The divine work in the world continues in the presentation of what took place then. The work of God is also the Word of God. The work of God began in the resurrection, continued in the activity of the Spirit, and moves toward the completeness of the whole economy in the final and universal appearance and revelation in Jesus Christ. He continues to exercise his prophetic work. Christ wills for others to join him in this activity. Thus, Christ commissions people to be Christians. One must hear this word from others, listen to that word, and obey that word. Prophets are not idle. They attach themselves to Christ, tread in the steps of Christ, and witness to the reconciliation of the world accomplished in Christ. The vocation of the Christian is to be a sign of the living Word of God. The existence of the Christian is to indicate and attest this Word. The point is not oneself. One is a hearer of the Word so that one may become a doer. One turns to the world that has not yet heard and make know this Word to them. Set at the side of God in the world, the Christian also is over against the world. Barth concludes by saying that he will want to fill out this concept of the Christian as witness in the doctrine of the command of God in the context of the doctrine of reconciliation (IV.4). The Christian as witness will be the controlling principle of the second form of Christian ethics.

The meaning of Christian service and ministry is the divine Word. Christian vocation is the accompanying and confirming sign of the living Word. One becomes a hearer of the Word to become a doer of the Word. He intends this idea to be the controlling principle of the IV.4.[69] He considered his ethical reflections in Chapter XII a prologue to his projected main statement here. His ethical reflection here informs his view in Chapter XII and supplies its end in the projected Chapter XXI. Since God is the gracious Father who has acted in the Son to reconcile sinners to God, our disposition ought to be filial engagement and trust. This trust should express itself in confident prayer for the coming of the rule of God and in the struggle against lordless powers. We should use our lives in the service of the rule of God and in revolt against the lordless powers. The advent of the rule of God has begun, and thus, one is already speaking of the Redeemer even as one is discussing the Reconciler. We hasten toward the consummation.[70]

For Barth, the reason ethics has the character of a command is that the command is an act of God. The command must work in the life of the human being to whom it comes.

In *The Christian Life,* Barth will remind us that ethics is an attempt to answer the question of what constitutes good human action. True church proclamation deals with God acting in relation to humanity and human acting in relation to God. It considers the goodness of divine and human action. The command of God is the source and norm of theological ethics. Human action is good when God commands it through the Word of God. He will want to deal with the significance of the command of God as worked out in the life of a human being. Considering the uniqueness of

---

[69] (K. Barth, Church Dogmatics 2004, 1932-67), IV.3 [71.4] 607-10.
[70] (Cambridge Companion to Karl Barth 2000), Nigel Biggar, "Barth's Trinitarian Ethic," 218-20.

each time and place, special ethics considers what constitutes a good human action. He summarizes III.4, Chapter XII, 52.1. 1) The Word of God is the speaking of the living God, the specific content of what is always a special event between God and the human being in its historical reality. He must point to that event in its uncontrollable content. 2) He refers to the one command of the one God, which has an event character. He must direct and instruct responsible humanity to the ever-new event of its encounter with the living God. He wants to expound on this kairos, this event between God and the human being. He finds the commanding God and the obedient and disobedient human being revealed in Jesus Christ. His approach will respect the immediacy of the dealings between God and humanity in a way that will not violate the freedom of God or humanity. He will respect the freedom, directness, particularity, and uniqueness with which it takes place between God and the individual in unique times and places. He will need to focus on the mystery of this encounter. He sees certain directives that can serve as witnesses to the Word of God. He will refer to the event of the encounter between God and individual human beings. He wants to help us understand this event in the context of a pilgrim theology in the light of grace and on the way to glory. This understanding is light of the coming of Christ in resurrection, in the power of the Spirit, and the yet unreached goal. This event occurs in the context of pilgrim theology.

For Barth the moral field is the circle of the covenant of grace. It involves the location and the event of the encounter between God and humanity, an encounter whose focal point is petitionary prayer. In tying together prayer and ethics, Barth explores a moral ontology and a moral anthropology. He discusses human dependence while being clear such dependence does not diminish the human agent. He discusses the importance of resolute action that does not lead us self-assertion. He holds to the unity in distinction we find in giving priority to God and the reality of the human agent.[71]

He will make it clear that he wants to preserve the event nature of ethics that he finds in the command of God. The encounter between God and the individual is the nature of a command because the will of God is an event that over-rides our resistance. Baptism and the Lord's Supper embrace the Christian life because both come from commands Jesus gave. The Lord's Prayer aids Barth in pointing toward what the Christian life looks like. His reflections will oppose the notion that the theologian ought to provide general principles that one could view as parallel to the attempts of moral philosophers to find general ethical principles. The effect is

---

[71] (Webster 1995), 114.

powerful. Christian ethics must not become a means by which Christian life imprisons itself in some pristine time in the past. It must always be free to hear a fresh word from God. Given his exposition of the Word of God in Volume I.1, we are aware that this does not mean an abstract word. It means a word inspired by the text and by Christ. Christians must always be willing to hear the Bible anew as new situations face the church and individuals. My own contention is that the flexibility of Christianity in this regard, as it moves into various times and cultures is a sign of its strength. As he turns to the Lord's Prayer, he finds a significant pointer to the concerns of Christian ethical reflection. Christian life begins in relationship with our loving and gracious Father and always as children of the Father. We are to have passion for the honor of God in our personal lives, in the church, and in the world. We are to pray for the rule of God to come. This means we clearly see the disorder of this world, fight the powers of this world, and welcome the rule of God that is still coming. Christ is the next new thing to come. We will seek the will of God. We will trust the Father for the sustenance we need every day. We will realistically face our propensity to do wrong to others and that others will do wrong to us. In response, we will release ourselves from the past and live with the freedom that offering and receiving forgiveness brings. We are to recognize the battle in which we engage evil, testing, and trial. Since we can give in and fail, we pray that we would not enter the worst of such tests and that we would resist evil. These themes of the Lord's Prayer will become the heart of living the Christian life.

Second, in *Christian Life,* Barth discusses the gracious God as the commanding God.

He begins with a brief survey. 1) The encounter with God is an encounter with Jesus Christ. We cannot look behind him or forward ahead of him. God has spoken and acted here. This means the commanding God is historical, among human beings, for human beings, and as a human being. In this new action, God encounters humanity. God is Lord of humanity, but in Christ is also Father and Brother. The coming of the rule of God means the breaking of judgment on the human being who violates it. Yet, the coming of the rule of God is for humanity in moving against the perversion of human thinking, willing, and being, against the darkness and confusion of the human situation, against the destruction of the human being, and against the power of chaos and nothingness. God is wrathful because God has urgent concern for humanity. Humanity has hatred for God, but God answers this hatred with becoming the friend of humanity. He stresses that the sin that brings human misery is that of trying to slip by God a thousand secret paths. God is special and different for each human being and even in each time and situation but is never other than who God is for every person, time, and situation. 2) If we consider the person responsible to the commanding God, we must also turn to Jesus Christ. The first and last word about humanity is in Christ. He finds no general picture of humanity. God affirms, loves, and elects individuals as a member of the people of God. God made this person free through justification, sanctification, and vocation (Volume IV). In reviewing III.4, human beings are fellow human beings, soul of the body, and creation in restricted time. In this context, humanity can use this freedom. The gracious God confronts humanity, making humanity responsible to God. Humanity has this Yes from God, even when humanity is impotent and unworthy of it. The ethics we consider is event rather than abstract law. Christians receive this Yes humbly, putting themselves in the place with other sinners who can only look to the grace of God and pray for it. Christians are in solidarity with all other sinners and is the responsible to the God who commands humanity. 3) He discusses the situation in which God and the individual stand over against each other, and confront each other, for they are two subjects in genuine encounter. Yet, they are partners inseparably bound to each other. God and humanity are together in Jesus Christ. In fact, they belong together, have a deep bond, and are in fellowship with each other. In Christ, the covenant has its irrevocable basis. In Christ, nothing can break this bond. God validates divine glory in divine love for humanity, in being the Father and Savior, and in being kind to humanity. 4) The central task is the consideration of the command that God gives to the individual in this situation. What does the gracious God want from humanity? The rule of God has drawn near and impinged upon humanity. God calls humanity to respond to divine action. What shall we do? We ask because God poses the question. To ask is to put one on the path of obedience. One must make the question one's own and put it as one's own. If one puts the question truly and genuinely, one will always ask it afresh and provide new directions. The question of the will of God should also be about a new event. The command of God is a dynamic reality because of the living God. The content of this action of God is a specific Word directed to humanity. It refers to the gracious God acting toward humanity; for this God says something to individuals that lets individuals know what they are to do. The command is the event in which God commands. The free human being is to receive the command of God as the concrete clam, decision, and judgment of God. What we shall do is the choice of God of the good today. This refers to the encounter and togetherness of God and humanity. We deal with a unique event or an ongoing and interconnected series of such events. Ethics cannot give direction. All it can give is instruction as to how to put the question relevantly and to look forward openly to the answer that God alone can give. He wants to explore the art of correct asking about the will of God and the hearing of it as the command of God.

In III, 4, Barth worked out the first part of special ethics as the final part of the doctrine of creation in the concept of freedom. He considers the possibility that he could continue with that theme, only now in the context of reconciliation. He will also consider an organizing theme of repentance, faith, thanksgiving, and faithfulness. He finds all of them insufficient as a way of grounding the ethics of the doctrine of reconciliation.

The organizing theme must be an action that characterizes the event character of Christian life. This leads him to consider the humble, resolute, frightened, and joyful invocation of the gracious God in gratitude, praise, and above all petition. This would be the normal action corresponding to the fulfillment of the covenant in Jesus Christ. Here is the individual calling upon God. The command comes from Psalm 50:15 to call upon God. This simple command is behind every command. He will follow the course of the Lord's Prayer in Matthew 6:9-13 and Luke 11:2-4. Prayer is the heart of his consideration, but surrounded by two other commands of God, that of baptism (prologue) and the Lord's Supper (epilogue).

Barth will consider the prologue and foundation of the Christian life in baptism (75). This part volume is a fragment of IV.4 published in 1967 as part of *Church Dogmatics*. He admits his dependence upon the work of Markus Barth, his son, for changing his views on baptism. The views expressed here are consistent with the view of the church and the sacraments as these matters arise in his discussion of the doctrine of reconciliation.[72]

Everything Barth has been developing concerning the Holy Spirit comes to fruition in this part-volume. He abandons the notion of sacrament as a means or instrument of grace. He regards both baptism and the Supper as essential to the unique ethical life of the Christian. Water baptism is a response or answer to the regenerating action of the Holy

---

[72] One of the issues in Barth studies is whether this volume represents mature thought or the reflections of an aging man. One can make a compelling case, however, that it is a sign of the direction Barth is heading. He would discuss both Baptism and the Lord's Supper within his discussion of Christian ethics. As I will show, Barth has a view of the church and the sacraments that is close to the Anabaptist and Zwingli position. W. Travis McMaken, in *The Sign of the Gospel: Toward an Evangelical Doctrine of Infant Baptism after Karl Barth* the author shows how IV.4 is a natural outgrowth of the mature thinking of Barth. It was not an aberration. However, like many postbarthians, he will also want to find a way to affirm the tradition of infant baptism within the Barthian tradition. My discussion here is to present my understanding of the argument of Barth.

Spirit. The Augsburg Confession (1530) had already declared the Spirit works faith in those who hear the Gospel as God pleases. As such baptism is the first act of obedience by the Christian. He will offer an exposition of the Christian life as one of active obedience, lived in the way of sanctification. God baptizes with the Holy Spirit and the believer responds in receiving baptism of water as an act of obedience. Throughout Volume IV, Barth has emphasized what Christ has done "for us." Only now does Barth focus upon what Christ does "in us." Barth is bringing baptism into line with the Reformation understanding of Word alone and faith alone. His teaching here is a result of his view of election. God demonstrates who God is through the actions of God in creation and reconciliation. Humanity shows who it is through action as well. In acting in response to the gracious act of God in Christ, the person responds to God and thereby becomes who God intends the person to be. Water baptism is the way church and believer establish the validity of the Christian life in a non-sacramental way, beginning with an adult act of obedience. The teaching on baptism we find here offers a positive interpretation of human action in view of human salvation. Water baptism is a petition for the Holy Spirit. This petition is redemptive human action. The person is the subject of his or her own action.[73] Among the concerns of some is that the theology of Barth here is not ecumenical. Granted, it challenges Reformed, Lutheran, Catholic, and Orthodox views of baptism. However, it has ecumenical significance in the growing global Christian movement that includes Baptist, Pentecostal, and Charismatic perspectives.[74]

First, baptism with the Spirit refers to the objective ground of the Christian life in the decisive act of God in changing and renewing our human nature in Jesus Christ. Baptism is part of the gathering of the church by the awakening power of the Holy Spirit. A change does take place in humanity in the freedom of the grace of God that enables humanity to become and to do what it had not been or done. However, the decisive change has already taken place in Christ. A Christian is the one in whom God has brought about a turning back towards God. He refers to the event of this change that marks the beginning of the Christian life as a mystery and miracle. He ponders how it is even possible for the rule of God to enter the sphere of human being, life, thought, will, and action. He grants the individual becomes different. One becomes a stranger to oneself, and thus different from what one was before. Yet, one is also aware of similarity. The question he ponders is how this person becomes the subject

---

[73] (Richardson 2004), 61-6, 176-89, referring to untranslated essays by Eberhard Jungel.
[74] (Richardson 2004), 208.

of this event of the awakening by the Holy Spirit, and thus to faith in God, love for God, hope in God, and one who lives as a friend of God rather than an enemy of God. In this way, the individual becomes serviceable to God and a witness for God. Scripture will write of this as a new garment or a new birth or even as the transition from death to life. Humanity clearly has a restlessness, an anxiety, a dissatisfaction, awareness of finitude and transience, the hunger for a new beginning, and convincing experiences of dramatic change in one's life. As the foundation of the Christian life, baptism first refers to the divine nature of this change. For him, then, the history of Jesus Christ is the foundation of Christian existence. In this sense, the Christian life begins between Bethlehem and Golgotha. The event of a change in an individual life today has its root in the history of Jesus Christ. He hastens to say, however, that a genuine change occurs in individuals today. Jesus Christ was faithful to God and faithful to us. The event of this change viewed from above is the history of the faithfulness of Jesus Christ to God and to us. The event of this change viewed from below is an event in time in which a specific person finds liberation and refashioning of one's life in the light of the history of Jesus Christ. He points out that the history of Jesus Christ has the power to be truly for us. This occurs as the work of the Holy Spirit applies the power of the history of Jesus Christ to an individual life through an awakening that makes these persons free, able, willing, and ready to give this event the principal place in their willing and thinking. The Spirit makes one subjectively open, seeing, hearing, and comprehending. God has genuine partnership with in individual. This divine change is the result of the baptism of the Holy Spirit. This divine change takes the form of the grace of God that reconciles humanity to God, but now addressed to the individual. The divine change demands the response of human gratitude. The divine change occurs in the context of a distinctive fellow-humanity united by the common experience of this divine change. Such a divine change as seen in the baptism of the Holy Spirit is a beginning that moves individuals toward a future as a new creature. This baptism will bear, in its season during a human life, the fruit of the Spirit (Galatians 5). Further, this baptism hastens toward a future that is coming to meet the individual. One receives nourishment for the journey in the body and blood of Christ. As a pilgrim people, they seek to be a people who hallow the name of God, who live in the rule of God, and who do the will of God on earth as it is in heaven. One is constantly running towards this future, constantly seeks to apprehend it, and lives in daily renewal.

Second, baptism with water refers to the subjective aspect of human initiation into the Christian life performed in the church in response to the faithfulness of God. The first step in the Christian life is the baptism with water. Such baptism is the first step taken in the Christian life in the actualization of that change. It occurs by the decision of the individual in a request made of the community and as an act of the community. One receives it in gratitude for what God has already done, in commitment to a life of obedient conformity to the reconciling and commanding Christ, and in the hope that is born in the promise of Christ and directed to its goal in the consummation. The sharp distinction shows that baptism is not a sacrament or work of grace. Baptism is a human liturgical work in recognition of what God has already done for us in Christ and in obedience to the commission laid upon us in the reconciling work of Christ. The basis and goal of baptism is union and fellowship with Christ. Baptism arises out of the commitment of individuals to no longer lead self-enclosed lives. Rather, they live their lives in reference to Christ and in fellow-humanity with the Body of Christ. They unite to a particular congregation. The meaning of baptism focuses upon hope. Baptism with water is a human work. We do not dignify it if we make of it an immanent divine work, such as the church has done in calling it a sacrament. His focus is upon the ethical meaning of baptism. For him, we are to seek its meaning in its character as a true and genuine human action that responds to the divine act and word. Formally, he can say that baptism points us to the liberated life of the Christian, directs us to participation in the life of the congregation, and one enters it freely as individuals and as congregations. Materially, the meaning of baptism lies in a strict correlation and distinction between the human and divine action from which baptism springs. In this sense, baptism is an act of obedience in its basis and an act of hope considering its goal. Baptism involves the common conversion of both community and candidate to God. The congregation is in solidarity with the one receiving baptism. Conversion of all involved in the act of baptism is at the heart of his consideration here. Conversion is the most human thing one can do, effected as it is by human knowledge, thought resolve, and will. He thinks it foolish to rob human action of its significance by looking for something deeper. Theologians, pastors, and congregations need to take this human action seriously as a decision of this individual. The command to which one obeys is from Jesus Christ. The promise to which one responds is from Jesus Christ. One becomes a disciple of Jesus Christ, forsaking a former life and entering upon a new life. One makes public confession, and the congregation listens and trusts. This first step in Christian life is a look to Jesus Christ. It will be the first of many steps. Baptism points to the justification and sanctification of the individual. It suggests renewal of life in the service of God. The third meaning of baptism, in addition to obedience and hope, involves the movement of one's life toward future glorification. In baptism, one makes oneself responsible for the witness and mission of the church in the world. Baptism pledges one to the daily repentance and conversion to God. This foundation of the Christian life will have its ambiguities as one leads a Christian life. We must remember that baptism occurs in hope, a human action that looks beyond self and toward the future. Jesus Christ is the future of their action. Such hope becomes real in the prayer of individuals and congregations. The meaning of baptism in prayer, knowing the spiritual hazards that are ahead, is overcoming worry about this future with calm and cheerful hope.

The Reformed churches retained infant baptism because they regarded baptism as acceptance of the covenant of the grace of God that is not for adults alone but for infants as well. John Wesley also defended infant baptism. In his Treatise of Baptism, he agrees that direct evidence from Scripture and the first century does not exist. However, its practice seems pervasive from the second century onward. Thus, his respect for the tradition of the church led him to defend the practice. He did have a sacramental view of baptism. Karl Barth overturned the practice of infant baptism in some reformed churches. Barth demanded that baptism should take the form of an expression of the free confession of the candidate in 1943. In this volume, he made his teaching even more pointed by distinguishing between Spirit baptism and water baptism and presenting the latter as a human act of the obedience of faith. The criticism Barth finds in the faith and free confession of the baptized a prerequisite for baptizing them. Is he right? Alternatively, can we defend the practice of infant baptism as in keeping with the nature of baptism? We cannot answer this question simply by a critique of the arguments of Barth. The reason is that churches that practiced baptism for believers only called for confession at baptism. This would still stand, even if the arguments of Barth for it failed. One can easily show that there is no adequate biblical basis for the distinction between Spirit baptism and water baptism made in this volume. Primitive Christianity had no Spirit baptism as distinct from water baptism. There is only the one baptism, administered with water normally linked to the gift of the Spirit. We see this in Mark 1:8, Acts 19:1-7, Acts 10:44ff, 11:16, and 1:5. These are the only passages that we might consider as serious arguments for the position of Barth. In contrast, I Corinthians 12:13 refers to the work of the Spirit, in baptism, but with no suggestion of a baptism without water. Mark 1:8 and John 1:33 are sayings of the Baptist whose distinction between Spirit and water baptism is outdated by Christian baptism in Acts 2:38, as we see from acts 19:2. The announcing of the baptism of the Spirit in Acts 1:5 simply takes up the formulation of the Baptist in Luke 3:16 because Luke could find no pertinent saying of Jesus himself in the tradition. When Peter takes up the saying in 11:16, however, the aim is precisely to show the connection between water baptism and reception of the Spirit, which Luke finds to be normal in Christian baptism according to 2:38 and 19:2ff, though as a rule the imparting of the Spirit is obviously by laying on of hands in 19:6, but not 8:39.[75]

Barth discusses the basis of Christian baptism as rooted in the life of Jesus. The simplest answer is a reference to Matthew 28:19 as a baptismal command utter by the risen Lord. This saying shows that the community sought to trace back the baptism that it so self-evidently practiced to a command of its Lord, and that it did not want any other basis or justification for it. Further, in the baptism of Jesus in the Jordan, Jesus submits to the baptism of John. By doing this, He did in fact give to His people in every age and place, as the Head of this people, the command to baptize that the community has significantly repeated and expressed. Each gospel narrates the event and the Christian world of the first century new the story. In this event, we find the true basis of Christian baptism that Matthew 28:19 declares and formulates. The way Barth formulates this matter is consistent with the evaluation of the text in Matthew 28:19 from an historical and critical perspective, as well as its marginal position in the history of the development of Christian baptism. For that reason, Barth rightly refers to the baptism of Jesus as the true basis of Christian baptism that Matthew 28:19 declared and formulated.[76]

Barth accepts the label of Neo-Zwinglian in his view of baptism, saying he thinks he understands Zwingli better than he understood himself. He considers the matter of infant baptism a tiresome matter. Theology can only advise the church. He wishes the church would occasionally ask for advice. No one has sought his advice on the matter, and he has only the faintest hope that the church will heed it. In a different essay, he is clear that he moved toward the "congregational" position regarding church polity. He prefers the term "congregation" to the term "church." The essence of the church receives its definition in baptism and the Supper of the Lord. The threat to the church is that it falls in love with itself and become blind even as it attempts to lead the blind. The congregation consists of people who can sin against the grace of God. His concern is for dead congregations, for they can only be congregations divided. He thinks that had the congregation in Rome wanted to serve rather than rule, dominate, and sit upon a throne as infallible judge, then we might all be Roman. He quotes approvingly Friedrich Loofs, who wrote in 1901 that one who knows whether it might not be the case when the established churches of Europe collapse and that the congregational form of church in

---

[75] (Pannenberg, Systematic Theology 1998, 1991) Volume 3, 259-60.
[76] (Pannenberg, Systematic Theology 1998, 1991) Volume 3, 279.

America may not yet have a future among European congregations. He considers that this may well prove to be prophetic.[77]

Many Barthian scholars have sought to work around this view of Barth. It seeks some a middle way. If one respects tradition and honors ecumenical relationships, one will need to find a way to do so. Further, I am not aware that Barth on a personal level submitted himself for baptism as an adult. An impressive effort in this regard is that of W. Travis McMaken. He agrees with Barth in his critique of infant baptism. He agrees that witness is the primary mode of the life of the church in the world. This means that awakening or conversion is the way we participate in this witness, of which baptism with the Spirit is the primary sign. For Barth, Christ encounters human beings in the proclamation of the church. Thus, what Barth says in his fragment on baptism in IV.4 is consistent with the thrust of CD. When the church, even in infant baptism, provides a setting in public worship for baptismal gospel proclamation and invites the Spirit to come, even upon an infant, we are to understand the prayer as a hope that the child will fulfill, even if the church cannot say how or when. McMaken then concludes that the New Testament does not require nor forbid the practice. Churches will need to make a decision in the variety of times and places concerning whether or not infant baptism applies to the missionary setting.[78] Pannenberg will move a similar direction, largely agreeing with the critique by Barth of infant baptism but concluding that the New Testament neither forbids nor requires. He clearly does so as he pursued his concern for the ecumenical nature of the church.[79]

Barth seems quite right to suggest that Reformed and Evangelical Protestants have defended infant baptism in a form that suggests a theological and biblical justification after the practice had spread widely.[80] The fact that Barth did not submit himself to adult baptism makes one wonder how deeply he held his position.

I will now offer a sketch of the rest of the volume on *The Christian life*. The basis is the lectures fragments entitled *The Christian Life*. However, I will also refer to other parts of *Church Dogmatics,* his *Gottingen Dogmatics,* his *Ethics,* and, in a text well worth pondering if one is beginning with Karl Barth *Prayer and Preaching*. Thus, I will not be guessing at what Barth might have said. I am placing here what Barth has said elsewhere in a way that I

---

[77] (K. Barth, God Here and Now 1964, 2003) Chapter 5, 1947.
[78] McMaken, W. Travis, *The Sign of the Gospel: Toward an Evangelical Doctrine of Infant Baptism after Karl Barth*, Minneapolis: Fortress, 2013. pg273-274, Print. (formatting slightly modified)
[79] (Pannenberg, Systematic Theology 1998, 1991), Volume 3, 262.
[80] Barth, CD IV.4 fragment on baptism, 179.

like to think is helpful to others in pointing us in the direction Barth was heading. He will depict the Christian life as an enacted prayer for the rule of God that surpasses all other possibilities of revolt against the disorder humanity causes by entangling people in a plethora of causes, systems, and ideologies. The Christian becomes a rebel against the disorder that oppresses true humanity. Human idolatry leads to the victimization of "lordless powers," whether spiritual (political powers, ideologies, economic systems) or chthonic (fashions, hobbies, etc). Acknowledgment of the true Lord will lead to genuine freedom from the preying idols that lead to various forms of oppression.[81]

The Lord's Prayer becomes how Barth brings together the analogy between divine and human action. It achieves its concrete relation in and through invocation. The grounding act of the Christian life is the invocation of God. We see a form of synergism in Barth based on faith, a cooperative labor of the Christian life arrives where being in action by the believer emerges as a genuine Protestant concept. In pointing to the Lord's Prayer, we see the Christological uniqueness of the Christian life.[82]

First, Barth discusses the phrase in the Lord's Prayer, "Our Father," focusing on the children and their Father (76). Barth says the obedience of Christians follows from the fact that in Jesus Christ they recognize God as their Father and themselves as children of their heavenly Father. Obedience is their action to the extent they venture it in invocation of God. Liberated by the Holy Spirit, they take God as their Father and themselves seriously as children of their heavenly Father. Barth is making it clear that the Christian life is a distinctive form by its unique reference to God as Father. It brings to our consciousness that God is the active subject and the subsequent human action relies upon our relation to God as Father. As scripturally grounded, we simply acknowledge that God is Father. Calling God Father is not expressivism, a human label placed upon God, as in nominalism, but becomes obligatory due to scripture. Such language is a matter of revelation, for God is the Father of the Son.[83]

Barth discusses the Father. The one invoked as Father is a Thou, a fatherly "I" taken seriously as such. Thus, God is not "It," or even Wholly Other.

Tertullian called this prayer a breviary of the whole gospel. It invites us to apply the adage that the law of prayer is the law of faith. The law of faith implicit in the law of prayer is a law of life, a criterion by which to answer our question concerning the obedience required of Christians.

---

[81] (McMullen 1988), p. 71-2.
[82] (Richardson 2004), 189-90.
[83] (Webster 1995), 176-80.

The first words of the prayer give us direction. The words are an invocation of God. People who pray it may have no desire for God. The Lord commands people to pray.

Christians do not speak about the Father, but to the Father. They put into practice this knowledge: I believe in God, the Father ... God is Father, independent of the attitude or disposition with which other beings encounter or do not encounter God. God acts as Father toward us. "Father" gives content to the word "God." "Father" suggests that God is the head and founder of a certain family or society. "Father" suggests complete dependence of all other upon God, something similar to what Schleiermacher called "the source of the feeling of absolute dependence." Of course, the problem with Schleiermacher is that the Father becomes "It." "Father" also signifies in the minds of many Christians, "dear," suggesting fatherly goodness. "Father" signifies the fatherly subject who bears and guarantees everything we have just mentioned. The Father is the personal Creator and Ruler, the origin and source of all good. Christians living in obedient encounter with God as Father in reality and truth. Such a notion stresses filial engagement in complete trust. This trust should express itself in confident prayer for the completion of the coming of the rule of God, and with it the secure establishment of just relations between human beings.

What is the meaning of the indicative in which this imperative to pray like this has its ground, and with it the Christian's obedient invocation of God as Father? In what sense does one who sees Jesus see the Father? In what sense does Jesus reveal God as His Father and therefore as our or the Father? The history of Jesus Christ in its totality is the only possible answer. The will that Jesus affirms is that of the Father. In His participation in the world and humanity, acts as He who is one with the Father. Jesus shows Himself to be the faithful and obedient Son as He exercises mercy.

Barth will then discuss the children. How can there be this invocation by a small group of people from among humanity? They can do so in anticipation of the future universal praise of God. To live in this prophetic minority is the destiny of Christians. "Father" suggests great closeness to the one addressed, having a familiar and intimate character. One must regard oneself as a child of God. How can one claim this right in practice? People have abandoned this right long ago. Their property would belong to the Father. They would orient their lives to the Father. They would have to love the Father. They would lift their heads to the Father. Christians are not fit for this childhood of the Father. They are not children of the Father because they have shown themselves to be such. They confess that they are sinners. Grace is the presence, event, and revelation of the simplest, truest, and most real of all things for those to whom God addresses it and who recognize it. Grace is the overcoming of the distinction between God and humanity, Creator and creature, heaven and earth. People become children of God by the grace of God, and thus, by the goodness of the Father. This grace comes through the history of Jesus Christ. As people awaken to the history of Jesus Christ that controls their own history, people become the children of God. They recognize that his birth, ministry, death, and resurrection took place for them. The history of Jesus Christ anticipates their individual history. Individual life has its end or goal in Jesus Christ. In Jesus Christ, world and God find reconciliation.

It will now be our task to make some statements elucidating the mode of existence of these children of God. 1) The grace by which they are what they are is always grace, the free kindness of God, and thus have the freedom to call God, Father. They have gratitude for this kindness. 2) Those who through the grace of God have the freedom to call upon God as their Father will never encounter God except as those who are inept, inexperienced, unskilled, and immature, and thus as children. They are always beginners. Even at the most advanced stage, and in the ripest form, it can never be anything better. Christians contradict themselves if their lives take the form of a trained and mastered routine, of a learned and practiced art. As masters and virtuosos, they would not live by grace. Children show readiness to learn and helplessness. Christians, who regard themselves as big, strong, rich, dear, and good children of God, are not Christians at all. For this reason, he is skeptical of liturgical worship or systematically constructed theory and practice of individual and spiritual formation. I am not aware that Barth deals seriously with the apostolic admonition to move from childishness in faith to maturity in faith. John Wesley would suggest that the Christian life is open to stages of growth on analogy with the stages of the natural growth of human life from infancy, childhood, adolescence, and adulthood. Some people stay too long in the childish stage of Christian life. However, in agreement with Barth, moving toward maturity in faith and discipleship means an increase of love to God and to neighbor.[84] 3) We think in terms of the plural, children of God, when we invoke God as "Our Father." We also affirm this in the article of the creed "I believe in … the communion of saints."

Barth then discusses the invocation. The Christian life is event, history, and action. The Father wills live dealings with the children. They must actualize the partnership in this history. The Father wills that their lives become invocation. That God is our Father, and we are children of God, is true as we respond to the work and word of the Father by calling upon God as Father. This response is what concerns us here in the context

---

[84] John Wesley, Sermon 40, Christian Perfection.

of ethics. Invocation is the movement in which the children bring themselves to the attention of their Father and cry to the Father. To call upon the Father is to take a place alongside the Father, to take the word of the Father as true, and to confess this before people. Children of God are free for responsible decision and action. Thanksgiving entails honoring, extolling, lauding, and praising of the Father as the giver of the gift of this relationship. Invocation becomes event in the lives of Christians as thanksgiving, praise, and prayer, and therefore as the primal form of the Christian ethos. We must note how extraordinary this event is. We stand before the mystery of the covenant. Something special has taken place. What must take place if people are to be Christians is a special movement and act of God in which God gives to the Word of divine grace the specific power to reach the specific people among the many to whom it goes out. The astonishing event that takes place in the invocation of the Father by human children is that of the fruitful meeting and the living fellowship of the Holy Spirit with them and with their spirits. In the Holy Spirit, God meets with the unholy human spirits.

We can see here that the priority of God as self-acting Subject, from which Barth will consider secondarily human subjectivity and action. In line with his discussions throughout *Church Dogmatics,* human freedom has its grounding in the grace of God. Only counterfeit freedom relies upon human worthiness. In the call upon God, the children recognize they are in God, not outside, and not without God. Barth is leaving room for human agency within a covenant with God in which humanity has a role freely and actively received. The basis of our invocation of the Father is the life of Jesus of Nazareth, who lived his life as one who called upon God as Father. He lived his life in this way vicariously for us, but also became an example of we are to lead our lives. The agency of Christ does not inhibit human agents as part of the covenant. God has chosen not to work alone, a prisoner within divine agency. Barth is boldly asserting that corresponding to the human act of invocation is the divine act of hearing. Prayer is a real movement from humanity to God. Revelation is the action of God toward humanity, and prayer is the responsive action of human agents toward the action of God. Prayer as petition entails an affirmation of the human agent as a voluntary self in relation to God.[85]

Barth now offers three elucidations. 1) The Christian life is a spiritual one, a life that in its distinctiveness is from first to last conditioned by the special movement and act of God in the work of the Holy Spirit. A life of invocation consists in the prayer for the Holy Spirit, as seen in Luke 11:13. The spiritual life is life in awareness of the immediate presence of

---

[85] (Webster 1995), 182-91.

God. When the Spirit blows where the Spirit wills (John 3:8), the Spirit blows in the dark valleys and well as on the bright mountains. The Spirit blows into the holes where Christians find themselves. The Spirit takes loving care that when they fall asleep, they will always awaken. 2) The freedom of Christians to call upon God as their Father is a personal matter, but not a private one. Such matters do not concern private salvation and individual bliss. Christians call upon "Our Father." Invocation is not an end, but a means to end. Christians live lives determined by the One who gives them to freedom to be children of God. They do not become an "island of the blessed," but precisely there where all other people live under the same conditions. In his resurrection and ascension, Jesus did not separate from the world, but acts and still acts in the world. The world needs this witness. They are salt and light in the world. Christians are aliens, exiles, and pilgrims, and thus affliction and distress unavoidably hangs over them. Further, the children of God are not what they are in vain or for their own sake. They call upon God as messengers in service to God. However, "Our Father" is not just the cry of the members of an exclusive club, but the recognition that others do not yet have this knowledge, and yet, they also have God as their Father. In this sense, it becomes a prophetic prayer. 3) The invocation of God by the children of God is an integral part of the history of the covenant between God and humanity. God hears the praise, thanksgiving, and petition of the people.

Barth discusses the first petition of the Lord's Prayer (77), Hallowed be thy name, under the theme of zeal for the honor of God. We should note that in his exposition of the first three petitions, the concern of the prayer Jesus taught us is to unite with him in our concern for the cause of God. To pray these first three petitions is to pray that we make the cause of God in the world our cause as well. Barth says that Christians are people who know about the self-declaration of God. Their beginning has already taken place and their consummation is still to come. As such, they suffer because they are so well known and yet also so unknown to the world, the church, and to themselves. They pray that God will bring divine self-declaration to its goal and the manifestation of divine light that destroys all darkness. They have a zeal for the primacy of the validity of the Word in the world, church, and in their own hearts and lives.

He discusses the great passion. Christians are people with a definite passion. They are not cowards, bored, boring, or commonplace. A passion is the suffering of a person from an unfulfilled desire that seeks fulfillment, the fulfillment in which it can transform itself and become delight and joy instead of pain. Christians are people suffer from such an unfulfilled desire that seeks fulfillment. The Christian passion is a great, unconquerable, permanent, and even dangerous passion. Christian passion has a close connection with their election and calling to active knowledge and attestation of the work and Word of God, and thus to their lives as children of God. As those who live in the world, they have other passions. However, this passion makes them uniquely Christian.

"Hallowed be thy name" will lead us to the goal of a further development of Christian ethics under this theme. Invocation in this form is decisively petition, asking for something that only God can do and give. The human attitude and mode of action of the one praying this prayer seriously is one that characterizes their whole being, life, and action in such a way that it necessarily must be that of children calling upon their Father. The concern is for the honor of God. The person who seriously prays for this suffers from the unfulfilled desire that in a way that has not yet happened in the world, the church, or his or her own life, one longs for the sanctification of the name of God. This desire fills, impels, and rules Christians.

In the title of this section, Barth has chosen to use the word "zeal," but one might also think of delight and desire. Christian life must have the Christian passion of zeal for the honor of God.

Barth discusses the known and unknown God. God is both known and unknown, within the world in general as well as within the church. Christians pray for the honor of the name of God so that they will develop that zealous quality. What they mean is the following: Father, do what you alone can do. See to it finally, perfectly, and definitively, that people will know you. See to it that no one desecrates your name. Dispel the fatal ambivalence of our situation.

The image Barth has in mind is three concentric circles. The outer circle is the world, the church is the middle circle, and the inner and outer personal life of the Christian is the inner circle. They touch and overlap. Yet, they do not coincide. Barth wants to look at each one separately.

One, moving from outside to inside, we begin with the world, the creation of God in its totality. In this sense, world refers to nature, but more specifically, to the human world. The relationship of the human world to God is not one ordered to God principally and teleologically. The world is still alien to the covenant of grace, not yet committed to it, not yet called to bear witness to it. Its relation to God is open and neutral. The world does not seek to honor the name of God. It has ambivalence, neutrality, and indecisiveness of its relationship to God. The church and Christians become guiltier by living in that ambivalence in which God is both known and unknown to them as well.

Our first thesis is that the world objectively knows God very well. This thesis would have some truth, just from the standpoint of the spread of Christianity in the world. Yet, it seems too strong. Further, the guilt of the world for God remaining unknown to so many is also too serious. Have the church and Christians really had concern about God? We come to a deeper level when we recall that God already hallowed the name of God in making a good creation. To know God is to honor and love God, living in obedience. The name of God is holy in every blade of grass and snowflake, in every breath we take, in every thought we think, in every effort of humanity. Whether it does it and is grateful or not, the world lives by the object fact that it is the world God has created, and that God is constantly open to it. The basis and constitution of the world is what God holds together and sustains by the perfection with which God loves those who are enemies. People cannot escape God. God is at the heart of the world events and world affairs. In all the secularity of the world marked by human subjective refusal, the world already objectively knows God. The objective reality of God does not change with the subjective ignorance of humanity. Christian activity will always be highly debatable. What God already does as creator is ever a subject for debate.

We must now raise the question of the guilt in which the world implicates itself because the God well known to it remains unknown subjectively. The world evades the witness of the church. The dubious nature of this witness may excuse the world. However, Barth can think of no valid excuse when people do not know themselves in their given nature with their orientation to God, when they should know God, do not know God. They should know God, but do not do so in fact. One may blame the church and Christians, but one cannot blame God. The world is responsible for this structural perversion.

We cannot take the course of natural theology. We cannot count on the objective knowledge of God the Creator as a fact, so we can count on a corresponding subjective knowledge of God that is proper to the world and humanity. We cannot claim that as God as creator hallows the name of God, so the world hallows this name to some degree. We must admit the concealment of the knowledge of God. We must admit the hidden quality of the knowledge of God. Knowledge of God as creator has a limit. The history of Jesus, His birth, life, death, and resurrection, are the place where we find the name of God hallowed. This knowledge of God becomes definitive.

We must turn the page and speak about the ignorance of God so typical of the world, as well as the desecration of the name of God that takes place so widely in it. Of course, this thought should never become a favorite theme of theology and ought never to have more importance than the New Testament. Like his view of Nothingness, such ignorance has no power, significance, or dignity of its own. It lives by what it negates.

The most primitive form of the ignorance of God in the world is intellectual godlessness or theoretical atheism: "There is no God." Not all theoretical atheism is practical atheism, just as not all theoretical knowledge of God is practical knowledge. It expresses its alienation from God directly. It cannot frame its negative statement to bring out the seriousness of its intention. It constantly breaks out in polemics. If the world were as devoid of God as the atheist says, why would it have need of the proposition? Why is it so unsettled by the confession of faith in God? The world is not as godless as the atheist says. Godlessness also appears in the form of religion. Disguises godlessness occurs in secular cultures in which they cultivate secular images in a religious fashion. Some religions maintain the form. Religions arise from the self-declaration of God in the world that we cannot escape. In religion, the world tries to domesticate the God is known and yet also unknown and strange.

Another form of the desecration of the name of God is to exalt its own cause as the cause of God, or to subject the cause of God to its own. This attempt arises when the world believes that God can be useful and indispensable to its own goals, aims, and aspirations. The world is with God consistently, earnestly, and zealously. The world integrates itself with God. It equates God with itself. Although he does not refer to process theology here, I wonder if that is his concern.

The human being who denies God in the above ways also desecrates the name of God by not knowing truly the fellow human being.

We must also speak of the knowledge and ignorance of God in the church. Since the church is part of the world, it participates in the objective knowledge the world has of God. The church has its origin the self-declaration of God in Jesus Christ and can therefore see the knowledge of God in creation. The church has its life from this origin. As the church lives by Christ and bears witness of Christ, it is faithful to the world to which it belongs, but into which God sends it.

The fact that ignorance of God in the church or the fact of the failure of subjective knowledge of God exists in the church ought to disturb us more than that ignorance of God in the world. The prayer to hallow the name of God is a prayer the church needs to make as well. One sinister motif is that the church neglects its nature and task, thus become unfaithful to itself and denying its being as the church. Apostasy is the result. One form of apostasy is excess, puffing itself up. It exceeds the limit within which it can be the church of Jesus Christ. It will serve its own needs instead of Christ. It will become its own means of life and glory. One might call it, in relation to its Lord, the introverted church. It recites that Jesus is its Lord, but much of its pomp and circumstance is for the glorification of itself. It incorporates the priestly, kingly, and prophetic office into itself. It has the Spirit. It expounds the Scripture. A second sinister motive is the church in defect, the church that does not take itself seriously enough because it is only half-sure of its cause. Such a church is also unfaithful to the world. One might call it the extroverted church. It looks to Jesus Christ but might find it dangerous to cling to Him. It wants to be the Christian church, but it finds itself frightened by the world. The favorite word of this church is "and," as in "revelation and reason," "church and culture," "gospel and state," and so on. In both, the church commits apostasy, falling away from its living Lord, and having ambivalence concerning its Lord. It will then equate itself with the world and accommodate to it. The world takes over the church. Further, a practical atheism exists in the church.

We also find that God is both objectively known and subjectively unknown in the life of the individual Christian. The Christian knows God well. The determination for God, for fellowship the Son, is what determines the existence of the Christian. One lives as a Christian and repeatedly becomes a Christian. What makes a person a Christian is what happens to the person in the Word of God. The church exists in the light of God, as well as in the darkness of the world. The Christian is open to the self-declaration of God in Jesus Christ. To the extent that we are Christians, we hallow the name of God. Living in the light of God makes the darkness even more strange.

Let us look at our own lives. Us Christians can know and live with a clear understanding that we brought nothing into this world and can take nothing out, that wealth is a great deceiver, and yet, we live with two masters. Us Christians have a profound sense that we are always in the wrong before God, whereas we are strongly in the right. We are confessing members of the Christian community, while finding it strangely hard to live in a real unity of spirit with fellow Christians. We clearly see the need to handle weak fellow persons in the church with special patience, and yet we do not bear with them. We believe in peace. Yet do not Christian fighters for peace of all schools compete with non-Christians for the honor of being the most difficult of all God's creatures? We are not to have anxiety about tomorrow, yet we regard our situation as special and in need of anxiety. The world and its lusts pass away, yet we ensure our fair share of it. We live in the joy of the Lord, and yet, when we must suffer reverses, we have the odd freedom to react if possible, with greater pessimism. We believe in the primacy of faith, and yet, every moment we think it appropriate to think and to take up positions according to the rules of some self-invented or acquired psychology, politics, aesthetics, or morality unaffected by theological considerations.

The list could go on. The point is that the Christian is righteous and sinner. Our knowledge of God and our ignorance of God are present equally in each of us.

Barth will then discuss the first petition, "Hallowed be thy name." The content and meaning of this first petition of the Lord's Prayer is as follows. The one bears the pain of our division, the One humbled and wounded by it, yet superior to it, takes this disorder and distress within the divine life, and removes it from the world. The prayer of the believer is that God would stamp out ignorance of God in the world, in the church, and in oneself. This request given by the church and the Christian occurs in a provisional way on behalf of humanity. Repeatedly, God will make God known. The hidden quality of God is such only where people deny, blaspheme, and dishonor God. The prayer arises out of genuine knowledge of God, regardless of how weak that knowledge may be. Only God can hallow the name of God. The one praying it, as part of human invocation of God, has a corresponding will and action. As Luther puts it in his Small Catechism, it becomes a prayer that the name of the holy God would become holy among us. However, the petition looks beyond human zeal, will, and action to a work whose subject is God. We ought not to view this petition as a pious wish. Rather, God must act at some future date to make this petition a reality. One can pray this petition only because one has at least some knowledge of this God shown in Jesus Christ, regardless of how weak it is. Coming from Good Friday and Easter Day, the Christian world knows what it is talking about when it prays for the hallowing of the divine name. It prays for the taking place of the unique and definitive divine act that it knows to have taken place already in Jesus Christ. Further, given the confidence of the resurrection of Jesus Christ, Christians know that God has already answered the prayer in Jesus. To what extent can the hallowing of the name be future? The confusion of the church, the Christian, and the world suggest the desecration of the name of God. Hallowing the name of God in this world has its only source in the cross. Therefore, it has validity for our time as well. God does not abandon us to the scandal. What must happen was done in the history of Jesus Christ, and it was done perfectly and definitively. Thus, the petition looks beyond the division of the present. With the promise, "I will glorify it again," it looks ahead to its future fulfillment. As in Revelation 21:5, "Behold, I make all things new." Between the yesterday and tomorrow of the redeeming work of God is today, our present time. We believe in the Word of God spoken in the resurrection of Jesus Christ from the dead. Yet, we cannot see it in the world, in the church, or in our hearts and lives. What we see is the misty landscape, the luminous darkness, in which people know God and people in whom God remains unknown. The hallowing of the name of God already accomplished in Jesus Christ presses toward the manifestation that will remove the veil. The petition relates to this last thing that God will do. It prays that the one who came yesterday will come tomorrow as the Victor over the division of the present. Along these lines, we say with Luther, "Help us in this, dear Father in heaven."

Barth will then discuss the precedence of the word of God. The law of prayer is the law of action. Calling upon God in this petition is an act of obedience. The people who pray in this way long for the great and final day, the Sabbath day of the light of God that abolishes all the division of the present. They turn toward the day with some movement of their lives toward it. As the command of God, this petition demands zeal for the honor of the name of God from us. It demands a movement in our lives. The Reformation understood this petition was that with the help of God, it might be that our works and words, through our lives and teaching, we would honor God. The petition is for God to act. Yet, as with all prayer, it implies human movement toward that which the person prays.

Our part can only be our part, taking place in due modesty and honesty. We adopt and validate the idea that we engage in active participation in the hallowing of the name of God. Of course, we cannot try to do what belongs only to God. Human beings cannot make the future envisioned happen through their word and work. The hallowing of the name of God is in the hands of God. We move toward this petition in personal life, in church, and in world. Such limits do not alter the urgency required for us to make this movement. The knowledge of God we do have is not idle. Living in obedience to the command of God, we move toward the command to hallow the name of God. With small steps or large leaps, with humility and resoluteness, we move toward its fulfillment.

What this petition requires is zeal for the honor of God. Those who pray for the future honor of the name of God cannot accept present desecration of that honor. The way forward is acceptance in all humanity of the present situation. We continually begin in our present resistance to desecration. We never become adept at it. To sum it up, Christians must confirm the precedence of the Word of God in what they will, choose, and do. By this, Barth means the Word of the living Christ. The precedence of the Word must assert itself over all other factors that may influence the life of the Christian. One must hear the Word of God first. The Word has distinction, majesty, and dignity that mark it off from all other factors that touch the lives of Christians. The Word of God hallows the name of God, and thus, living by it, we will hallow the name of God.

When Barth says, "precedence of the word of God," Barth might use a word too weak for what he means. Yet, to give the Word of God precedence over other constitutive factors in our lives is something we can do. The Holy Spirit can enlighten, command, and help. The Word of God differentiates itself from all others in that it does not just stand alongside these factors but puts itself ahead of them. Other factors will influence

Christians, of course. We can make that assumption. We cannot ignore or eliminate them. As those who pray this first petition, our thoughts, words, and actions do not result in mere sanctioning of the status quo.

In what acts will one have to be zealous for the honor of God? The person who prays this petition lives in three circles: as a child of the world among children of the world, as one of the members of the Christian church, and in the relative isolation of personal Christian life. Each circle represents unity and particularity. The general answer we must give if we give it with reference to each of these three circles.

One, Barth begins with those acts in the personal life of the Christian in which the Christian will need to be zealous for the honor of God. The Christian exists in the intolerable contradiction of Yes and No. The contradiction is between election and calling as one who knows God on the one hand, and the being and conduct of a person to whom God remains unknown. The contradiction is between acting fully out of sin and darkness on the one hand and fully out of knowledge of God as a saint on the other. The Christian life is fully neither extreme but is both. We must respect the limits and borders of this place for Christian life. Christian life is both courage and humility in the presence of such realities. The Christian life neither rises too far nor sinks too low. Christian life is neither demonic nor angelic. Christians will venture to contradict the contradiction in which they find themselves entangled, even if in a provisional and relative way.

Two, we need to consider those acts in which the church reflects its zeal for the honor of God. Christians experience the same division in the church that they experience within their lives. The church is unsettled. Yet, the church is not Babylon, nor is it New Jerusalem. One can pray for the one, pure, holy church, of the New Jerusalem.

Three, Christians as citizens of the world also have zeal for the honor of God. A Christian concerned only with self and church, and not for the world, would be a contradiction in terms. Of course, the fact that the churches are so unsettled within themselves suggests that they should attempt only the smallest of steps in the world. If Christians have no shock of the lack of the knowledge of God in the world, something would be wrong. Further, is the Christian as shocked and pained by the lack of knowledge of God within self and church? 1) Christians in the world should not act as if it is their responsibility to set the world in order, since so much ignorance of God exists in it. One could become monastic, holding itself aloof from the world so that the world will something alien in it and create a desire for it. One could also become a crusader, passing over people in the world and in the church in the favor of militant acts, aiming to do harm to the worldliness of the world. The monk and the crusader are the extreme forms of life to avoid in this regard. They underrate the knowledge of God in the world. They overrate the knowledge of God in the individual Christian and in the church. They obscure the positive content of the Christian witness in the world. 2) Christians could affirm the world as it is since God has already reconciled the world to God through Christ. They modestly join it and adapt to it. This liberal possibility takes solidarity of the church with the world. Such a position is gullible and innocent toward the world. It makes the Christian keep the secret of his or her message from the world. It refuses to give the No of the gospel message to the world. This approach lacks the courage that must characterize Christian obedience in the world.

Christians must steer a middle course between these two extremes. The Christian will need to give witness as one who is a person of the world who, in distinction from the rest, has heard the Word, recognized its value, lives by its authority, and lives by its promise. It would be better if Christians confine themselves to speaking only about what one may say and do at the human level. In what they do or leave undone, they can make themselves known to the world as understanding hearers of the Word, and thus draw attention to the Word in their lives in the world. This Word will give their choosing and willing specific character so that their lives will become a text accessible to Christian and non-Christian alike. So long as they do not have the vocabulary, grammar, and syntax, the non-Christian may not understand it, but it becomes legible to them as written by a human hand. The Word is present to non-Christians in the person of Christians as bearers of the Word of God. To make this witness fruitful and successful is the affair of God. The affair of the Christian is to be unassuming and resolute doers of the Word, and in this way to be witnesses to it. Christians will respect the freedom with which God acts in the world. Christians cannot take part in the great vacillation contained in the ambivalence of its knowledge of God. Christians present themselves to other people of the world as nonconformists, as those who are zealous for the honor of God, as a witness to what they have to advocate to others of their kind. They do this by offering to them the image of a strangely human person – Jesus Christ.

Barth is granting that the actions of Christians have a limited and fragmentary character. They lack the finality and absoluteness one can only attribute to the revelation of God in the Incarnation of the Son. Yet, precisely for this reason, he does not want to trivialize human action. The acts of Christians are interim steps, provisional, and relative in significance and range. One would do well to re-read the section in IV.2 on sloth. Barth is now calling upon Christians to rebel and resist this expression of sin. He affirms the eschatological orientation of the Christian life, midway as it is between reconciliation and redemption.[86]

Barth will then discuss the second petition (78), "Thy kingdom come," under the theme of the struggle for human righteousness. He says that Christians pray to God that God will cause divine righteousness to appear and dwell on a new earth under a new heaven. They are to act in accordance with their prayer as a people who are responsible for the rule of human righteousness. They pray for the preservation and renewal, the deepening and extending, of the divinely ordained human safeguards of hum rights, freedom, and peace.

Barth has a discussion of a revolt against disorder. The genuineness of human zeal for the honor of God needs testing. It has the character of obedience to the command of God within the sphere of ethical discussion. The command of God summons Christian to a revolt, and therefore to enter a conflict. Christian life as a warfare is not so evident in the New Testament. The New Testament refers to the conflict of an athletic contest. Ephesians 6:11ff shows Christians in need of armor for battle. I Timothy 6:12 and II Timothy 4:7 refer to their good fight. Such a revolt rejects a specific possibility. They say No here because they will say Yes there. They fight for more than simply their lives. The affliction Christians experience in the world cannot separate them from the love of Christ. Such affliction can strengthen their perseverance, deepen their self-confirmation, and renew their hope. A war-like attack is not something the New Testament ever envisions.

Christians cannot avoid the struggle involved in such a revolt. They become fit for such a battle as they leave behind them the personal revolts and conflicts and use their freedom for life. The militant revolt demanded of Christians does not have a direction against any people, a fact that distinguishes it from other types of revolts. They revolt against the disorder of this world caused by its rebellion against God.

Barth discusses the lordless powers. The point here is that community confidently prays for the secure establishment of just relations between human beings. It should also find expression in corresponding engagement in the struggle for human justice. The struggle is largely negative in that it remains revolt against these lordless powers. Such powers are human potentialities in rebellion against the primary order of creation and have become oppressive idols. He will see these powers in political absolutism, materialism, ideological dogmatism, and chthonic or earthly powers (technology, fashion, sport, pleasure, and transportation). Turning aside from God, humanity uses nature in a way in which humanity becomes their slave.

---

[86] (Webster 1995), 200-201.

Barth describes the human situation as one that suffers, that loses its proper agency in grasping for a form of self-mastery and self-competence that leads humanity to slavery and oppression. Human agency has led to robbing humanity of its dignity and freedom. Christians reject the regime of lordless powers, witnessing to the disenchantment of the world by the mighty action of God. Given his previous generous reading of the political order, this analysis comes as a surprise. The point of this revolt against lordless powers is the actualization of a different possibility. It entails repudiation of bondage of this historical moment and a positive assertion of human work involved in the actualization of a quite different reality that participates with God in the revolt of God against the lordless powers. The root of this revolt is prayer. The prayer, "Thy kingdom come," acknowledges that our act occurs within the prior act of God in Christ.[87]

Christians call upon God to set aside evil powers.

The adversary is the great disorder that controls the state and course of human things. It consists in human unrighteousness. It consists in the plight that plagues, disrupts, and devastates humanity. The basis of this disorder is human alienation from God that the fall of humanity presupposes. Alienation from God results in self-alienation and alienation from other people. Humanity tries to live a lordless life. Yet, people do not become lord and master of their lives. In escaping the lordship of God, they find it hard to become little gods. God can make use of the lordless powers. God is their creator, and they stand at the disposal of God.

World history is the history of innumerable absolutism of various kinds, of forces that are truly autonomous. They are powerful despite their impotence. They are powers, sovereignties, influential spiritual beings, dominion, authorities, world rulers, and so on. The world still needs a good deal of de-demonizing. In praying for the kingdom of God to come, negatively, we ask for the gracious unmasking, overcoming, and abolition of these absolute powers that rule us.

Although the New Testament does not usually name these powers, they primarily refer to political absolutism such as the first Christian communities saw at work behind and diversified governments of the day. One might note Revelation 13:1-8 in this regard. A question of the demonic is at work in all politics. Government exercises authority, one group of people over another. The New Testament freely uses mythical language about political powers.

Mammon is another of the lordless powers. It refers to material possessions, property, money and resources that have become like an idol. In Matthew 6:24 and Luke 16:13, Mammon competes with God for love,

---

[87] (Webster 1995), 204-9.

devotion, and service.

Ideologies and intellectual constructions are another prominent form that the lordless powers take. Humanity has the remarkable ability to grasp in the form of concepts its perceptions of inner life, that of other people, and that of the world. One can put these together in definite pictures. One can arrange impressions and ideas in thoughts. One can make them into exact knowledge and then bring this into inner connection with other thoughts one has. One can convince oneself of the need to begin with certain theoretical and practical ideas in all that one knows, wills, thinks, says, and does individually, to make these ideas the solid presuppositions underlying actions, and to approach solutions to problems determined by them. Yet, fallen humanity has a problem in all of this. One no longer views this ability as provisional, but rather, as permanent. The ideology becomes so fascinating that, rather than freedom, it brings enslavement. The ideology that a person creates exerts power over the individual. It receives loyalty from the individual. One now ventures to ask and answer only within the world of the ideology. One orients one's life to it. Individuality disappears behind the mask created by the ideology. One evaluates others on the basis adherence to an ideology. Such "isms" become dictators, in which individuals cease to experience freedom of spirit. They lead to slogans or catchwords, usually with a menacing ring. They do not enter conversation with the other. Rather, they speak about the other in a massive surprise attack. It does not teach, instruct, or convince. It aims to exert a drum-roll influence and issue marching orders. Ideology must also put out propaganda with a swing on its own behalf and with varying degrees of violence. Propaganda puts things in black and white. They must how the valueless and harmfulness of their rivals. Truth needs no propaganda and does not engage in it. Truth speaks for itself and opposes falsehood. Propaganda is a sure sign that truth is not at issue, but an ideology.

There are such powers as Leviathan and Mammon, and spiritual and chthonic powers, that we must not ignore. We must not overlook their false lights. We have had to speak of them. The fall of humanity brings their disorder into human history and life. The Christians who prays the second petition prays rebels against them. They bring no help to humanity. Humanity thinks they will give liberation, strength, ease, simplification, and enrichment. They do not do so. They do not intend the best for humanity. On the contrary, they break away from humanity, even as they break away from God. They are inhuman. They are the enemy of God. They are hostile to humanity and the enemy of humanity. They disrupt human life. They are fictions, illusions, and lying spirits. They oppress people. They tear apart individuals and society. Giving rights to no one, they make it impossible for any to grant mutual rights. They care nothing for human dignity. None of them can have peace; none of them can grant peace to others. Their dominion reveals the plight of humanity.

Barth discusses the petition, "Thy kingdom come." Humanity would like to break itself free from God. In so doing, it overreaches itself. Humanity cannot succeed. Lordless powers find their limit in God. The prayer for the kingdom of God sets a limit to the lordless powers. The petition points to an act of God that is a once for all act. It points to the occurrence of a specific history inaugurated anew and brought to its goal by the Father. It opposes the demons and the disorder of human history. This kingdom referred to in Luke 2:14, is peace on earth, actualized when God comes as King and Lord and creates and establishes it. The kingdom defies expression. Only in the reality and truth of the coming of God does that beautiful morning light dawn on the margin of the horizon of our experiences and thoughts. The second petition looks toward this. The New Testament compares the kingdom to a house (John 14:2), to the future world of God, the New Jerusalem, and to the royal action of God in history (Luke 17:20-21, Romans 14:17, I Corinthians 4:20).

The rule of God escapes intellectual systematizing. It is independent of human will and action. The kingdom is the new thing toward which we pray, not the completion of what we already are doing. Luther said this petition prays for the kingdom to come to us. For Calvin, the petition refers to the expansion of the kingdom among us. Pietism saw the kingdom arriving in various renewing movements and in the deepening of the Christian life. The Enlightenment saw it as the expansion of the fellow feeling among human beings, including expansion of ethical life. The point is that J. Weiss, A. Schweitzer, and F. Overbeck are pioneers in viewing the kingdom of God as future.

The one who prays engages in pure prayer. 1) God is the One the prayer invokes. 2) Such persons turn to God. 3) It carries it with the certainty that God will hear the prayer.

How does such a prayer enter the lips of the Christian? It has eschatological content and character. It has its basis and meaning in this history. The kingdom has already encountered those who offer the prayer. The new thing for which they pray has already entered their lives. It already terrifies them as judgment and comforts them as grace. The kingdom is already an event. The new thing coming is the history of Jesus Christ. He is the mystery no system can contain. He is God acting in human history. He calls people to obedience. He is the limitation of human disorder and the limit on the demonic. He was in his history the immanence of the rule of God. 1) The past act of the coming of Jesus and the drawing near of the kingdom had the power to present itself to the Christians who looked back to it as also their future, and the future of the entire world. 2) The first Christians were still able to find a place for and to follow the impulse that came to them from the history. Such an apparent impossibility became actuality in the Easter history. It also became actuality ever since through the work of the Holy Spirit, the power of God to open blind eyes to see this light. The Holy Spirit is the forward that majestically awakens, enlightens, leads, pushes, and impels, which God has spoken in the resurrection of Jesus from the dead. One could give no answer without reference to Easter and Pentecost.

Barth closes this discussion with a section on fiat lustitia (let justice). Barth offers a less tightly argued section than that of the preceding sections. He will argue that since prayer as prayer is responsible human action, we cannot divorce it from our way of life. He will sketch a way in which the world of grace and the world of the rebel can exist alongside and in relation to each other. He rejects the antithetical alternatives of autonomy and heteronomy. He prefers to think of a set of analogical relations between the action of God and human acts. He remains deeply suspicious of human autonomy, which he views as an evasion of the problem that faces humanity rather than its solution.[88]

The unassuming action of prayer is still a movement toward that which one prays. When some turn bravely to God with this petition, then with their hearts and lips, caught up by what they pray, their whole life, thought, and deed are set in motion, oriented to the point to which they look with the petition. They established themselves on that for which they pray. Christians live toward the kingdom and the new heaven and new earth it promises. They wait for the kingdom, but they also run toward it. As such, God claims them for action in the effort and struggle for human righteousness. At issue is human righteousness. Such righteousness is imperfect, fragile, and problematic. What can one mean by kingdom-likeness and therefore human righteousness? The aim is to help people. Christians can look only where they see God looking and try to live with no other purpose than that with which God acts in Jesus Christ. The concern of Christians is with humanity, and therefore they are humanists. The question is whether any cause will serve the improvement of the human condition in a provisional way. Devotion to a worldview ought not to get in the way of such a concern. Christians, looking always to the only problem that seriously interests them, must allow themselves the liberty in certain circumstances of saying only a partial Yes or No where people might expect another answer. They will not become prisoners of their own decisions. God loved humanity. Christians owe to humanity whatever righteousness

---

[88] (Webster 1995), 211-3.

they have. In praying for the kingdom, in praying, "Come, Lord Jesus," they do not abandon humanity. They see in every person a companion and future brother or sister and treat the neighbor as such.

In his lectures of 1962, Barth says that one can gaze beyond the ambiguity of human life in the petition, "Thy kingdom come." Theology cannot here and now become a reality without being accompanied by its deeply internal endangering through this contradiction. Its character remains fragmentary, a knowing in part. The theologian deals with doubt in the gospel. Paul praises the gospel in Romans 1:16-17 as the power of the God. However, what is the power of the gospel compared with the powers of world economics, natural science, and technology? The gospel does not even seem as powerful as the arts, sports, fashion, ideology, mystic, rationalism, or ethics. People seem to live by these things rather than the gospel. Further, the community of faith in terms of its feebleness and disunity can also be a source of doubt. Flaw in individual life can also lead to doubt.[89]

If we live in the light of the command of God the Reconciler, we worship God as Creator and as gracious Reconciler. Therefore, we should use our lives in the service of the rule of God and in revolt against lordless powers.[90]

When we pray for the rule of God to come, we pray that we may also receive the insight to see the first signs of this new age, of the victory that God has already won in Christ. We pray to see the events of our history in the light of the universal day that is ahead of us. We have this insight because of the event of the past, which looks toward the Day that is coming that will reveal the universality of the work of God. We receive the gift of living in that hope. In praying for the rule of God to come, we have hope for our time, for today, for tomorrow. The great Future is also future. This fact is enough to help us see the insufficiency of present works, the pettiness of our conflicts. It sets in context our personal, psychological conflicts. We see such tensions differently considering the rule of God to come. Such a hope helps us live in tranquility, good humor, and in love that may attract some people. He notes that in Luke, a variant reading asks the Holy Spirit to come upon us and purify us. The variant is a proper commentary on this prayer. If one prays for the coming of the rule of God, one is praying that the Holy Spirit may come within us.[91]

---

[89] (K. Barth, Evangelical Theology: An Introduction 1979, 1963), Chapter 11, "Doubt."
[90] (Cambridge Companion to Karl Barth 2000), Nigel Biggar, "Barth's Trinitarian Ethic," 218-20.
[91] (K. Barth, Prayer: 50th Anniversary Edition 2002), 35-41.

Barth planned to discuss the third petition, Matthew 6:10, thy will be done, on earth as it is in heaven (79). We return to the present, which belongs to the realm of the will of God, the realm in which God carries out the plan to glorify God as Creator and Lord land to justify and glorify that which God has made. We are small, weak, and threatened by many dangers. We are prone to failure, contaminated by sin and lost. The fulfillment of the will of God is not up to us. It belongs to God as all categories of time belong to God. We pray that God will be patient with us until the end. While praying like this, we have the confidence that God is already engaged in carrying out the will of God. We pray in communion with Jesus Christ, and thus know the will of God is already carrying out the divine will. The reference to the will of God already done in heaven refers to creation and the history of the covenant. We do not see it, and thus its already dimension is not visible in time. We pray for the execution of this will in our world and in our lives. Our prayer is that is that the confusion between heaven and earth will end. We pray for the end of the imperfection of our obedience. We pray for our freedom from the contradictions that exist within us. In all of this, the focus is the cause of God. We pray urgently, for so much of our brief time is lost time.[92] The will of God is to maintain and save that which God has created. The will of God is to fulfill the work of God by the manifestation of the rule of God. In praying for the will of God to be done, we are praying for the execution of the plan of God. We cannot fulfill the plan. We ask God to turn toward us in loving concern for us and for our world, patiently working with us until the end. Yet, God is already engaged in carrying out the will of God. We pray in communion with Jesus Christ for the fulfillment of the will of God.[93] In Gethsemane, Jesus would ask that the cup of suffering pass. However, he wants the will of God rather than his own will.[94] In Jesus, the will of God is done on earth as it is heaven.[95] Barth would have us note that the emphasis of the first three petitions on "Thy," referring to the Father who is in heaven, becomes the basis of the following three petitions.[96] This petition is of crucial importance. The will of God should be done on earth as the end and goal of the divine purpose and activity as it is done in heaven as its origin and commencement. The will of God should be done on earth today, tomorrow, and always, as heaven already does the will of God. The will of

---

[92] (K. Barth, Prayer and Preaching 2018; 1952; 1932-3 Lectures on Exercises in Sermon Preparation and 1947-9 Lectures on Prayer), Kindle edition, 564ff.
[93] (K. Barth, Prayer: 50th Anniversary Edition 2002), 41-43.
[94] CD IV.1, 270.
[95] CD IV.2, 167.
[96] CD I.1, 387.

God should be one on earth by the obedience of the earthly creature as it is done in heaven by the obedience of the heavenly. The will of God should be done on earth with the same self-evident necessity as it is done in heaven. The point is that heaven should come to earth. From heaven, God should cause the will of God to be done on earth as in heaven. The petition presupposes that heaven and earth are still divided or at least distinct. It asks that this differentiation should cease in the day of consummation. It presupposes that the will of God is done in heaven. Heaven is the created sphere in which the will of God is done. Such obedience is still to come on earth. We must orient our lives toward the will of God. Thus, we know that for which we ask when we ask for the will of God to be done. Chrysostom paraphrases, "O Lord, let us be so zealous for the heavenly kingdom that we may will as it does." Luke 19:37-8 and Luke 2:13-4, are good commentary on what this petition means. Both passages reflect the biblical emphasis upon the movement from heaven to earth.[97] Here is the substance of all prayer. What do we pray for when we pray like this? We clearly pray God will make us obedient. We want nothing other than the will of God done to us. We pray that in some way God will deal with us in the gracious, holy knowledge, and will of God. Yet, we must not dispute with God, as if it is not the will of God done to us, or as if the will of God is not gracious and holy. At what point and in what position will we stand to offer such a dispute? Rather, we stand on the side of the will of God rather than dispute with God. The will of God is not our fate. We adore the will of God, for the will of our Lord is always justified and right. We are not speaking of the will of God at all if we do not grant it this range and adore it.[98]

The first three petitions have focused upon the glory of the Lord. They correspond to the first four of the Ten Commandments. In them, we are to pray that the cause of God reaches their fulfillment in the hallowing of the name of God, the coming of the rule of God, and in the doing of the will of God. The cause of God becomes our cause as well. Our prayer for these things is to issue forth in an altering of our lives so that we become part of the fulfillment of these petitions. God invites us to participate in their fulfillment in our work, church, and world. The freedom, joy, and alacrity of the second set of three petitions have their basis in the first three. The first three are the ground on which we walk so that we can pray the second set of petitions. They assure us that we live with God as we align our cause with the cause of God. As we do so, the second set of petitions assures us that God aligns with our cause as well. Thus, the second set of

---

[97] CD III.3, 444-5, 447.
[98] CD II.1, 558.

petitions concern us directly. Our prayer concerns itself with our comfort, good pleasure, and physical and spiritual wellbeing. We can appeal with simplicity on behalf of our cause. We entrust the baggage we have accumulated during our lives to God. Our baggage is temporal, material, secular, eternal, Christian, ecclesiastical, and theological. We must remember that Jesus of Nazareth prays this prayer. We join him in this prayer. In this prayer, we take part in the action of God. God is busy for the glory of God and for our salvation. We benefit from this divine action by uniting with it in prayer. The cause of God and our cause have an intimate connection and unity. The "us" of these petitions involves those who wish to unite with Jesus Christ, the fellowship of the people of God, the fellowship of all those who share the human condition, and thus those who share the misery of human existence. The prayer becomes direct, explicit, and imperative. The prayer shifts toward boldness and temerity. We are asking God to have a concern for human affairs. God has accepted us as co-workers. The first three petitions involve us in the cause of God, and the second three boldly invite God to have concern for the human cause. Christ has vanquished the enemy, inviting us to participate in the victory.[99]

Barth planned to discuss the fourth petition, Matthew 6:11, give us this day our daily bread (80). Barth notes that when we ask for daily bread, Luther suggested that "bread" means the necessities and requirements of life. In biblical language, it can refer to the minimum nourishment without which the poor cannot survive. It can also refer to a sign of the grace of God. Bread becomes something sacred. We pray that would God give us the minimum requirements of life but doing so as a sign anticipating the wholeness of life. We receive in the gift of the minimum requirements of life the sign of eternal goodness and the assurance of life with God. We are a people in the wilderness, surrounded by the glories of creation. God is faithful to us as our creator. God desires that we live.[100]

This prayer has a close relationship to Matthew 6:25, where we are not to worry about our lives.[101] He reminds us that Jesus wants us to pray with the same confidence for our daily bread as we do for the forgiveness of sins, the revelation of the divine name, the coming of the rule of God, or the doing of the will of God on earth as it is in heaven.[102] To pray for our daily bread acknowledges God as the giver, removing anxiety from our

---

[99] (K. Barth, Prayer: 50th Anniversary Edition 2002), 26-31,43-47 and (K. Barth, Prayer and Preaching 2018; 1952; 1932-3 Lectures on Exercises in Sermon Preparation and 1947-9 Lectures on Prayer), Kindle edition 612-28.
[100] (K. Barth, Prayer: 50th Anniversary Edition 2002), 47-52.
[101] CD II.2, 692.
[102] CD III.1, 39.

concern for that which sustains our lives. It transforms anxiety into prayer.[103] Jesus acknowledges the relationship between humanity, animals, and vegetation that God established in creation. God provides necessary food for humanity. God abundantly spread the table for all.[104] The basic motive of work is the earning of our daily bread. Without it we cannot exist at all for the cause of God. We cannot pray for the hallowing of the name of God, the coming of the rule of God, and the doing of the will of God. The first three petitions place us at the service of God and summon us to be witnesses for God. The fourth petition is an immediate call to work. This petition refers to the existence we are to receive from God in prayer and maintained by work. In our work, we preserve, develop, and fashion our existence. If we do not work, neither should we eat. Daily bread refers to that which is indispensable or at least highly desirable for the existence of each of us. They are the object of our prayers and the aim of our work. Of course, our work reminds us that others are seeking to earn their existence by their work. How will we understand our work in relation to them? They are our fellow human beings. We cannot be human beings unless we see them as our fellow human beings as we receive assistance from them and as we assist them. If our work is genuinely the command of God, then we must ask in what way it is human. We need to consider the humanity of our work. If we reflect upon our actual practice of work, we can see the distance between the human quality of the command of God on the one hand and our observance of it. Even in our best activity, we are perverted people in a perverted world. Human work takes place in co-existence and co-operation. However, human work also takes place in isolation and mutual opposition. Human work should provide each of us with our daily bread in peace. It offers us an opportunity for the development of our abilities and the corresponding accomplishments. It would then liberate us for the service of God, which is our real work in obedience to the command of God to work. Yet, our reality of work is that reflects the struggle for human existence. It affirms our existence, in the isolation and abstraction of our needs, wishes, and desires and in the ignoring, thwarting, and suppressing of those of others. We express our inhumanity in isolation from and opposition to fellow humanity. Ecclesiastes reveals the shadow that hangs over work. The Reformers gave some approval to the notion of work as worship. Barth cannot yield to this type of enthusiasm for work. In his view, the economic arrangements of the modern era have intensified the inhumane quality of work. If we are to experience work as the command of

---

[103] (K. Barth, Prayer and Preaching 2018; 1952; 1932-3 Lectures on Exercises in Sermon Preparation and 1947-9 Lectures on Prayer), Kindle edition, 698ff
[104] CD III.1, 207.

God, we must avoid the thoughtless opinion that one can work to procure daily bread in isolation from fellow human beings. Nourishing bread derives from work gained from the bread broken and shared with fellow workers. The vital claims of become part of our lives. If we are to experience work as the command of God, we must guard against the thoughtless opinions concerning the claims that each of us advances. What tears people apart and incites them against each other is the various wants, desires, and claims that have such a slender foundation. We experience the revolution of empty and inordinate desire. We have lust for superabundance. We have lust for possessions. We have lust for power over others. Work in the service of genuine and vital claims will have the character of peaceful co-operation. In any case, these two evil roots in human work is not something that either capitalism or socialism can eradicate. We can do much to remedy these two thoughtless approaches to work. The competition can be fine, invigorating, and exciting. Yet, the means becomes an end as people compete for the necessities of life. The struggle for existence seems deeply embedded in nature. It may be behind what we think of as progress of civilization and culture. We may ease the situation by people who engage the context with degree of decency and generosity. We can place limits on the struggle with a system of justice that sets limits between freedom and caprice, between legitimate and illegitimate competition, between admissible and inadmissible seizure for one's own advantage. The command of God will always gravitate toward such counter-movements to the thoughtless approach to work. Yet, work under the sign of this competition is always inhuman. To the socialist mind of Barth, modern industrialization can only rest upon the principle of exploitation, where benefits accrue to the owners of the means of production. He acknowledges arguments in favor of free competition but seems not to take them seriously. He admits that pure capitalism does not exist. Employer and employee can develop mutual loyalty. One can remove its worst features. One can mitigate its greatest severities. Yet, to his mind, capitalism makes people a means to end. He admits, however, that state socialism can reflect the same bitter root and thoughtlessness as does capitalism. Socialism will not end the class struggle. His basic point is that the church must stand against exploitation that arises from the two thoughtless approaches to work. The command of God is a call for counter-movements on behalf of making economic arrangements increasingly humane. Christianity in the West needs to comprehend the disorder and assert the command of God. It must stand with the exploited and the victim. We must not forget our fellow-humanity nor forget our genuine and vital claims. The fact that we do forget, giving precedence to isolation and inordinate desire, we express our basic disobedience to the command of God. In any case, the decisive word of the church does not tie itself to a specific program. Its decisive word is the proclamation of the revolution of God against ungodliness and unrighteousness and in favor of the proclamation of the rule of God that has already come and is yet still to come.[105] In this prayer, we act in such a way that we receive daily bread as we may receive it as God gives it to us as a sign and promise. Why we are using the fruits of this sign, while we are blessing God, we enjoy beforehand the presence of the things God has promised to us and has allowed us already today to participate in the feast prepared in eternity.[106]

Barth planned to discuss the fifth petition, Matthew 6:12, forgive us our trespasses (81). Barth agrees when Luther says the church admits its sinfulness when it prays the Lord's Prayer.[107] We are in default in our relation to God. We owe to God the totality of our person. Even if we seek to live as Christians, and thus in accord with the Lord's Prayer, we increase our debt, for we aggravate the mess of our situation. To forgive is to regard our debtor as having done no wrong. This petition recognizes the effect of divine pardon upon our relationship with others. Those who know they depend upon divine mercy can do nothing other than extend mercy to their fellow human beings. We acknowledge that we are debtors to each other daily. Human forgiveness is a beautiful thing. Let us not settle down to enjoy the offences against us. Let us not nurse grudges against others. Rather, we need to retain some humor regarding those who offend us. When we receive pardon from God, it enables us to extend pardon to others. Even before we ask for pardon, God has pardoned us in the cross. We need not constantly gaze upon our own sin. Rather, we look to Christ who has severed from the bondage of this past. God has commanded us to look ahead. We do not treat lightly what we have been and done. We do not trust what we shall be. We shall live by being on guard but also trusting what God has pronounced in the death of Christ. God has set us on the road of our destiny in Christ, with forgiveness giving us the freedom to travel upon it.[108]

Barth planned to discuss the sixth petition, Matthew 6:13, do not lead us into temptation, but deliver us from evil (82). Barth can refer to the fact that we experience some minor or provisional temptations that God sends daily. Such temptations will vary according to our stage in life,

---

[105] CD III.4, 534-45.
[106] (K. Barth, Prayer and Preaching 2018; 1952; 1932-3 Lectures on Exercises in Sermon Preparation and 1947-9 Lectures on Prayer), kindle edition, 727.
[107] CD I.2, 747.
[108] (K. Barth, Prayer: 50th Anniversary Edition 2002), 52-59 and (K. Barth, Prayer and Preaching 2018; 1952; 1932-3 Lectures on Exercises in Sermon Preparation and 1947-9 Lectures on Prayer), Kindle edition 761ff, 808ff.

whether for the youthful or for the aged. Such temptations come to us because they are necessary for us. We endure them. They work together for the good of those who love God. Temptation came through the trials of Job or David. We must not ask God to not pass through the trials through which all saints have had to endure. However, the prayer here involves the great, eschatological temptation. The infinite menace of nothingness that opposes God, the supreme temptation, can be of no use to us. It can produce no fruit. The threat exists and manifests its presence. Since we must speak of the Devil, us modern Christians pass over this temptation too lightly. He does not want to become an expert in demonology. We must be aware that the Devil exists, and we must hasten to get away from it. The Devil has only pseudo power. The Son revealed the sinister wickedness of the enemy. For that reason, the Lord's Prayer ends with *de profundis*. Jesus taught us to end with a prayer for deliverance, to snatch us from the jaws of death. We are to think of many psalms in this regard. We are in the jaws of death. We complain of it, we suffer from it, but we cannot break loose. God directs us in the paths and gifts that lead us to pardon, to reliance upon God for our necessities, and to participate in the cause of God. When we follow the written word, we shall avoid the great eschatological temptation. The Son shall shield us from the aberration of the Devil. God alone is our liberator. Christ is victorious over the shadows by the resurrection. The signs of such deliverance are present, if we open our eyes through faith and see them. We proclaim such deliverance in baptism and the Lord's Supper. Christ is already our victorious leader. We know that our paths would never be the right paths. Only God can snatch us away from the jaws of death. Because God is our liberator, we have the freedom that God grants us. God has annihilated the one who wished to annihilate us. The love of God is efficacious and delivers us.[109]

    Barth will say that knowledge of God is knowledge of the grace of God. In this context, we can more closely define prayer, which is the essential determination of the knowledge of God. The Lord's Prayer has God as the object, and we become those who know God. In this petition, we must pray that we do not succumb to the temptation to treat God objectively, as if we were disobedient observers that hold back in a place that we think is secure from obeying God. We must not succumb to the false opinion that God is object like other objects in the world we know freely and from differing perspectives. We must not succumb to the temptation of wanting to know God as if we were spectators and thus do not need to take part by corresponding our knowledge of God to obedience. We can change into the world of dead gods or all too living

---

[109] (K. Barth, Prayer: 50th Anniversary Edition 2002), 59-64.

demons, in which contemplate the essence of the world without giving ourselves into the hands of God. We enslave ourselves to these gods and demons. Such are the characteristic directions of those whom God has already called to the people of God. If we give way to this temptation, we will lose true knowledge of God. That which proceeds from us will always succumb to this temptation. We must pray to overcome this temptation.[110]

The prayer concludes with the statement that to God belongs glory. Barth acknowledges the phrase is not in some good early manuscripts. In one sense, the Lord's Prayer concludes that the kingdom belongs to God rather than the evil one of the final petition. However, it may also summarize the entire prayer. We pray in the way we do in the Lord's Prayer because the kingdom, the power, and the glory belong to God. All that ask in this prayer only God can do. "Amen," so be it, leaving no room for doubt.[111] We have here a simple statement of fact. In the Old Testament, "glory" refers to the essential value of a thing. It is light as both source and radiance. It constitutes the worth God creates for the divine self. Glory is the divine presence in Israel. The revelation of glory is always in the future, but we can affirm it today. God reveals divine glory in grace and mercy, in condescending to humanity and in friendliness toward humanity. In the New Testament, we behold the glory of God in Jesus Christ (John 1:14). The love of God becomes event and person.[112] Yet, "Thine is the kingdom, the power, and the glory" means more than the statement of a fact. "Kingdom" suggests something broader than power. For Barth, the concept that lies ready to our hand here is beauty. God is beautiful. God enlightens, convinces, and persuades. The revelation of God is a revelation of the rule of God and the power of God. Yet, to say that God is beautiful is to suggest the form in which revelation of the rule of God and the power of God takes place. God has superior force in the power of attraction, which speaks for itself, which wins and conquers in that fact that God is beautiful, divinely beautiful, beautiful in a distinctive way. God is beautiful in a way that only God is beautiful. Such beauty is unattainable primal beauty, while also having genuine beauty. God acts in a way that gives pleasure, creates desire, and rewards with enjoyment. God is pleasant desirable, full of enjoyment. God alone is that which is pleasant, desirable, and full of enjoyment. God love sus as the one who is worthy of love as God. We mean all this when we say that God is beautiful. He refers to Augustine, Confessions X.27. He refers to Pseudo-Dionysius De div. nom

---

[110] CD II.1, 26-27.
[111] (K. Barth, Prayer and Preaching 2018; 1952; 1932-3 Lectures on Exercises in Sermon Preparation and 1947-9 Lectures on Prayer), kindle edition, 907ff.
[112] CD II.1, 642-3.

IV, 7. The beautiful becomes the ultimate cause of movement. Such comments are a form of Platonism. Rarely has such thinking entered Protestant orthodoxy, although we might refer to the hymn "Fairest Lord Jesus." He admits that the concept of the beautiful tends to be a secular one. Dangers abound if we go the direction of considering God beautiful. We may jeopardize or deny the majesty, holiness, and righteousness of the love of God. We may bring God into human oversight and control. We bring contemplation into a form of self-contemplation of an urge which does it recognize its limits. Yet, he thinks we need to take this step if we are to appreciate knowledge of God. Divine glory is the sum of the divine perfections. The divine self-declaration is superior and irresistible. He has no desire to allow a form of aesthetic to speak in a way that would lead to false and unchristian dynamism, vitalism, and so on. Yet, the danger here is no greater than any other form of "ism" to invade the church. The concept of beauty is not one of the leading attributes of God that he would discuss. The subject remains the glory of God. He will speak of the beauty of God only in the context of the glory of God. Yet, the concept helps us to dissipate the idea that the affirmation of divine glory is only a statement of fact, effective only through power. Rather, the rule and power of God are effective as they are beautiful. Such an understanding is essential. Of course, the idea of the beautiful is not an outstanding part of the Bible (Psalm 104:1-2, 45:2, Song of Songs). Yet, the philological fact is that glory in Hebrew, Greek, and Latin includes the idea of beauty. Glory includes the pleasant, desirable, enjoyable, and beautiful. The glory of God is overflowing self-communicating joy. Its nature is to give joy. The objective meaning of divine glory is grace, mercy, patience, and love. Divine glory is worthy of love. In the quality of beauty, it speaks, conquers, persuades, and convinces. Where we recognize divine beauty, and its peculiar power and giving of pleasure, it awakens desire and creates enjoyment. As God stoops down to us, God becomes an object of desire, joy, pleasure, yearning, and enjoyment. "My soul magnifies the Lord, and my spirit rejoices in God my Savior," as Luke 1:46-7 puts it. Paul urges us to rejoice in the Lord always (Philippians 4:4). The good and faithful servant will enter the joy of the Lord (Matthew 25:21). Paul desires to be absent from the body and present with the Lord (II Corinthians 5:8). We are to have legitimate delight in the Law of God (Psalm 1:2, 112:1, Romans 7:22). We may find pleasure in its commands (Psalm 119:4). We are to delight in the Lord, who will give us the desires of our hearts (Psalm 37:4). If we give our hearts to the Lord, we will have pleasure in the ways of the Lord (Proverbs 23:26). The hand of the Lord is open in a way that satisfies the desire of every living thing (Psalm 145:16). The right hand of the Lord has pleasure forever (Psalm 16:11). We receive the invitation to taste and see that the Lord is good

(Psalm 34:8). We could recount the many times Psalms and Proverbs urge us to take delight in and find our joy in the Lord. The Lord is the object of joy and delight. God radiates joy. God would not be understandable apart from joy. Thus, we are saying nothing strange or excessive when we say that God radiates joy because God is beautiful, for we are speaking only of the form and manner of divine glory, of the persuasive and convincing element of divine revelation. God is glorious in the self-declaration of revelation. Thus, awe is not enough. Gratitude, wonder, submission, and obedience are not enough. We are to respond to God with joy, desire, pleasure, and yearning for God. Divine glory awakens joy in us. Such glory is solemn, good, and true. Joy before God has an objective basis. Something in God justifies our response of joy, desire, and pleasure toward God and is the basis of the summons to do so. Something in us attracts us to have this response. That which attracts us is divine glory. If so, we cannot dispense with the idea of the beauty of God. God is beautiful in love in all the works of God. The form of revelation has this beautiful quality that elicits from us joy, delight, and pleasure. Without this dimension of divine glory, we run the risk of being joyless and humorless as a people of God. What is the beautiful element in God that makes God the object of joy, desire, and pleasure? We need to remember that what is beautiful arouses pleasure. Divine revelation and therefore divine being is that which is beautiful. We must learn from it what is beautiful. We see this beauty in the doctrine of the Word of God and in the themes of *Church Dogmatics*. Theology is a peculiarly beautiful science. The theologian who has no joy in the work of the theologian is not a theologian at all. Anselm makes occasional reference to the beauty of theology. Thus, all we can do is indicate by several examples they fact that the being of God speaks for divine beauty in di vine revelation. One would need to review the discussion of the reality of God (II.1, Chapter VI, 28-30), and thus, the attributes of God as one who loves in freedom, from the standpoint of its beauty. The being or essence of God in revelation is beautiful in the sense that grace and holiness, mercy and righteousness, patience and wisdom, cohere in the way they do. The being or essence of God is beautiful in the way unity and omnipresence, constancy and omnipotence, and eternity and glory, cohere in the way they do. The perfection of the attributes of God is beautiful. God shines out in this beauty. Only the form of the divine being is beautiful. Yet, this means divine being itself is beauty. Where we recognize divine revelation of divine being, we will feel it as beauty. When the perfect divine being declares itself, it also radiates joy in the dignity and power of divinity. It releases the pleasure, desire, and enjoyment of which we have just written. This form is persuasive and convincing. This persuasive and convincing form is the beauty of God. A second example is the Tri-unity of God (I.1, Chapter II,

Part 1). We find here the three modes of being, simplicity and multiplicity, divine space and time. We have here a perichoresis, in which the three modes of being are always together. The tri-unity is the basis of the power and dignity of the divine being, and therefore also of the divine self-declaration in revelation, and therefore of divine glory. Of course, this glory is what makes this power and dignity enlightening, persuasive, and convincing. The form of divine revelation is radiant in radiating joy. It attracts and therefore conquers. It is beautiful. In fact, the tri-unity of God is the secret of divine beauty. Thus, we cannot escape the fact that God is beautiful. A third example is the Incarnation (I.2, Chapter II, Part 2). We are at the center and goal of the works of God, and therefore the hidden beginning of all the works of God. The prominent place the Incarnation receives correspondence to the essence of God. The Son forms the heart of the Trinity. The Son is the locus of the divine work. Therefore, the work of the Son reveals the beauty of God in a distinct way and in a supreme degree. The Son displays this beauty in a unique way as the eternal Logos. The divine being becomes flesh in the Word. The divine being becomes one with humanity in Jesus Christ. God adopts humanity into unity with God. God does this while remaining divine. God becomes human while remaining God. God condescends to humanity in a way that is not strange to God and without creating estrangement within God. The beautiful in the being of God is the fact that God is one and yet another. The Incarnation is the form of divine revelation, and as this form reflects the beauty of divine being. Since the Son is beautiful in this way, God is also the source of all truth, goodness, and beauty. We will need to recognize the beauty of God in Jesus Christ. The beauty of Jesus Christ is the beauty of what God is and does in Christ. We see the majesty and condescension of God in the Incarnation. We see the love of God in the Incarnation. If we see this, believe this, and this seeing happens to us, we will see the form of this event, the likeness of the essence of God in Jesus Christ. We will see this likeness as beautiful.[113]

Barth planned to discuss the Lord's Supper (83). The Supper takes us back to the event of revelation that founded the church and constitutes the promise of God to the people of God. The Supper is an action physically and visibly performed. The Supper is the sign of the event of revelation turned towards the future for which the people of God wait. True preaching occurs between the grace of the event of revelation we find in baptism and the hope of the event of revelation we find in the Supper. Isolating preaching from baptism and the Supper exalts preaching and the

---

[113] CD II.1, 650-66.

preacher beyond what is proper in the church.[114] The Supper, far from being an instrument of grace, answers the Word of God in the form of thanksgiving as an act of obedience.[115] My goal here is to summarize what Barth has already said about the Lord's Supper. John Wesley acknowledged that many people neglect receiving the Supper and that we have a duty to receive it regularly. He argued that Jesus commanded it, it communicates forgiveness of sin, and it refreshes the soul for the journey. He did view it as a sacrament and a means of grace.[116]

Barth refers to the Supper as the "crown" of his ethical reflection. The Supper is a thanksgiving that responds to the presence of Jesus Christ in His self-sacrifice and which looks forward to His future. The Lord's Supper relates to the continuation of the history begun in baptism, the sustaining of humanity in the fellowship of that life and therefore in calling upon God.[117] He will say in other parts of *Dogmatics* that the Supper typifies the union of Christ with community. As Baptism was the unity of a divine action, baptism in the Holy Spirit, and human action, baptism in water, he would have undoubtedly wanted to approach the Supper in an analogous way. However, as I have suggested, Barth is advising the church to dispense with its talk of sacraments, recognize Christ as the one sacrament, and recognize the Supper as a human act with the signs of bread and wine that testify to the unity of the community with Christ. He would want the church to focus on the Supper as a human action that sustains the Christian life in response to the command of the Spirit. Barth says that the Supper is not an extension of the Incarnation. Rather, the Supper is an extension of the prophetic work of Christ. The Word of God takes up residence in those who have accepted responsibility for their vocation. The living Christ gives such persons His life. This is the mystery and miracle of the union of Christ with them. The Christian does not lead the Christian life alone.[118] Barth stresses that the Supper confirms the fellowship of the community with its Lord, its participation in the body and blood, and therefore, its attachment to Christ.[119] Barth makes it clear that the Holy Spirit is the one who unites this people with its heavenly Lord. The community imparts and receives the body and blood in and with their human fellowship as realized in the common distribution and reception of bread and wine. One can perceive

---

[114] (K. Barth, Prayer and Preaching 2018; 1952; 1932-3 Lectures on Exercises in Sermon Preparation and 1947-9 Lectures on Prayer), kindle edition, 11170.
[115] (Richardson 2004), 62, 64.
[116] John Wesley, "The Duty of Constant Communion," Sermon 101.
[117] CD IV.4, ix.
[118] CD IV.3, 543.
[119] CD IV.3, 737.

this only in faith.[120] The unassuming action of the Supper is a sign of the goal that ends the conflict of economic classes. The Supper is the repeated and conscious unification of this people in new seeking and reception of the free grace of God. The Supper is a sign in which people are together in fellowship. The fellowship of the Trinity has a mirror in the fellowship of God with the world. The Supper is a sign full of meaning and power. It is simple and eloquent, containing elements of the witness the community owes to the world, especially the witness of peace on earth among human beings, with whom God is well-pleased.[121]

We may regard the Lord's Supper from the perspective of Easter as well, since we can view it as the marriage feast of the Lamb. The Supper is a joyful meal, in which the eating and drinking are eternal life during our life. We are guests at the table of the Lord and so no longer separated from Christ. We are no longer separate from Christ. In this sign, the witness of the meal unites with the witness of the Holy Spirit. It tells us you shall not die but live and proclaim the works of the Lord. We can allow Christ to conquer all that is deadly around us, and with it our sorrow and melancholy. One who believes that we shall live with Christ is beginning here and now to live the complete life. Since we receive the testimony of the Supper we already live here and now in anticipation of the eschaton.[122]

I suspect that Barth is moving in the direction his son, Markus, promoted.[123] He states his goal as reducing outdated and divisive disputes over the table to which Jesus Christ invites sinners such as we are. He affirms that the Lord's Supper is something good and great, simple and deep, moving and practical. Christ invites to his table. We are guests of the Crucified, who has promised to come again. We have overshadowed the meal with a somber and depressing mood. Religious self-concern and egotism have gained the upper hand, contradicting the essence of the meal. The language of the tradition has sought to focus upon the mystery: sacrament, transubstantiation, consubstantiation, transignification, or symbol. The tradition has wrapped the Supper in a smokescreen of difficult language. Theologians will focus upon the relationship between spirit and matter, eternity and time, visible and invisible. Many traditions exploit the Supper as a means of excommunication. Often, Greek dualism and the practices of ancient mystery religions have contributed to the confusion. It

---

[120] CD IV.3, 761.
[121] CD IV.3, 901.
[122] (K. Barth, Dogmatics in Outline 1947, 1949), "The Resurrection of the Body and the Life Everlasting."
[123] (M. Barth, Rediscovering the Lord's Supper: Communion with Israel, with Christ, and Among the Guests 1988, based on lectures in 1986-7).

highlights the contrast between spirit and mater, clergy and laity, holy and profane, religious expression, and daily conduct. The reality is that is an expression of thanksgiving to God, the love among brothers and sisters, and the common witness to reconciliation and peace for all the world. The ethical implications of the meal that focus upon a Christian life of service, love, and mission are in the background.

Markus Barth reminds us of the Passover root of the Lord's Supper, suggesting that Christians have communion with Israel. Christians can learn from the Jewish people how to celebrate the Lord's Supper and serve God in the process. He points out that Jesus practiced the Passover in a form consistent with his time. This means it was joyful, using comfortable couches, a lamb, and wine. It was a time for including children. They even invited non-Jews to the celebration as a witness to the liberation of the nations. The celebration focused upon remembering an historical act of deliverance from God. In the Passover, "this is" refers to the service of remembrance of deliverance from slavery in Egypt. An altar was necessary for the sacrifice of the lamb, but a table was necessary for the meal, which included other items than meat and the wine. Finally, the Passover was a communal affair and did not focus upon individual guilt, sin, and forgiveness. In applying such thoughts to the Lord's Supper, the presupposed question of the disciples revolves around why they are celebrating this meal. Jesus re-orients the Supper to refer to his body and blood as the sacrifice. We see that Christ is the lamb of God that takes away the sins of the world (John 1:29, 36, but also I Peter 1:19, Revelation 5:6, 9, 12). Paul refers to Christ as our Passover lamb (I Corinthians 5:7). Hebrews refers to the one great sacrifice of Christ. He thus rejects the sacramental interpretation of the saying of Jesus, in which Jesus was offering himself along with the bread and wine. Rather, he is referring to his sacrificial death on the cross for the benefit of others. Jesus reveals his priestly function and the sacrificial nature of his death. In this case, sacrifice refers to an act, a gift, a revelation, from God. To know the death of Christ as a sacrifice is to know that regardless of the depths of human guilt and weakness, one has died for us out of love for us and intercedes on our behalf before God. In that sense, the Supper remains a good, joyful, hopeful, act of gratitude by the people of God. The Supper represents a new covenant. The newness of the covenant is first renewal of the covenant God has with the people of God. The covenant is new because it is open to all, not just the circumcised. It fulfills the promise that Israel was to be a blessing to the nations. The table represents the reconciliation of all people before God. The eschatological outlook of the Supper anticipates the fulfillment of the promise of God and the hope of the people of God. Children are an important of the meal. Clerical officiating over the meal adds nothing to its celebration, for Christ is the priest offering the meal. He urges the removal of any hint of altars in favor of the table. He encourages a joyful celebration.

Markus Barth will move from his discussion of the synoptic portrayal of the Lord's Supper to the discussion Paul has in I Corinthians 10-11. His theme is communion with Christ crucified and risen, focusing upon public joy based upon the death of Christ. We find Paul introducing Supper, table, and communion (koinonia) into the tradition of the church. Paul combines elements of confession, narrative, commentary, and ethics. What we do not find are doctrinal inductions and deductions, definitions and systematizing. The text does not contain a timeless doctrine on the Eucharist. Rather, we find specific practical problems taken up and met head-on. The theology of Paul is practical in that it deals with the worship and conduct of the congregation. In this case, the congregation had a security arising from its sacramentality and spirituality. They neglected their social bonds and obligations (10:32). The chief example is that the gathering for the Supper had become an occasion for dividing the rich and poor (11:22). Thus, in 10:1-12, we have sharp words. His point is that Israel, while in the wilderness, had a form of sacramental baptism as well as spiritual food and drink. Yet, God judged them. Thus, the congregation has no sacramental security, for observance of a sacrament is not an alternative to ethics. They are to have exclusive communion with Christ. God does not tolerate their divided allegiance (10:21-22). The first commandment is still valid. You shall have no other gods. You cannot serve God and mammon (Luke 16:13). He points out that 10:16-17 is an important but partially obscure text. Paul refers to the cup as communion with the blood of Christ and the bread as communion with the body of Christ. Verse 18 asks the rhetorical question of whether those eating sacrificial meat are in communion with the altar. The answer is yes. Communion, fellowship, is an act of unity, participation, and sharing. It signifies communion between persons that may have its foundation in sex, friendship, educational, or economic bonds. Such bonds may arise out of a communion of lofty ideas or ideals, common possession of certain things, or common interest (plays, sports, or weapons). Such communion is spiritual and interpersonal. The Supper is intimate existential communion between the participants in the meal and the person of Christ crucified. In sharing the Supper, participants accept that the death of Christ means their death, that his suffering makes them willing to suffer with him, that his resurrection promises their resurrection, that their life is in Christ and Christ is in them. In fact, Christ is their life. In the future coming of Christ, they will be with Christ. Sharing bread and cup expresses and confirms intimate communion with Christ. He notes that we do find mention of the Holy Spirit neither in the Synoptic

Gospels nor in Paul. Yet, he thinks the tradition and theologians have many good reasons to emphasize the essential and creative function of the Spirit in the Supper. He points us to 11:26 as the final part of the church tradition that Paul cites. The verse is key to what Paul means by communion with Christ crucified. The conclusion is simple and clear, free of obscurities and ambiguities. Its three parts are rich sources for describing the essence of the Supper. 1) You proclaim the death of the Lord. This death is good news. The Supper celebrated at this table express the pleasure and joy the crucifixion brings. It announces publicly and clearly what has happened as well as the meaning of the event. The Eucharist shows and confesses that that the death of Christ is different from a natural event, a criminal act, or a tragic loss. Nor is the Supper and occasion to accuse, moan, or complain. Further, the Supper is not an example that anyone can imitate. The sacrifice to which Paul refers signifies the greatest gift of God to humanity (Romans 8:32, 3:25, and I Corinthians 5:7). Granted, those celebrating the supper know the pain and shame, the horror and scandal of the death of Christ. Yet, they also rejoice in the slaughtered Lamb because God has raised him from the dead. The Crucified is also the raised and living Christ. The crucified is the one who rules the church and the world. The crucified is the one who will come again. In this way, the godless receive justification and reconciliation, salvation, and peace. As participants in the Supper, we have abundant reason to rejoice. When Paul emphasizes that we proclaim the death of Christ, he is focusing upon this joy. Such proclamation forbids narrowing the celebration of the Supper to private and ego-driven observance. The proclamation demonstrates the love of God. The Supper is a missionary event and action. The Lord's Table is a center for evangelism. The proclamation occurs as the community breaks the bread and share the cup. The Supper encourages us to continue the proclamation. The congregation, not just the clergy, becomes a herald of Christ together. To have communion with Christ is to give thanks to God for the gift of Christ, to join in the bond of mutual love with the congregation and to signal to the world that work of God embraces all creatures. Communion with Christ at the table of the Lord is something the participants are doing, after they have responded in faith to the Word of God and the Holy Spirit has invited them to come. The Supper is a human work that God has commanded us to do. The Supper is work of faith. The language of "do this, take, eat, and proclaim" give human activities surprising weight. Eucharist, thanksgiving, is an appropriate name for the Supper. 2) The proclamation of the Lord's death occurs until he comes. Thus, the Supper is the meal of pilgrims, the provision of God for people on the way. 3) As often as you eat this bread and drink the cup. The communal eating and drinking are actions by which followers of Jesus remember and proclaim the death of Christ. Thus, the Supper is how they publicly demonstrate their communion with Christ crucified and risen. In this way, the eating of the brad distinguishes the Supper from other meals. Our daily bread is a gift of God in the company of persons who have heard of the gracious acts of God and want to give thanks for them. Gratitude for the gifts of God is the basis for eating and drinking. The Supper is a common meal and thus a community affair. Participants demonstrate their hope that Christ will return. The sharing, serving, and loving demonstrated at the Lord's Table verify in our lives the truth of our confession of faith. Such sharing of bread is a hint of our social responsibility and actions are the essence of the meal. The cup of wine in the Bible gives participants permission to be glad, relax, and forget the misery that often besets life. The cup insists upon the festival and joyful character of such sacrificial meals. Yet, to drink this cup means to suffer. It presupposes the cup of suffering. Those who drink are aware of the price Jesus paid for liberation of Jew and Gentile alike. Through his suffering, Jesus entered glory. Disciples express their readiness to suffer with Christ. A Christian is a joyful herald of the crucified Lord, a brave witness to the necessity and glorious effect of the terrible death of Christ. Thus, eating and drinking are not too little, trite, or contemptible to serve a magnificent purpose. The Supper invites us to share bread with the neighbor. The Supper invites us to acknowledge that the only path to promised glory is through suffering. The Supper proclaims the death of the Lord and demonstrates living and true communion with Christ.

Markus Barth goes on to discuss the importance of the Supper as an expression of communion among Christ's guests, stressing the honor of those despised. While I Corinthians 10 focuses upon communion with Christ, as over against idols, I Corinthians 11 focuses upon the disruption observance of the Supper has brought to the fellowship Christians are to have with each other. Flagrant social misconduct has entered the Corinthian congregations. Division between rich and poor is offensive to Paul. In 11:20, Paul asserts that they have no communion with Christ when the divide the community in this way. Love of God and neighbor, while we need to distinguish between them, have such a profound link that you cannot have one without the other. Paul seems to be boiling with anger over what he has heard is happening among them. The Christology of Chapter 10 applies to the Ecclesiology of Chapter 11. In fact, Paul practically identifies Ecclesiology with social ethics. He forbids disassociation from fellow Christians. The Supper in Chapter 11 is primarily an ethical act and event. We might say that ethics identifies the essence of the Supper. Ethics is its home, framework, and purpose. Each Christian has a vital role to play in the common praise of God and public witness to believers and unbelievers. Paul will make an analogy in Chapter 12 of the church with the human body. However, his primary point is that the church is the body of Christ. The church is the missionary manifestation of the prophetic life of Christ upon which Karl Barth expounded in Volume IV.3. One way to examine the famous expression of love in Chapter 13 is ask ourselves of the kind of neighbor Paul calls upon us to love. This neighbor requires patience and kindness. This neighbor needs zealous observation and radical correction. The neighbor is irritating. The neighbor is a "load" we must be willing to bear. The neighbor has a burden to heavy carry alone. We are to help with that burden. The neighbor may well be a pain the neck, but Paul praises the kind of love that reaches out to the neighbor anyway. If we read Chapters 8-14 in this light, then some members of the community may well be inferior and some may feel superior, but Paul protects those considered inferior. We could go as far as to say that the weak and poor have a special connection to the crucified and risen Lord and come under the special protection of Christ. Christ is present in a distinct way among the weak and poor. They are personal gifts of God. In a comparable way, Luke has gathered his various accounts of Jesus at meals during his life and allowed the Supper to be a special concentration of the rays of light we find there. The meal itself is not a mystery. The meal does not convey salvation. Rather, the meal proclaims the goodness of Christ and his association with sinners, such as we are. His death on the cross, placed between two criminals, is a special sign of that proclamation. We can show love for Christ only as we gladly accept that irritating neighbor. The social and ethical nature of the Supper radiates outward toward the everyday lives of those who participate. The Supper is a missionary and social event. Christian ethics is Eucharistic in this sense. The Supper demonstrates love for others, especially the little ones, sharing of earthly goods, witness to Christ, and orientation toward the future return of Christ. The Supper is a gift that orients us to love of God and neighbor. The Supper is evangelical ethics in the context of praise to God and testimony to others.

  Markus Barth has a final discussion of the unique issues involved in John 6, where he will emphasize that Christ is the one and only sacrament. Bread and eating in this Chapter refer us to two events. One is the objective giving of the Son as the bread and the other is the subjective reception of the bread in eating. Such eating is to believe in Christ (Augustine). Flesh, blood, eating, chewing, drinking, is coherent elements of imagery. We can understand John 6:32-58 only as metaphor. Only by his death does Jesus become the Bread of life. Only by giving away his life does he extend eternal life to others. Christ is the sacrifice, the sacrificial meal, to which Old Testament sacrifices could only point. Only in his death do we find the eternal life promised by God. Hebrews 7-10 also draw this distinction between Old Testament sacrifice and the sacrifice of Christ. In this case, "to chew" means to eat with joy and pleasure. Taken in this way, John 6 speaks of the Incarnation and the sacrifice of Christ rather than the Eucharist itself. The text of John 6: 52-58 provides ample reason to give thanks to God and to live a life of gratitude. At the Supper, participants remember, proclaim, and praise Christ crucified. Nothing we do in our ritual deserves to share in the glory reserved only for the Lamb of God. In John 6:63, the sense of the statements on the quickening of the Spirit and useless flesh is Christological. The fate of the historical Jesus would be useless without the Spirit, who raised Jesus from the dead and who transforms the preached Word into the Christ of faith. The Logos becoming flesh (John 1:14) finds its completion in the work of the Spirit, who raised Jesus from the dead and is the promised gift to the apostles to hear and proclaim the truth revealed in Christ. The Word and the Spirit apply the work of God to the people of God. Word and Spirit demonstrate objectively that God has included human beings in the work of Christ and draw human beings into their subjective enjoyment of its effects. In this sense, the means of grace are what God has provided in Word and Spirit. Martin Luther (1517, commenting on Hebrews 2:3, 10:19 and in 1520 in his disputation regarding infused and acquired faith) insisted on using the word "sacrament" only for the death of Christ. The cross alone is the sign, cause, instrument, and means of salvation. None of the seven sacraments identified by the church of his time has the name sacrament in the New Testament. Jesus Christ is the one sacrament. Eberhard Jungel affirmed that baptism and Eucharist celebrate Jesus Christ, the one sacrament offered by God.

At one level of discussion, John Wesley would defend baptism and the Lord's Supper as means of grace. John Wesley noted that the Church of England referred to sacraments as a means of grace. He points to the church in Acts as continuing in the teaching of the apostles, breaking bread (the Lord's Supper for Wesley), and in prayer (Acts 2:42). Such devotion to the Scripture, to receiving the Lord's Supper, and to prayer are means of grace. He understands the term to refer to outward signs, words, or actions ordained by God with the purpose of being the ordinary channel to humanity of prevenient, justifying, or sanctifying grace. At another level, he would share some of the concerns Karl Barth and his son had regarding the misuse of sacrament. Thus, some mistook the means for the end. The point is not to perform the outward work, for the outward work has no intrinsic power. The benefit of the outward work relies upon a heart renewed after the image of God, growth in love for God and neighbor, and purification from pride, anger, and evil desire. Performing the outward work will be of no benefit if one is not practicing justice, mercy, and the love of God. Separate from the end or purpose, they are nothing. As important as they are, however, Wesley reminds us that God is above any means. We must not limit the way God works, even to the means of grace. While one is practicing any means of grace, one needs to be aware that it has no power in itself and that one receives no merit in doing it. We practice them because God commands them. Our salvation is only through the Holy Spirit, the blood of Christ, and trust in God alone. He urges us to seek God alone through the means of grace, for nothing by God will satisfy the soul.[124]

As we conclude this attempt to suggest the direction of Karl Barth might have gone in IV.4, I want to say that I have found this way of understanding the Christian life challenging and helpful. I have studied philosophical ethics. I find it tempting to study Christian ethics in a comparable way. What I like about Barth is that his approach combines intellectual acumen with devotional and prayerful consideration. It gives proper place to baptism, the Lord's Prayer, and the Lord's Supper as communal acts that influence the lives of individual believers. Thus, it moves us away from abstracting Christian ethics from theology and worship. The living of the Christian life in all its aspects is to arise out of the fellowship we have with Christ, signified in our baptism, and is to move us toward deeper fellowship with Christ as signified in our giving and receiving of the bread and cup. Both acts are witnesses to what matters most in living the Christian life. Approaching our daily lives as a prayerful invocation of God for help and in praise is something for which we can be grateful in the theology of Karl Barth.

If one were to follow Barth in affirming that Christ is the only sacrament, one would have a profound ecumenical problem. I wonder what would happen if the churches could affirm Christ is as the primary sacrament or means of grace. At the same time, they could allow that certain practices (baptism, the Supper, marriage, worship, small groups, study, prayer, service, and so on) open us up to the impartation of grace into our lives in such a way as to lift us into deeper communion with Christ, with each other, and with service in the world. Of course, children and non-Christians would receive an invitation to participate in such practices. Of course, clergy do not need to officiate, as if only they could confer grace to others.

---

[124] John Wesley, "Means of Grace," Sermon 16.

VOLUME V
DOCTRINE OF REDEMPTION

III.4, 56 (1951)
The basis of the holy day is eschatological. It points us to the ultimate consummation of this history the omnipotent grace of God rules the whole of time and all times. However, it does so towards a special history and time that will in their particularity be the last history and time, the end of everything that we know as history and time. The concluding judgment of the world is also the grace of God, for accompanying the judgment is the establishment of the new age in which everything that has been will be as it was in eternity, that is the time of God and therefore before God. Eschatology is the grace of revelation in the light of which everything that is now dark will be bright. In its future power, it is secretly present already. The particularity of the last day is the mystery of all the other days hastening toward it. The particularity of the holy day, interrupting and placing limits on our working days, also has the inner connection with the particularity of the last day. It undoubtedly corresponds to it each individual human life, the day of the death of each individual, concerning whose particularity for the individual we hardly need to speak. ... The goal, set by God, is toward the being of all creatures, which means also the inexorable

end of the form of their present existence.

III.4, 384-5 (1951)
Joy is a provisional fulfillment of life received with gratitude. Our joy today is anticipatory. Our life is provisional in that we live in expectation of eternal life, the revelation of the union of our lives with the eternal life of God. We are not joyful or grateful in vain today. This hope sustains our present faith. Faith clings to the accomplished moments as the future in every present. Here and now is the great prelude to what will one day be revealed and constitute the goal.

III.4, 510
Prophetic service to the community refers back to the death and resurrection of Jesus Christ as the beginning and his coming again as the end of all things it anticipates what is still to be consummated. It attests that Christ alone reigns in eternity and therefore in time.

IV.3, 606 (1959)
Commencing in His resurrection, continuing in the presence and activity of His Holy Spirit, and moving towards the completion of the whole economy in His final, universal and definitive appearance and revelation, Jesus Christ is also the Proclaimer of His being and action as the one High-priest and King. He is also the one Prophet of the kingdom of God drawn near in Him.

As we conclude with a reflection on the doctrine of redemption, I invite you to offer two prayers.

> Lord, you are everlasting. The span of my life, long or short as it may stretch ahead of me today, is brief, a mere candle flame burning to the edge of the taper, when compared with the vastness of creation and the eternal quality of your divine life. My life is temporal. Regardless of when the end of my time comes, the end is always close to me. The end troubles me. The sense and awareness of the eternal quality of your divine life gives me some assurance and peace. In quiet moments, I ponder the seasons of my life, its progress and its steps backward, its dramatic changes or its slow but persistent change over time. I see mysteries around me. I ask your help to look and listen to your creation. I am uncertain

of what the end of my life will bring. Yet, when I look to your Word, your Son, and his life, death, and resurrection, I approach my end with hope. Is death really a birth into a fuller life than I can imagine here? I trust your Word. Such trust will lead to life on earth with greater readiness to follow where your Spirit leads me. Amen.

Lord, the pain and suffering of this world are overwhelming. I turn on the TV or open the newspaper, and I see death, disease, and despair. At what point do I just throw my hands in the air and quit? However, this present suffering cannot compare with your future glory (Romans 8:18). When I pay attention to the other parts of nature, I see it also struggles with its pain and suffering. I wonder if at some level, its creatures long for its pain and suffering to end. Lord, how much longer must humanity wait, how much longer must humanity suffer? No matter how deeply I hope, hope does not cure the sick or end wars. Lord, many of us in the community of the faithful seek your glory, your presence here and now. We want the power of your Spirit to fill our entire being to be overflowing. We are simply one part of your vast creation. As part of your faithful community, we long from the depths of our souls for the lifting up and revelation of the children of God. What this means, of course, is that I must wait. I am impatient at times. I wait with pain. I wait as I move toward death. Yet, I also wait with the firm hope in your Son, who has already experienced the glory to come in resurrection. So today, I wait and offer thankful praise for the glory to come. Amen.

In his fragment on IV.4 preface, Barth says people have asked anxiously about the remaining parts of *Church Dogmatics*. Despite its bulk, it remains incomplete. People have challenged him on the question of redemption or eschatology. To such persons, he challenges them to note how much he has already written regarding the sphere of eschatology, both indirectly and directly.

I am taking this statement as direction for us. I will grant that Barth took some turns in Volume IV that one might not have anticipated after reading his commentary on Romans or Volume I. At the same time, Barth has suggested that he has given us some quite solid hints and directives. Throughout *Church Dogmatics*, in his "lecture fragments" and in his *Ethics,* he gave hints as to what he intended. Most of this section devotes itself to those hints. It will mean re-reading some of the previous material. I hope this section proves helpful, as Barth completes his theology with reflections on the Holy Spirit, on eschatology, and on hope. He suggests that in redemption, the dialectical reasoning in which he has engaged in his *Dogmatics* will end. Christ will reach his goal through the Holy Spirit. Berkouwer relies almost entirely upon the Church Dogmatics Vol. III/2 §47 as his source of Barth's eschatology, with a few quotations from the Church Dogmatics II/1 §39 as well. You can re-read the following sections if you want to remind yourself of the place eschatology has had in the journey that is *Church Dogmatics*.

#1 "Ending Time" (CD III/2 §47.5)
#2. "The Promise of the Spirit" (CD IV/3.1 §69.4)
#3. "The Condemnation of Man" (CD IV/3.1 §70.3)
#4. "The Subject of Hope and Hope" (CD IV/3.2 §73.1)

In I.2 [24.2], Barth outlines some of the concerns for this volume.

Barth clearly thought he explained the role of the future and eschatology in his own concepts of threefold time in Chapter X, III.2, 47.1 and the threefold Parousia (in the resurrection, the coming of the Holy Spirit, and the return of Christ at the end) in Chapter XVI, IV.3, 69.4. Barth thought that overemphasis on redemption and eschatology would lead to theological imbalance. Just as clearly, neither Moltmann nor Pannenberg could travel with Barth in this assessment. In fact, in his *Systematic Theology*, Pannenberg will insist upon the importance of eschatology with each doctrine of the church. I would encourage review of the Barth material here for the reader to assess this matter. Clearly, Barth thought he had explained the role of the future and eschatology in these reflections.

I begin with looking upon the general theme of redemption in XVIII. I will point to the subject-matter of the doctrine and some of the issues with which Barth would have dealt. I will offer a personal judgment on decisions I think Barth would have made. In Chapters XIX, XX, and XXI, I will stay close to what Barth has already suggested would be the theme of his final volume on redemption. This will mean some repetition of what I have written. Yet, I will reconsider these materials in a way that will refocus our attention upon the themes of redemption and hope. Previously, as seen in the quotes that begin this chapter, Barth has offered brief hints of the difference between the event of reconciliation and the event of redemption. I will consider other writings of Barth as I suggest directions he seemed heading. A place I continue to wrestle is how he fits within the broad categories of theological reflection upon eschatology. My tentative conclusion is that he fits within the realized millennium or a-millennial position quite well, although in a typically unique and fresh way. He wants to avoid apocalyptic speculation or any approach to eschatology that would empty each moment of its significance.

I offer a few biographical exchanges Barth would have with two young theologians that have helped provide hints of the direction I think proper as we consider what Barth intended in this final Volume.

In 1964, Barth drafted a brief self-presentation that includes a glimpse into the future. He is aware of the weaker aspects of his capacity and achievement. He thinks someone can surpass his achievement. In fact, he has reckoned with the likelihood that one day other means and methods may do it better. He would not object. He would rejoice for the sake of the cause were this to happen. He also laid out what a fresh theological program must accomplish to surpass him. First, it must carry out the source, object, and content of all theology worthy of the name. Second, it must point forward, inviting and encouraging the continuing Exodus from Egypt rather than something like the program of the Jews back to that land in Jeremiah's later years. Third, it must be consistent and complete in form. His assessment at that point was that while he may have become hard of hearing, he has not heard the new song to the Lord. He only wishes for systematic theology to remain in its mode yet free, critical yet joyful enquiry that has become dear to him through all wanderings and temptations, and well worth all the trouble.

Barth was in the hospital toward the end of 1964. He wrote letters to two great theologians, both men writing major theological works. In the background is his hope for someone to have a worthy theological program. We find him disappointed in both theologians.[125]

On November 17, 1964, Barth wrote a letter to Jürgen Moltmann after he read *Theology of Hope*. Again, we see that Barth is looking for the "child of peace and promise," someone in the next generation who would go beyond *Church Dogmatics*. The varied scholarship, spiritual force, and systematic power of the book impressed him. He does not see the book as the hoped-for refinement of his *Church Dogmatics*. He wonders if Moltmann subsumes all theology in eschatology, especially baptizing the principle of hope of Ernst Bloch. Theology becomes an eschatological principle, a path down which Barth toyed going but rejected, a decision for which Moltmann criticized Barth. He thinks Moltmann should accept the immanent Trinity. He is challenging Moltmann to embrace the protological move that Barth makes. Moltmann will not do this. He puzzles whether Moltmann found his own concepts of threefold time in III.2, 47.1 and the threefold Parousia in IV.3, 69.4 made such negligible impact on him that he did not give them critical consideration. Clearly, Barth thought he had explained the role of the future and eschatology in these reflections, while Moltmann did not. In any case, Barth offers the opinion that the God of Moltmann is a pauper.

---

[125] A twitter follower @postbarthian has been very good to post such material.

Thus, Moltmann is not the "child of peace and promise" for which he had hoped, although he would like to think that Moltmann could become that child. He hopes Moltmann will outgrow the "inspired" one-sided character of his first book. He has the stuff from which a great dogmatician can arise who can further help the church and world.

On April 4, 1965, Moltmann responded that Barth has inspired preoccupation with this one eschatological or messianic idea. He admits the book is a prolegomenon and that he lacks a concrete eschatology. The challenge from Barth to put eschatology behind him and replace it with the immanent Trinity has given him much room for thought. While that may be the case, I do not think Moltmann will take seriously moving toward the protological perspective Barth adopted. The work of his friend Kasemann has compelled him to work through eschatology. His plan is to focus on the economic Trinity in the foreground, and later work on the immanent Trinity. He clearly wants to focus on the Holy Spirit as the one involved in raising Jesus from the dead. Eschatology grounded in the cross and resurrection opens to the eschaton where God will be all in all.

On December 7, 1964, Barth wrote a letter to Wolfhart Pannenberg after reading *Jesus-God and Man*. The book remains a major contribution to Christology. We see in the letter the same concern that he hopes he will hear a new song to the Lord in terms of a theological program. Barth will criticize Pannenberg for taking the historical studies of the Synoptic Gospels so seriously. He prefers his own approach of taking the text as it is. In a conversation with Moltmann, he told me that he does the same thing with the biblical text. Barth quite likely did not see that if one were to surpass Barth, one would have to take seriously new exegetical studies in the gospels.

In a personal visit, Barth advised Pannenberg not to write for a decade. Instead, he realized that he had already written his "great work on Christology." He sees that Pannenberg knows well where he wants to go. In fact, he knows that direction too well. He has acted upon the program that he shared with Barth in his visit. Pannenberg cannot reverse course. "We are theologically ... very different if not separated people." He respects and admires his achievement. His breadth of reading in exegesis, history, and philosophy is impressive. He stayed on his course. He shows critical acumen that never fails. He can establish and safeguard himself on both the right and the left. His book is a venture of unusual significance. The key point, however, is that he read the book with the hope that at last he might be dealing with "the child of peace and promise" who would represent a superior alternative to his *Church Dogmatics*. He has been waiting for this better option. He hopes he will be alert and humble enough to recognize it. He does not see that superiority in the work of Pannenberg. For all the originality, he finds his writing a serious regression to a mode of thinking he does not regard as appropriate. Barth read with horror of the idea of pursuing a path from below to above that would orient Pannenberg toward a Jesus one can find historically. Pannenberg seems to manage resting the doctrine of the revelation of God enacted in Jesus based on the historical figure Pannenberg accepts. He suggests that building the resurrection on objective vision and the empty tomb is to build a house on the shifting sand of historical probabilities. He may think he is on solid rock because of Jewish apocalyptic. Pannenberg thinks that considering this we find a general orientation of humanity to a being that transcends life and death. He presupposes a general anthropology, cosmology, and ontology. He refers to the shadowy figure of his historical man Jesus. He thinks the Christology of the early church more promising than that of Pannenberg. Barth remains committed to a path from above to below, from the particular to the general. He views the path of Pannenberg as reactionary.

On May 9, 1965, Pannenberg responded to the above letter. As was typical of Pannenberg, he does not think Barth has understood him. He had hoped Barth would see that Pannenberg continued the basic thought of his theology of revelation in a changed intellectual climate. He stresses that his concern is to begin with the highly particular and unique fact of the historical event of Jesus of Nazareth. He thought he had to begin with the historical question of Jesus of Nazareth. His taking seriously the historico-critical biblical investigation for theology is the prominent sign of the change of intellectual climate in comparison with that of Barth. If Barth does not see this shift in the intellectual climate, then he can understand why he would respond to the book as superfluous and reactionary. He thinks Barth might have a limitation in his original justifiable antithesis to the theological historicism of Troeltsch or Harnack. He stresses that his intent, even with his critical turn, is to continue his concentration of theology on the truth of the revelation of God in Jesus Christ, which transcends all our human questioning and speaking. He will always be grateful that he learned from Barth to focus all theological work on this center.

Given these exchanges with Moltmann and Pannenberg, both rightly considered as post-Barthian in their respective theological work, it may well be that no one could continue the program as Barth outlined it, for the historical setting had changed so much.

Before we begin, allow me to share a couple of Karl Barth anecdotes that provide some clues as to direction this volume would be heading. After a lecture, someone asked him if he thought we would see our loved ones when we die. His response was that he really did, but then added, "If I know anything about Jesus, we will also probably get to see everybody we hate." Dale Moody says he tried to corner Barth with the question of whether he thought God would save everybody. His reply was, "You wouldn't get mad if he did, would you?"

CHAPTER XVIII

The Work of Redemption

Chapter XVIII would have dealt with the work of redemption. Barth could make the philosophical themes of the true and the good a theme of *Church Dogmatics* in a way that he could not make the philosophical theme of beauty a theme. Yet, he also makes it clear that the rule of God and the power of God radiate divine glory and therefore divine beauty. His picture of the end intends to help us appreciate its beauty. This beauty has been present in Trinitarian relationships and in the exposition of the works of God as creator and reconciler. In the work of redemption, the beauty of God will become clear to all persons and will attract all persons. Barth reminds us that we will not draw people to Christ by loudly discrediting what they believe. We will not bring them to Christ by telling them how wrong they are. We might witness in a way that will show others a light so lovely that they will want with all their hearts to know the source of it.[126]

When we look upon reconciliation and redemption as events, we need to exercise some proper caution. In his discussion of the resurrection of Jesus, Barth distinguishes between *historie* and *Geshichte*. If *historie* is objectivity and likeness to other events, then neither reconciliation nor redemption are *historie*, but they can be *Geshichte*, events understood theologically as acts of God. Hence, he will take the biblical text regarding

---

[126] Madeline L'Engle, Walking on Water: Reflections on Faith and Art (Macmillan, 1995), 122.

Jesus of Nazareth as it is (*Geshichte*) rather than *historie*, which the gospel narratives clearly are not. Barth is also clear that the resurrection of Jesus is not a meaningless appendix to Christology. In an analogous way, the event of redemption is not an appendix to dogmatics with which the theologian can easily dispense. However, if we think of the event of redemption as a definite and objective event, describable in terms like other events within *historie*, we will be traveling a path Barth will not travel. To put it in terms of the analogy of faith, the event of Jesus of Nazareth (birth, life, death, resurrection, and ascension) is a unique and unrepeatable event of *Geshichte*. Yet, the event of the resurrection of Jesus determines Christological thinking. In a comparable way, the event of redemption will be a unique and unrepeatable event of *Geshichte*, not describable in ways available to the modern historical method or to science. Yet, the event of redemption determines fullness of Christian teaching concerning the destiny of humanity and creation. I grant that I may be making the distinction sharper than Barth would want, but I also like to think it shows that his eschatology is nothing like the popular variety we find in dispensationalism or the classical view of the first centuries of the church in its chiliasm. Yet, when Barth is describing the event of redemption, he does so in a way that suggests the secret history of Jesus Christ becomes observable for all to see. He shows no interest in how or when it will happen, interests he thinks distracts from the potential fullness of the present. His focus is upon the hope for this event in such a way that it fills the present with the living Christ through the sanctifying and redeeming work of the Spirit.

We need to consider the criticism Barth offers toward the view of eschatology in the theology of his time. Barth had mentioned to Moltmann that the young theologian should have spent more time reflecting upon these texts before he took up the theme of eschatology. I also find some comfort in seeing that Christopher W. McMullen, in his thesis presented under the guidance of John Webster, follows a similar pattern. His thesis is readily available on-line. If the reader is interested in specific criticisms of Barth, his thesis is well worth considering. Some of the criticisms I hope to dispel in the way I explain the direction I think Barth is heading. I am not confident enough in my grasp of the immanent Trinity as Barth understood it, but I do hope to make it clear that a focus upon the Spirit as Redeemer brings the Trinitarian structure of his *Church Dogmatics* to its proper conclusion.

Barth thought it was a disaster for dogmatics when eschatology became a suspicious closing chapter next to other things. Dogmatics that has not seen and respected the eschatological character of revelation from the beginning will stand before closed doors when it approaches this topic. Christian truth is eschatological from the beginning. As he stated in his

Romans commentary, Christianity that is not altogether thoroughgoing eschatology has nothing to do with Christ. He often criticized the Protestant theology of the 1800s for de-eschatologization of Christian teaching. The distinguishing mark of Christian eschatology is its basis in the threefold form of the Word of God. Its primary interest is not last things, but in the person who is coming. The motivation is not curiosity, but fidelity to the Word of God. In fact, he rejects premature eschatology. He emphasizes Christians are still amid conflict and are not already at the goal.[127]

Barth criticizes neo-Protestant theology because it dispenses with the coming redemption he was to discuss in this volume. In neo-Protestant theology, redemption became a vague goal of a gradual progress in the direction of the memory of Christ. Coming redemption has no real significance for those existing in the interval. The faith necessary in the interval is a special mode of human capacity and is therefore not Christian faith. Such faith is a religion. Such faith expects progress, but this faith only influences the individual. One becomes master of oneself. Such a fellowship of religious people is a club that people join for certain enterprises.[128]

Barth explores the shift that occurred in his lifetime with eschatology. The Reformers focused on what God did in election from eternity. Unfortunately, the result was that what happened in time became an appendix and eschatology became an appendix of an appendix. He wants to add a teleological element that the Reformers did not have.[129] Then, in a version of liberal Protestant theology, the temporal became primary, dropping what God had done from eternity and what God will do in the future, for the moment became eternal. This led to secularization. Then, at the end of the 19th century and beginning of the 20th, certain sects emphasized individual hope for the future. Through scientific exegesis, some looked upon Jesus and the disciples as entirely consumed with looking for the coming age. Their opponents were a church-centered Christianity and pietism, both of whom focused on an individual hope for a future life. Some identified eschatological hope with the socialist Labor movement. He admits to focusing upon the futurity of God and the real

---

[127] *The Gottingen Dogmatics: Instruction in the Christian Religion* consists of lectures delivered in 1924-5. It covers many of the same themes as does *Church Dogmatics*. Barth scholars will have some fascination with the shifts in his thought. My concern is only to see the ways his discussion of the doctrine of redemption in these lectures might provide some hints as to what Barth might have said had he had the time to do so.
[128] CD I.2, 21.1.
[129] CD IV.1, 58.4.

end of all things. He refers to his commentary on Romans 8:24, where he stressed that the visible is not hope. Genuine Christianity is eschatology. Hope is what sets free. Hope is grace. We cannot see redemption. Christians must be people of hope. His comment on all of this was, "Well roared, lion!" He refers to the danger of cultural Protestantism. He refers negatively to the Kairos-philosophy of Tillich and to the attempt of Bultmann to reduce the New Testament to anthropology. He now felt the need to guide theology out of its "theology of crisis," which he helped create, a theology that could have existence only for a moment. He then has an interesting discussion of the domination of compelling ideas in theology. We will eventually tire of them. Some thought of the whole of primitive Christianity chiefly concerned with the end of all things, a reaction against Ritschl and Harnack and embodied in Weiss and Schweitzer. It emphasized the unfulfilled word of Jesus and the hope of the return of Jesus. Secularization followed, as the tedious became all too interesting. Vitality and freshness in theology departs where the focus becomes one dominating insight. The pathetic monotony of such emphases became instruments with which to beat up others. He looks at his later theology as attempting to bring together the emphasis the Reformers had on the decision of God in eternity with eschatology. He has sought to do this with his exposition of the notion of the three forms of eternity as pre-temporal (the decision of God in eternity), supra-temporal (time), and post-temporal (eschatology).[130]

Barth saw dangers in eschatology that this volume would seek to expose and correct. The danger of Reformed teaching of the 1500s and cultural Protestantism of the 1800s was its removal of eschatology from profound influence upon dogmatics. He also saw dangers with the evangelical church in its focus upon individual piety, church community, and individualized hope for a future life with God. The danger of the latter was its concern for the preservation of the self.

As much as many of us, as modern Christians, might want to dismiss eschatology and apocalyptic, their basic themes are part of core statements of faith and liturgy. In the Nicene Creed, we read, "He will come again in glory to judge the living and the dead, and his kingdom will have no end." The same Jesus of Nazareth, whom human beings crucified and rejected, but whom God raised from the dead, and who now is the with his Father, will be the one who comes at the "end" of human history as its judge. He will judge me – and you, as a reader. The creed concludes by affirming, "We look for the resurrection of the dead and the life of the world to come." Such a statement affirms that the life we have lived here on earth, in the body, remains significant for any notion of life after death. It

---

[130] CD II.1, 31.3

also signals that whatever such a "life" is, it will be quite different from the life we now lead. In the United Methodist Church, "A Modern Affirmation" and "The World Methodist Social Affirmation" look upon the "kingdom" as something human beings bring about by their actions of love, justice, and reconciliation. The Lord's Prayer is part of the liturgy for many congregations. "Thy kingdom come, they will be done, on earth as it is in heaven" is an important part of that prayer. Christians pray for a future that influences the way they practice their discipleship today. They are to live in a way today that reflects the desire for this future. In a baptism liturgy of the United Methodist Church, the prayer over the water includes that those baptized receiving the clothing of righteousness so that, dying and rising with Christ, "they may share in his final victory." In the liturgy of the great thanksgiving used by many denominations, the church proclaims the mystery of faith: Christ has died, Christ is risen, Christ will come again. We pray to be one in ministry to the world, "until Christ comes in final victory and we feast at his heavenly banquet." In the funeral liturgy used in many denominations, the church affirms that "Christ will come again in glory." Later in the same prayer, we affirm "What we shall be has not yet been revealed; but we know that when he appears, we shall be like him, for we shall see him as he is." Even as one whom people have loved had died, Christians affirm that Jesus is the resurrection and the life. Because Christ lives, we shall live also. Such statements affirm that the same Son of God through whom God created all things, through whom God worked in reconciling love, is the same Son of God who will come at the "end." He is Lord, and therefore the source of life, Christians affirm in their teaching on creation. He is Lord, and therefore the "end" will be a saving end, one that brings creation as a whole and human history to a meaningful conclusion.

    C.H. Dodd concludes that the core proclamation of Paul focuses on the facts of the death and resurrection of Christ but placed in an eschatological setting that gives significance to these facts. Christ himself marks the end of the evil age and the coming of the age to come. He identifies this proclamation in its essentials in the following way. First, Christ has fulfilled the Old Testament prophecies. He was a descendent of David. He died in accord with the Scripture. He was buried. He rose on the third day. He is exalted at the right hand of God as Son of God and Lord. He will come again as judge and savior of humanity. He sees enough similarity of the preaching of Paul with the Jerusalem preaching in the opening chapters of Acts to suggest that Paul derived his basic teaching from it. As he puts it, the expectation of a speedy advent must have had extraordinarily deep roots in Christian belief. New Testament authors are all using language that implies that the final and decisive act of God has already entered human experience.[131]

Rudolf Bultmann has given a searching exploration into the nature of myth and the modern world.[132] His essay ponders what we as modern readers of this literature can learn from texts governed by such a world view. He admits that modern thought can be shallow and may need to recover the truths the ancients saw more clearly (p. 3). The mythical view of Jewish apocalyptic, especially as it found its way into the New Testament, is untenable because the return of Christ never happened (p. 5). The modern world is "naturalist" (p. 7). He thinks the academic theologian and the parish priest need some clarity and honesty here, something he clearly thinks Karl Barth lacks in this regard (p. 9). For him, then, myth does not present an objective picture of the world as it is. Rather, it expresses the understanding that human beings have of themselves in the world in which they live. As a criticism of Bultmann at this point, I think apocalyptic writers themselves took their imagery as expressing their understanding of themselves and their world. They used a disciplined and fanciful imagination to convey to their readers precisely what Bultmann says we as modern readers need to do. Bultmann will spend the rest of the essay presenting his program for viewing the mythical images of the New Testament through an existentialist interpretation of them as read in the philosopher Heidegger. For him, the life of faith is the authentic life, grace and forgiveness brings deliverance from bondage to the past, and thus opens us to life in the Spirit. For him, this suggests an eschatological life. For him, however, the "event of Christ" is not a relic of mythology. His life is a human life that ended in the tragedy of crucifixion. In his life, we have a unique combination of history and myth. This event is a revelation of the love of God, free humanity from self and to be self. Humanity becomes capable of self-commitment, faith, love, and therefore an authentic life. Bultmann grants that for those who think all talk of God is myth, his project is not satisfying.

Bultmann brings up an interesting point when he suggests that the "event of Christ" is not a relic of mythology that he has kept within his theology. The Christian canon itself shows that, regardless of how mythical its writing becomes, it keeps coming back to this non-mythological "event of Christ." We can see this in I Corinthians 15, where it begins with Paul making it clear that the basis of Christian teaching is the non-mythological account of the death and resurrection of Christ. Yet, he will go on to explain to these Greeks several Jewish apocalyptic notions of the resurrection body and the expectation of a general resurrection. However,

---

[131] (*The Apostolic Preaching and its Developments,* 1935, p. 13, 17, 31)
[132] (*New Testament and Mythology,* 1953)

most significantly, we can see this in the highly mythological presentation in Revelation 12. The imagery of the dragon and the woman ready to give birth. The dragon is ready to kill the child, but "her child was snatched away and taken to God and to his throne." For the Christian reading this, what the author has done is summarize the life, death, resurrection, and ascension of Jesus. A mythological presentation like this still cannot eliminate the grounding of the myth in a non-mythological "event of Christ."

The Book of Revelation is an important aspect of the apocalyptic character of early Christian preaching. Taking a literal reading of Revelation was an approach that Augustine, Roman Catholic teaching, and John Calvin had dispensed with in their theological reflections. This fact should alert us to the direction Barth would have headed in his final volume. If the church is to have an eschatology that has application to Christian discipleship today, it will need the courage to put aside some of the most popular religion of our time. Any notion of making the image of the beast relevant to a predetermined plan of world empires today shows an attempt to force Revelation into typical Jewish apocalyptic thinking which, I think, John resisted. He resisted it because the primary event of the end times, the last things, has occurred in Jesus Christ, in his suffering, death, and in his resurrection. As such, the primary end time hope of Jewish apocalyptic, that of resurrection, had already occurred. It is not like other world events must occur for the "end" to come. All attempts to identify the name behind the number 666 are a waste. As writers in the second century already indicated, it was a waste of time then, as it is now. Friederich Schleiermacher stresses that anything the theologian says about the end must have everything Chiliastic purged out of it.[133] Barth would agree with this. Chiliasm means painting a picture that decidedly envision the return of Christ to defeat armies on earth and establish a kingdom on earth for one thousand years. This view, adopted by early authors like Papias, Justin Martyr, and Irenaeus, envisioned Jesus ruling the earth from a restored Jerusalem. Augustine set aside this notion in favor of what we now call an a-millennial view, in which Christ has already bound Satan so that the church will not experience the full onslaught of the forces and evil and therefore be allowed to carry out its mission and ministry. Christ now reigns with the saints (the church), although this is reality seen with faith. In the terms of Barth, Augustine is proposing a secret history seen from the perspective of the event of faith in Jesus Christ. My point here is that beginning with Augustine, the church put aside chiliastic teaching in favor of its form of a realized eschatology. The church focused upon the

---

[133] (*The Christian Faith,* par. 160)

blessings the church and individuals experience now because of what God has done in Christ. It focused upon the church militant and its spiritual battle today and placed the church triumphant into the distant future. The Reformation continued this emphasis. Thus, for over a millennium, some version of a-millennial thought was dominant. In his *Institutes of the Christian Religion* (Book 3.25), John Calvin calls chiliasm a "fiction," and says that it is "too puerile to need or to deserve refutation." Well, it may seem harsh to call something that seems to have grabbed the imagination of so many Christians in the modern era as childish. On the other hand, human history shows that human beings have the capacity to believe such things with great ferocity. As we shall see, Barth will have similar concerns with certain types of popular eschatology that lean toward the transformation of this earth in a way that borders upon or embraces a modern form of chiliasm. However, his recovery of eschatology in dogmatics means he will want to restore the priority of the future and the dynamic power of hope in Christian living.

In his Gottingen Dogmatics, the portion not yet translated into English, he contrasts Christian eschatological statements with secular eschatologies, such as historical-sociological (Marxist), the geological-astronomical (the scientific end of the universe), parapsychological, and ontological eschatology. As I read Barth, eschatology provides us with the proper framework for approaching the question of meaning regarding world-historical events, the history of the people of God, or our personal history.

The resurrection of the flesh was a major theme of the early church. It could speak of the literal collection of the particles that would occur in the return of Christ in a way that preserves the individuality and identity of the person. We see this view in Jerome, Augustine, and Aquinas. Another way of describing the resurrection of the flesh was that it occurred as God takes fleshly existence into divine life and allows flesh to participate in that divine life. We see such views in Origen, Athanasius, and Maximus. Both views can treat the flesh as an appendage to a process of increasing spiritualization of the notion of resurrection.[134] Barth can speak of the resurrection of the dead in a way that invites a focus upon participation. God takes human existence into the presence of God, thereby we (the dead) become what we are not (resurrected). The resurrection of the flesh occurs because we who are in the flesh now receive the miracle of resurrection now in life with God.[135]

I think Barth would have dealt with the basic creeds and especially

---

[134] (Hitchcock 2013), Chapter 1.
[135] (Hitchcock 2013), Chapter 2.

the confessions of the Reformed tradition.[136] The Interrogatory Creed of Hippolytus (c. 215 A.D.) asks, "Do you believe…in the resurrection of the body?" Similarly, the Creed of Marcellus (340 A.D.) declares: "I believe in…the resurrection of the body." The Creed of Rufinus (c. 404 A.D.) is more explicit and declares "I believe in the resurrection of the flesh." The Apostles' Creed proclaims belief in the resurrection of the body, but the Nicene Creed states only a belief in the resurrection of the "dead." Other creeds and confessions holding to the resurrection of the flesh include the Athanasian Creed and the second London Confession of 1689 (Baptist). Although the term "body" is ambiguous and elastic enough to mean spiritual bodies, we may assume that physical bodies was intended and understood.

The heirs to the creeds were the articles and confessions of faith of later centuries. For example, chapter XXXII of the Westminster Confession - Of the State of Men after Death, and of the Resurrection of the Dead - states:

1. The bodies of men, after death, return to dust, and see corruption: but their souls, which neither die nor sleep, having an immortal subsistence, immediately return to God who gave them: the souls of the righteous, being then made perfect in holiness, are received into the highest heavens, where they behold the face of God, in light and glory, waiting for the full redemption of their bodies. And the souls of the wicked are cast into hell, where they remain in torments and utter darkness, reserved to the judgment of the great day. Beside these two places, for souls separated from their bodies, the Scripture acknowledgeth none.

2. At the last day, such as are found alive shall not die, but be changed: and all the dead shall be raised up, with the self-same bodies, and none other (although with different qualities), which shall be united again to their souls for ever.

3. The bodies of the unjust shall, by the power of Christ, be raised to dishonour: the bodies of the just, by His Spirit, unto honour; and be made conformable to His own glorious body.

Another doctrinal statement holding to the resurrection of the flesh is the Belgic Confession (Reformed Church):

---

[136] The references are from Kurt Simmons:
http://preteristcentral.com/The%20Resurrection%20of%20the%20Flesh.html

> "Finally we believe, according to God's Word, that when the time appointed by the Lord is come (which is unknown to all creatures) and the number of the elect is complete, our Lord Jesus Christ will come from heaven, bodily and visibly, as he ascended, with great glory and majesty, to declare himself the judge of the living and the dead. He will burn this old world, in fire and flame, in order to cleanse it. Then all human creatures will appear in person before the great judge-- men, women, and children, who have lived from the beginning until the end of the world. They will be summoned there by the voice of the archangel and by the sound of the divine trumpet. For all those who died before that time will be raised from the earth, their spirits being joined and united with their own bodies in which they lived. And as for those who are still alive, they will not die like the others but will be changed 'in the twinkling of an eye' from 'corruptible to incorruptible.'"

I doubt that Barth would have given much consideration to the Book of Revelation. However, as we turn our thoughts to the doctrine of redemption, I would like to explore briefly approaches to the book. Those who study the book seem to arrive at one of four general schools of thought.

One is the preterist position. In this view, an interpreter will refer to the events of the time of the writing. It assumes that the symbols and images meant something to the readers and writers. The seals, trumpets, and bowls refer to Jews, Christians, and Rome in the first century. For this perspective, the fulfillment of the prophecies occurred with the fall of Jerusalem in 70 AD. The book would have the purpose of encouraging Christians to live their faith in the Roman Empire as Christians experienced it in the first century. This approach has the advantage of relevance to the original readers, timing (must soon take place), and consistency with what Jesus said in Mark 13. Yet, this position must deal with the appearance that all the prophecies could not possibly all be fulfilled in the destruction of Jerusalem. My own thought is that such an interpretation of the book would be acceptable, had it not become part of the canon of the church. Had someone recently discovered the book, and we interpreted it in isolation from everything else, one might find such an approach acceptable. However, another issue with this approach is that the relevance of the symbols and images would seem non-existent. The fact that the book is part of the sacred text of a religious community says to me that the book has had continuing significance to readers. I do not think this approach offers us a valid reason for that significance. If a religious community were only interested in history, such an approach would make sense. However, a religious community looks upon its sacred writings to help shape the life of worship and discipleship today. At the same time, I do not think that this approach takes seriously the import of myths, symbols, and images from pre-modern cultures. All ancient texts use language and thought in a way different from an era influenced by the science and technology. We can alienate ourselves from these ancient texts, if we have superior knowledge and insight. I think such an approach is arrogant. It also denies the common bond modern readers have with the ancient reader. We have common human aspirations, hopes, and dreams. The ancient thinker often used myths, images, and symbols that reflect a profound insight into human nature. The "modern" person will use novels, poetry, and scientific method to arrive at such insight. Thus, I have high regard for the notion that the images and symbols must have meant something specific to the author and reader. Yet, as one reader of the Book of Revelation, I cannot stop there.

Two is the historicist position. In this view, the Book of Revelation provides an insight into the entire sweep of church history until the return of Christ. It expands the historical period covered from the preterist view of the first century to the whole sweep of history. This position does see God as in charge of history. It looks upon historical events as fulfilling some dimension of prophecy in Revelation. John Wesley (based upon Bengel) offered such an interpretation in his notes on the New Testament. These notes are readily available on the Internet. I invite any reader to look them up, for it shows the danger of moving down this path. We can "imagine" many connections to history, when we set our imaginations free from the first century and biblical context of this book. True, it can give some assurance to those who believe it that God is fulfilling biblical prophecy. Yet, the fact that it must keep shifting the meaning of the symbols discredits the approach. Not surprisingly, given Christian history, the fulfillment of prophecy is quite centered upon Europe.

Three is the idealist position. One could also call it a spiritual, allegorical, or symbolic approach. Personally, I do not like any of the terms, for none of them communicate what I want to suggest. For such a view, the correlation between the visions and any historical reality is not strong. The symbolism has an "overspill" of thought and reflection that one can apply to any time and culture. The images and symbols refer to the continuing struggle in human history between good and evil. Therefore, in Daniel 7-12, beastly power exhibited itself in Babylon, Persia, and the Greek Empire. For John, Rome may have been the beast in the first century. Yet, any government may display beastly characteristics, especially as it attempts to have absolute loyalty from its citizens and persecute the church. For me, if we ground our understanding in the first century, this position allows us to see the continuous nature of the battle between good and evil. The battle is cosmic, and thus greater than the battle in my heart or in my church. The battle is continuous, and thus not reserved for the "end." "Idealist" does mean divorced from real life, but rather, exposing the intensity of the struggle in which we can engage. This position does not look for the fulfillment of prophecy in historical events. Rather, the book is an encouragement to believers that God will gain eventual victory over evil. It calls upon them to persevere during the toughest times. As Paul put it in Ephesians 6:12, our struggle is not against enemies of blood and flesh, but against cosmic powers. The seals, trumpets, and bowls are recurring themes of natural and human history. This view is consistent with the apocalyptic nature of the book. For this position, apocalyptic literature is not a code to actual events. It becomes an artistic and dramatic expression. It becomes relevant to any age. The literal undertones of the text are satisfied if one includes a preterist dimension to this approach. If the idealist grounds the interpretation of the imagery and symbols within the first century, it avoids one potential shortcoming, that of the imagery meaning anything the interpreter wants it to mean. Incorporating a preterist dimension will also ground the imagery and symbolism in its early Christian, Jewish, and Old Testament context. This approach respects the notion that ancient writers often utilized myth, symbol, and image to convey profound thoughts and insights concerning human nature and history that will have continuing significance for every age.

Four is the futurist or dispensationalist position. In this view, the Book of Revelation describes events immediately preceding the return of Christ. This position is quite weak and has least integrity with the text, in my view, but it is popular. It assumes a secret rapture in 4:1, and then the rest of the book has no relevance to anyone until we are at the point of the last seven years before the return of Christ. Such a rapture interprets John as a symbol of the whole church, a position that I would suggest is questionable in the extreme. This view identifies a seven-year period of judgment (great tribulation) in Chapters 6-18, the return of Christ in Chapter 19, a literal thousand year reign of Christ on earth (chiliasm) in Chapter 20, a final judgment in Chapter 20, and the creation of new heaven and earth in Chapter 21. This view has captured the imagination of many Protestant evangelical churches. Now, what this view considers as a "straightforward" approach to an interpretation of the text would be valid only if the text itself invited us to do this. Yet, their interpretation of key parts of the text show that they are not true their own principle. For example, it would be quite a stretch for any first-time reader to think of the letters to the seven churches in Chapters 2-3 to be anything more than what they claim to be, that is, letters to specific churches in the first century. Yet, dispensationalists and historicists want them to identify ages of church history since the first century until "now," which usually means that we are in the age of the seventh church, and therefore at the end. Further, to think of "John" as receiving this vision by being brought to heaven as symbolic of the whole church being "raptured" is quite a stretch as well. The threefold repetition of judgments in seals, trumpets, and bowls is far more likely to be a recapitulation of one "judgment" upon sin, than it is a specific event of the last seven years before the return of Christ. In other words, for all their attempts to offer a "plain" reading of the text, their reading is far from such a description. The text clearly uses images, symbols, myths, and so on, to convey its point. I would add that the many occasions in which the New Testament says that we cannot know when the end will occur seem to conflict with dispensationalists. They think they can read the signs of the times. Yet, as Jesus put it, if the householder knew when the thief could come, he would be ready. Jesus himself says that no one will know when the end will come, not angels in heaven, not even the Son. The day will come like a thief in the night. People will be going about their daily activities, and then the end will come. Further, Christians in the Lord's Prayer have said, "Thy kingdom come." If the dispensationalism is right, it makes a lie of the prayer itself.

The purpose of the Book of Revelation is to reveal the nature of world events in such a way as to encourage the faithful to accept martyrdom, if necessary. The hope of the writer is that the readers will recognize the claims of Rome as deceptive. God is the true sovereign in their lives. The writer sets the present battle in the context of a cosmic battle, in which God will soon gain victory over the forces of evil and establish the rule of God over the earth. In that sense, then, the battle within the first century becomes the battle of every century. There are threats to the health and vitality of the church that arise from within and without. Political powers can become "beastly" in that they persecute believers and collect earthly power in themselves. In such a situation, believers need to remain faithful to Christ, accept martyrdom where necessary, and live with the hope that God will triumph, even when human means for victory seem exhausted.

One needs to remember that this is an apocalyptic work, however. It sees an "end" to the cosmic battle. In theological circles, we often refer to the notion of an "already" and a "not yet." The "not yet" refers to the fullness of the reign of God in the future, of which Jesus preached. The "already" is the presence of the reign of God through the work of the Holy Spirit here, in our lives, community, and world. It seems that the forces of evil, the Dragon, Satan, have their own version of this eschatology, in which the beast, false prophet, and prostitute are the historical images and manifestation of an evil seeks to bring itself to completion and fulfillment.

As Revelation reminds us, it will be "soon," but it will also come like a thief, at a time when we do not expect. In that sense, an important aspect of discipleship is to learn to recognize the signs of the beast, just as we need to learn the signs of the reign of God.

I need to offer a caution. Other parts of the New Testament did not take the approach to government that this author does. Granted, he (or some later prophet in the church, as some scholars would suggest) warned of governments persecuting believers in Mark 13. Yet, Jesus taught to render to Caesar to what belongs to Caesar. I Peter 2 encourages honor offered to the emperor. Paul took a quite different approach to Rome from what we see in Revelation in Romans 13:1-5.

> 1 Let every person be subject to the governing authorities; for there is no authority except from God, and those authorities that exist have been instituted by God. 2 Therefore whoever resists authority resists what God has appointed, and those who resist will incur judgment. 3 For rulers are not a terror to good conduct, but to bad. Do you wish to have no fear of the authority? Then do what is good, and you will receive its approval; 4 for it is God's servant for your good. But if you do what is wrong, you should be afraid, for the authority does not bear the sword in vain! It is the servant of God to execute wrath on the wrongdoer. 5 Therefore one must be subject, not only because of wrath but also because of conscience.

Paul reminds us that governments do not have to be beastly. In fact, in his time, in the 40-50's, he did not describe the government that way.

Let us approach the teaching of the end in another way. Some writers will focus upon how one interprets the notion of the millennium that we find in Revelation 20:1-6.[137]

In the interpretation of some thinkers, the millennium is either already present or an emerging reality. The millennium is now emerging on earth. What the people of God can expect is the fruits of that emerging but secret reality. The emerging millennial rule of God will conclude with the return of Christ and the judgment that will accompany it. this view resists detailed speculative explanations of present history as the fulfillment of specific prophecies, as if they are signs of a literal end of the times. It rejects

---

[137] Thomas C. Oden, *Classic Christianity: A Systematic Theology*, HarperCollins, New York, 19887), 805-11.

all forms of Chiliasm and Millennialism. We see this view in Augustine, *City of God* (20.7-14). His view prevailed in various forms, such as Clement of Alexandria, Origen, Dionysius, Tyconius, Aquinas, Luther, Calvin, and Roman Catholic teaching. In this view, "thousand" refers to the entire age of the church (Aquinas, B. B. Warfield). Although sometimes called a-millennialism, such a name suggests no interest in the millennium. This view would criticize all forms of premillennialism for depending too much upon a literal ready of a highly symbolic passage in Revelation 20:1-6. Conservative authors like A. Kyuper, H. Bavinck, G. Vos, A. Hoekema, and Jay Adams support such a view of realized millennialism. This view has the political tendency to unite the institutional church with the protection of the state.

Postmillennial teaching suggests that Christ will return after the church has proclaimed the gospel to all and has taken full effect among the nations. The glorious return of Christ will occur after the people of God establish the millennial rule of God. The general resurrection of the dead and divine judgment will accompany the return of Christ. It takes the Lord's Prayer seriously: Thy will be done on earth as it is in heaven will be a growing world-historical condition. Joachim of Fiora, Daniel Whitby, Cocceius, Witsius, and Walter Rauschenbusch reflect such a perspective. The difficulty of this approach is that the New Testament tends to see the time before the end as one that will include apostasy, persecution, and suffering. It seems optimistic to assert that an earthly messianic rule of God woud directly emerge out of the shambles of the history of sin, or that peace would reign under the present conditions of finite history. Even the Augsburg Confession (art. 17) rejects the view that before the resurrection of the dead, the saints will possess a worldly rule. This view tends to have the ethical implication of a transformational view of the civil and political order, tending to see the church as actively engaged in the responsibility to change society in conformity with the divine claim. The political tendency is the transformation of society from injustice to justice as an act of eschatological accountability.

Premillennial teaching expects a literal fulfillment of the unconditional promise to Abraham and David. They expect Christ to return before the millennium to institute the kingdom promised to David. On the basis of Revelation 20:5-6, they expect a first resurrection at the beginning of the millennium, the saints ruling with Christ on the earth for a thousand years, and then a second resurrection that will occur after God releases Satan from the bondage he endured for that thousand years. Satan will fail again, and God will bring judgment. Irenaeus (Against Heresies, 5.25.1 and 28.3, 33.2) was an early proponent of this view. This view was dominant with Justin Martyr, Hermas, the Letter of Barnabas, Methodius,

Commodianus, and Tertullian. Recent premillennial teaching comes tied with the dispensationalism we find in Darby, Schofield, and Gaebelein. This view divides the return of Christ into different spheres. The first sphere is the rapture as Christ comes for the saints. A seven-year period will follow in which there will be the gathering of Israel, the great tribulation, and the Antichrist. The second sphere will be the coming of Christ with the saints to rule on earth. This view tends to have the political implication of a realistic ordering of a country toward restraining evil, which will not likely diminish until the return of Christ.

My purpose in offering this background is not to suggest that Barth would have discussed all of this. I am suggesting that he would have dealt with this material in his unique and powerful way. His concern with the work of Moltmann and Pannenberg was that they might open the door to a too literal interpretation of the end. I think his comments would have been quite close to Augustine and Calvin in these matters. In fact, as I will show, the comments he makes in his public writings are quite close to the Reformed tradition. At the same time, he will want to restore the role of eschatology, the future, and hope, that he believed the Reformers lost in their emphasis upon faith in Christ and the Bible.

In the doctrine of redemption, Barth would want to let the Word of God as the Son speak to us as the Word of the end toward which humanity moves. God the redeemer is first and last. As the redeemer of humanity, the rule of God is coming to vanquish the rule of discord that defines human history. This event will happen in the dawning of the new heaven and the new earth. As the Word of redemption, the doctrine of redemption will comprehend humanity from the standpoint of eternity. Death shadows humanity along its course in history. Illuminated by the resurrection of Jesus, God has swallowed up death in victory in the revelation of the life of God. The promise of resurrection and eternal life allows humanity to move toward this end.[138]

The revelation of God described in the event of redemption will be new. If it were not, neither God nor humanity would have need of it. However, it will not be new in an absolute or abstract way. When it comes, it will fulfill that which God wants fulfilled as he explained in his doctrine of Reconciliation/Atonement.[139]

The Trinitarian structure of *Church Dogmatics* would have become clearer had Barth completed his project. Of course, throughout this work, we have seen the Spirit at work. The Spirit is the life-giving Spirit of creation. The Spirit is the one who gathers the congregation by awakening

---

[138] CD I.2, 24.2.
[139] CD III.1, 119.

people to the event of faith, who builds up the community in love, and who sends the community as a faithful witness with hope. Thus, the one whole God is the Subject and Author of creation, reconciliation, and redemption. Yet, the work of the Father relates specifically to the work of creation, the work of the Son relates specifically to the work of reconciliation, and the work of the Spirit relates specifically to the work of redemption.[140] The Holy Spirit opens the Triune life of God to be a free act of majesty. The history of Father and Son culminates in the Holy Spirit, the Lord of life, who proceeds from the Father. God is the free Lord on the inner union of this triune life. The triune life of God is the basis of the will and action that God directs to us. The triune life of God is the basis of the work of God, which includes the final goal of redemption to eternal life with God.[141] The good and the best within the created order await their future glorification.[142] The history played out under the lordship of God is the execution of the election of grace resolved and fulfilled from all eternity. God establishes fellowship with humanity and accomplishes its completion in the divine self-giving to humanity until its manifestation at the expiration of the last time. As the creation of all the reality distinct from God took place based on this purposed covenant and with a view to its execution, the meaning and purpose of the creature will have its course and reach its goal. The church is the community comforted by the Holy Ghost, proclaiming the name of its Lord, and awaits the manifestation of its Lord.[143] The history of the covenant will reach its divinely appointed goal. Our salvation and future glory do not have their source in anything we can read off nature or history.[144] The fact that God alone rules means that God is the only goal that God has appointed for the creature and towards which God directs it. Proceeding from God, accompanied by God, the creature must also return to God. The movement toward God is the meaning of its history. The glory of God is the salvation and glorification of the creature.[145]

The history of the covenant involves creation and reconciliation. When the interim period of proclamation of this work is over, it will culminate in the perfecting or redemption that consists in the general revelation of the creative and reconciling act of God. Here is the line, direction, and meaningful sequence and context, and therefore form and character, of the rule of God. Christ reveals the center and goal of this

---

[140] CD III.4, 52.2.
[141] CD IV.2, 64.4.
[142] CD III.1, 366.
[143] CD III.3, 36-7.
[144] CD III.3, 48.
[145] CD III.3, 158-9

economy. God will finally perfect creation in Christ. The love of God revealed in Christ moves toward its own perfection and therefore to the end of the age in the still future revelation of Jesus Christ. World-occurrence has a direction, even if we cannot read it off world historical events. Thus, even if we can see no trace of a sacred history, everything does move from the gracious creation, by way of the reconciliation accomplished in Christ, to its final revelation.[146] The prophetic service of the congregation refers to the death and resurrection of Jesus Christ as the beginning and his coming again as the end of all things it anticipates what God is still to consummate. It attests that Christ alone reigns in eternity and therefore in time.[147] Commencing in His resurrection, continuing in the presence and activity of His Holy Spirit, and moving towards the completion of the whole economy in His final, universal and definitive appearance and revelation, Jesus Christ is also the Proclaimer of His being and action as the one High-priest and King. He is also the one Prophet of the kingdom of God drawn near in Him.[148] The final revelation will show that God has already overcome the threat of Nothingness.[149] When Jesus Christ shall finally returns as the Lord and Head of all that God has created, it will also be revealed that both in light and shadow, on the right hand and on the left, everything created was very good supremely glorious.[150] The rule of God coming to us on earth is the rule of heaven. When the earth does the will of God as heaven already does it, it will be both a divine and heavenly happening. The angels as ambassadors of God will accompany God in that rule. Earthly encounter with God and the angels will find its fullness. Where God is, heaven and the angels are present.[151] The overthrow of the demonic is a genuine overthrow. Its final manifestation will be its destruction. The eternal fire will consume them.[152] The commanding God will liberate humanity for eternal life, redeeming and perfecting humanity in the final act and revelation of divine love.[153]

Barth discusses the Holy Spirit first as God the Redeemer. The Redeemer sets us free and makes us children of God. Such a statement arises from the knowledge and praise of God. We become the redeemed, the liberated, and the children of God in faith. This act of God in our

---

[146] CD III.3, 195-7
[147] CD III.4, 510.
[148] CD IV.3, 606.
[149] CD III.3, 289.
[150] CD III.3, 296.
[151] CD III.3, 477.
[152] CD III.3, 521.
[153] CD III.4, 24.

redemption encloses our being. We can contemplate our redemption only from the divine aspect of faith. Faith understands our redemption, or our beatitude or eternal life, as posited, fulfilled, and consummated by God. We cannot understand it fully, for then faith would be sight. We cannot see things with God in eternity. We cannot anticipate what lies beyond revelation and faith. Our redemption implies our being in addition to an act of God we can regard only as future. Our redemption comes to us from God. We have it in faith. Redemption in faith means that we have it in promise. We accept the promise given us in the Word of God in Jesus Christ even as we do not understand it or see it fulfilled or consummated in our present. We have empty hands with which we stretch out to God in the process of our redemption. We believe our future being. We believe an eternal life even while in the valley of death. In this futurity, we have our redemption. The assurance of faith is the assurance of having this redemption. The assurance of faith means the assurance of hope. Anything one can say about one who receives the Holy Spirit is an eschatological statement. In this case eschatological is in relation to the eschaton, which means to that which from our standpoint and for our perspective has still to come. It refers to eternal reality of the divine fulfillment and consummation. Such statements claim meaning as statements about temporal relations. Truth in this relation is important for humanity. Further, he says that the call, reconciliation, justification, sanctification, and redemption of humanity are eschatological statements in the New Testament. It speaks of reality in a proper way. God is the measure of what we consider real and proper. Eternity comes first, and then time. The future comes first, and then the present.[154]

We will explore the teaching within *Church Dogmatics* regarding time and eternity has important implications regarding the final destiny of humanity. Knowing that he would not complete his massive work, Barth invited others to continue his "pilgrim theology" (*The Christian Life,* p. 8). I will attempt to do that, looking at certain sections of the works of Barth from the perspective of eschatology and redemption.

Barth has discussed the secret involved in Christ, the event of reconciliation, and the church arising out of the outpouring of the Spirit and as the Body of Christ. In the event of redemption, the hidden God during the time of revelation and reconciliation openly shows who God is.[155] While a new world breaks through in Jesus Christ, explained in the doctrine of reconciliation, Christ points the way to the consummation of this new world. The consummation will mean removing of the things that

---

[154] CD I.1, 12.1.
[155] CD I.2, 16.2.

cause humanity to suffer.[156] The freedom of God shows itself in God being our redeemer.[157] The meeting of God with us, as explained in the doctrine of reconciliation, will find its fulfillment in the action of God as our redeemer.[158] Further, in Volume IV, he can say that the theology of the cross has a secret theology of glory. The priestly office has the secret of the kingly office. He describes the Christian as the new human being and the new secret of divine majesty. The community has a theology the resurrection and therefore a theology of glory. The glory of God shows itself as the resurrection lighting up the riddle of the existence of Jesus. Redemption is the completion of creation in its new form of peace, its being in the glory of God. The secret of the existence of Jesus Christ is that he is the true witness. The community exists in world-occurrence by virtue of its adherence to the open secret it has in its calling from Christ and in the power of its word in the Holy Spirit.

The final truth that *Church Dogmatics* would have considered is that God is the redeemer. God as creator considered faith in the Father. God as reconciler considered the love of the Son. God as redeemer considers the hope that comes through the Holy Spirit. The One who has made humanity and reconciled humanity to himself, encounters humanity in the Word of God in order that God may be the entire future, fulfilling and consummating what God promised in the creative and reconciling work of God. Again, one must recognize this in the action of God as creator and reconciler. It is only here that God meets us clearly as the God of everlasting faithfulness, who neither seeks us, nor allows God to be sought by us, without allowing us to find God. Following the rule of grace is the rule of glory. God will be our entire and perfect future. Jesus Christ comes again. The presence of the Holy Spirit is a pledge of the faithfulness of God to us and the coming of God. Barth will not want eschatology to become an appendix to the doctrine of atonement, as did Schleiermacher. We can understand Jesus Christ in the New Testament only as the Savior who is to come. If God is not the one who comes, God is not the one who has already come. If we do not understand the atonement that has taken place in God in the future tense, we cannot understand it in the perfect tense, which means we cannot understand it at all. What we have now in Christ we have in hope. In the Bible, God is the redeemer. Barth wants to offer a faithful account of the content of the Word of God. The atonement has its place and longing for the coming redemption has its place. The church has its place, and the coming of the rule of God has its place. Faith and love

---

[156] CD I.2, 18.3.
[157] CD II.1, 28.3.
[158] CD II.1, 31.2.

have their place, and hope has its place. Recollection of what God has done in Christ has its place; expectation of what God will do in Christ has its place. We need to combine gratitude and longing, patience and impatience, final peace and final disquietude, fidelity to the church and a passionate desire for the new aeon. Our regeneration, justification and sanctification, the church and its practice of baptism and the Lord's Supper, the whole existence, and the whole work of Jesus Christ in the present are eschatological, that is, they are actual only in the coming Redeemer.[159]

God promises the presence of God as the content of the future of humanity. God is the One who meets humanity on the way through time as the end of all time. God is the hidden Lord of all times. The divine presence through the Word is the presence of the coming One, coming for the fulfillment and consummation of the relation established between God and us in creation, confirmed in reconciliation, and a final Word of fulfillment. Of course, human words are never final, so only a divine word can have finality. The Word of God is the Word of our Redeemer. As Redeemer, the Lord keeps faith with the divine self as well as with humanity. Whatever God says is this final, consummating, and eschatological relation.[160]

Barth will stress that we have no analogy in which God the Redeemer becomes accessible to us. His discussion gives us some hint of what he would have discussed in this chapter. We know something about goals and attempts to attain them. The future is an empty form of the time that is still ahead of us. We know as an empty form the idea of a perfection that is prior to becoming. Yet, this has nothing to do with God the Redeemer. God is not the X at the end of our world picture. Redemption does not mean the world evolves in a certain direction. It means that Jesus Christ is coming again. Redemption means the resurrection of the flesh. It means eternal life as deliverance from eternal death. His point is that analogy does not work because any prior knowledge of hope and redemption must deal with the fact that humanity has had many false hopes. Real, confident, and joyful hope is an active looking to the future of God the Redeemer. Our expectations will obscure and cover up the expectation of Jesus Christ, resurrection, and eternal life. Only through the revelation of the divine future do we have knowledge of God the Redeemer. Such knowledge has its basis in the good-pleasure and free initiative of the divine mystery. The only human response to such knowledge is gratitude.[161]

---

[159] CD I.2, 24.2.
[160] CD I.2, 5.3.
[161] CD II.2, 26.1.

The basis of Christian hope is in the event of the grace of God in Jesus Christ for rebellious sinners. Christian hope rests on the love of God for the world that resulted in the giving of the Son. The living God loves with freedom. He will discuss the presence of Jesus Christ in this context. The event of the Parousia is something new. The dialectic of revelation and hiddenness characterizes the self-disclosure in history. He thinks many errors in theology have been the result of trying to achieve a premature eschatology. One does this when Christian hope thinks it has already reached its goal. The object and content of hope is what we do not yet possess. The event of the Parousia is the undialectical and unparadoxical coming of Christ, without opposition of form and content, end and means, eternity and time. Barth insists that there are signs of the reign of God here now but warns that these signs are not what they signify. We must not allow any great historical event to hold us prisoner, whether the Roman Empire, socialism, or the cause of one's own people. One may see such signs in a movement, as Barth could do with socialism. However, one must never affirm the sign for its own sake. One needs to direct fear and love to God.[162]

Barth will refer to the event of redemption as the unveiling of the purpose of the free love God for humanity and the world, the annihilation of all that would hinder this purpose. Redemption is the revelation and the manifestation of the new heaven and the new earth. He related the event of the creation, the event of the covenant, and the event of redemption is the reality in which God exists, lives, acts, and makes God known. In these works, God is the Person who expounds divinity and is thus the subject of this work as the event of the free love of God. In fact, the freedom and love of God shown in the works of God are the twin realities that expound divinity. We know freedom and love through the works of God.

---

[162] (K. Barth, The Gottingen Dogmatics: Instruction in the Christian Religion 1990, 1991, based on lectures delivered in 1924-5), Section 36.

CHAPTER XIX

The Life of Humanity and Hope

Chapter XIX would have dealt with the life of humanity in hope. The life of humanity in hope has the presence of the objective content of faith, Jesus Christ.[163] Humanity is the one whom God has determined for participation in divine, eternal life. Through the Spirit, God moves humanity to an end in which humanity lives in hope in the presence of the future of God and final revelation that will fully reveal humanity as the covenant partner of God. In the present, humanity is already expectant and certain the eternal future of humanity.[164]

The statement concerning Christian hope tells us negatively that the future to which the Christian looks and moves is not an obscure, neutral, or ambivalent future. It tells us positively that the future to which only the Christian can look is the *Parousia* of Jesus Christ in its final form, His coming in completion of His prophetic work, and to His consummating manifestation. The expectation of the Christian of the future is the expectation of this event. The question of the Christian can only be that of his or her self-authentication in the light of this future, in expectation of this universal, exclusive, and conclusive Word of Jesus Christ. This question is meaningful, legitimate, and fruitful, and demands an answer. We must now attempt an outline of an answer that we will give.

---

[163] CD I.2, 24.2.
[164] CD III.4, 25-6.

The answer can consist only in the being, thinking, speaking, and acting of the Christian in hope. Striding as Christians into the future, they approve themselves as witness of Jesus Christ when what they do becomes a work testifying to the Lord who has come, is present, and will come again.

Barth stresses the importance of hope as giving strength to faith and giving wings to love. This hope is in Jesus Christ, who will bring the presence of reconciliation into full view in redemption. The coming again of Christ removes the veil from that which the present period keeps hidden.[165] Further, joy is a provisional fulfillment of life received with gratitude. Our joy today is anticipatory. Our life is provisional in that we live in expectation of eternal life, which is the revelation of the union of our lives with the eternal life of God. We are not joyful or grateful in vain today. This hope sustains our present faith. Faith clings to the accomplished moments as the future in every present. Here and now is the great prelude that one day God will reveal and constitute the goal.[166]

Barth deals with humanity as the creature of God. He concludes with an insightful discussion of human beings in their time (III.2, 47). Barth will proceed to discuss humanity as having given time, allotted time, beginning time, and ending time. I invite the reader to reflect upon this section again, but this time, with the hope humanity has in God being there at the end of creaturely life.

I would invite the reader to Chapter XIV, IV.3, 73.2, on human life in hope. Although I will repeat some of what I discussed there, I will expand as appropriate to our desire to understand what Barth had in mind in thinking of the life in hope considering redemption.

First, in hope, Christians are not acting for private ends or the private affair of the Christian. Christians have supremely personal participation and commitment, of course. For this reason, the problems of faith, love, and hope always are personal. Yet, Christian hope does not primarily address the individual. Personal interest means personal acceptance of the function assigned, rather than concentration of individual will, desire, and striving on personal advantages that might accrue. We are not really Christians if we do not point beyond ourselves, liberated form glancing aside at the personal glory, rewards, or advantages that we might secure. What do Christians expect as they hope? What will specifically determine their lives in Christian hope? We have already seen that Christians expect the coming of Jesus Christ in glory. This implies something forceful and decisive for their personal future and expectation of it. It means glory, reward, and gain. It means pardon. It means departing to

---

[165] CD IV.3.2, 73.1.
[166] CD III.4, 384-5.

be with Christ. It means transition out of darkness into light. It means transformation. It means all these things in the context of the final redeeming act of God in full manifestation of the reconciliation of the world accomplished in Jesus Christ, of the conclusion of peace between Creator and creature, of the establishment of the reign of God, of the alteration of human and cosmic reality in Christ. The object is the whole community and of creation, and not just the individual. Christian individuals can expect all of this, but not in isolation from the redemptive work of God in human history and in creation. Christian hope is not a private event. Jesus Christ was a true witness to the world, and thus was not engaged in purely private affair. The calling of Christians to witness and service is to humanity, and not simply a private affair. Christians who hope represent the witness and service of God in the world through Jesus Christ and represent surrounding humanity that seems to sleep. The Christian can only work to wake people from sleep.

Second, the life of Christians in hope is their existence in expectation of the coming of Jesus Christ to judgment, and therefore of the end and the dawn of eternal light. Christians look and move toward their goal, which is this horizon. What they see is what is before the eyes of all. God has not lifted the veil. God has not yet redeemed creation. Human history is full of confusion and entanglement. Their lives as Christians participate in this confusion. They see continuing sin, even though they see their sin forgiven. They see death. In the face of all this, Christian hope could become hopelessness, based upon appearance in the world. It might become resignation. They could live only in expectation of this final event. They might fail to do what they might do. Transfixed by the thought of the last goal, Christians would move toward the future with hopelessness. Such hopelessness for penultimate developments is a pious illusion. Christians would participate in a gross deception if they had warm love for the eternal and a cool contempt for the temporal. It would suggest that only the end matters; what comes before the end does not matter. If the sphere of the penultimate is empty and hopeless, demons of the crassest sort will exult, dance and triumph because uncontrolled and undisciplined worldliness that has always proved to be the consequence of too rigidly eschatological versions of Christianity. Only Christian hope is strong enough in this sphere to match these demons. Christians who lose this relation to the penultimate hope have, in all probability lost their freedom to hope in the ultimate. Christian hope looks initially to the sphere of penultimate developments in the temporal life still lived by the Christian and the world. If they do not serve the Lord here and now, in the time God still gives them, what prospect is there for future service? If Jesus Christ is the goal and end of time, then this time has partial determination in the fact that it moves towards this end. If this is the case, Christians will look for visible signs of His coming, for indications of the impetus or flow of time to its goal. Precisely because Christians have ultimate hope, they have hope for the temporal and provisional. Precisely because they hope with joy for the dawn of the great light, they hope with provisional joy for the little lights they may see now. Precisely because they hope for the Last Day, they hope for the next day and the New Year. Barth will make three concluding observations on this point. Such hope does not focus upon either the lighter or darker side of human existence but looks at human existence with freedom. Such hope assumes the form of an action corresponding to its object. Such hope is not only for the individual, but also for the world, as it stands with the public ministry of Jesus Christ.

In another work, Barth famously suggests it would not be free grace if we could absolutely deny it. The sacrifice of Christ is for the sins of the entire world. He says it would be a "strange Christianity" whose most pressing anxiety would be that the grace of God might prove to be all too free on this side, that hell, instead of so many populating it, might someday prove to be empty. He stresses that we do not know what we are saying when we speak of the coming of Jesus Christ in judgment and the resurrection of the dead, eternal life and death. Scripture makes it clear we ought to prepare ourselves for it. We do not know what God will reveal when God removes the last covering from our eyes. We know that Jesus Christ is the same in eternity and the grace revealed endures through eternity. Such grace is unconditional and therefore tied to no purgatory, tutoring sessions or reformatories in the hereafter. Grace will come with the Judge. The one who will come is the one who has already come. He shall be both the coming of grace and judgment for everyone. Christ is the Redeemer of the world Christ has also reconciled. Christ is the one who reveals the good will, the plan, and the council of Christ who created heaven and earth. Christ is the answer to the great and small questions of our lives. Grace means we have the privilege of knowing the end of all things and their new beginning. Christ is our hope.[167]

Third, life in hope is life that derives from God. Our present concern with Christian hope is decisive with its reality, with the act and life of Christians in this hope. The concern is with their existence in the corresponding orientation, peace, and movement. The concern is with a hope that has solidity by its origin, theme, and content. The concern is with a life entirely lived in hope. Paul reminds us in Philippians 2:12-13 that God is the one who works in Christians, willing and doing the divine pleasure. The reference is to the mighty activity of the Holy Spirit. The Spirit

---

[167] (K. Barth, God Here and Now 1964, 2003) Chapter 3, (1947).

awakens people to become Christians, to be the kind of Christians who hope in God, and who hope for the ultimate. The only One who can secure and introduce this reality of Christians who hope is God. God is the Holy Spirit who awakens Christians to life in hope. God is Spirit, and therefore God truly awakens humanity to freedom. God treats humanity as a free subject. God sets humanity on its own feet as a partner with the divine. God wills that human beings should stand and walk on their own feet. God wills that they should believe, love, and hope. The Holy Spirit is God in the divine power that enlightens the heart of human beings, convicts the conscience, persuades their understanding, and wins individuals from within. The work of the Spirit can only be the freedom of humanity for life by Christ and therefore for life in hope. In this life in hope, awakened by the power of the Holy Spirit, humanity really comes to itself and may be itself. People born of God or of the Spirit, called to service, and living in hope, are people no longer self-alienated. They are true humanity.

The Christian is looking back and looking forward, thereby defining the life of the Christian. This look involves forgiveness of sin in the past and looking seriously at the death that lies ahead. If we have no terror or fear of the end, we have not experienced the joy of the gift of life. The resurrection of the body means the completion of a human life. The Christian hope does not lead us away from this life. It uncovers the truth in which God sees our life. Christian hope is the conquest of death. Eschatology, rightly understood, is the most practical thing that one can think. In the *eschaton*, the light falls from above into our life. We must believe in the completion of our lives despite the reality of death. One who does not know the power of death does not know what resurrection is. We need the witness of the Holy Spirit and the witness of the Word. The Spirit through the Word tells us we can live with hope.

CHAPTER XX

The Promise and its Future Realization

Chapter XX would have dealt with the promise and its future realization. The theme of this chapter would be the content of the faith as also the content of the promise and its realization.[168]

We can look upon IV.1 in these matters as focusing upon a form of participatory eschatology and eternalization. God has the freedom to lift the temporal into divine eternity. The resurrection of Jesus is the verdict of the Father upon the historical course of the life of God. The finite arc of a human life from conception to death has its completion only in the eternity of God.[169] We can look upon IV.2 in these matters as focusing upon a form of participatory eschatology and manifestation. The Incarnation of the Son in Jesus of Nazareth is the full fellowship of the human with the divine. The exaltation of human essence stems from the communication of divine essence in the Incarnation. In that sense, the resurrection of Jesus adds nothing that the Incarnation had not already communicated. Rather, the resurrection manifests the reality of the life of Jesus as the event of reconciliation on behalf of others. By analogy, our resurrection will be the manifestation of our hidden glory in Christ. The reality of our lives is unveiled in the three-fold Parousia of the risen Lord in his resurrection, in the outpouring of the Spirit, and the full manifestation that occurs in the

---

[168] CD I.2, 24.2.
[169] (Hitchcock 2013), Chapter 3.

return of Christ.[170] We can look upon IV.3 in these matters as focusing upon a form of participatory eschatology and incorporation. The Holy Spirit orchestrates the movement toward communion, incorporating the expansion of divine power and the retrieval of people into communion with God. Jesus is the prophet of incorporation, calling, upbuilding, and sending out the community so that all persons might gravitate toward Christ. Human existence suffers from its alienation caused by its sinful pride, sloth, and deception. The promise of resurrection of the flesh overcomes such alienation by incorporating people into the living body of Christ.[171] In all these profound reflections, Barth is seeking to retain a sense of the redemption of the body and therefore the redemption of creation. Even if we may think about these matters in a way different from him, we can respect his attempts to affirm the classical formulation of eschatology in the historic creeds.

Combining eschatology with ontology is an interesting Christian way of handling matters related to the end. If Jesus of Nazareth in life, death, and resurrection is the appearance within our space-time of the destiny of humanity, then he is the arrival of that destiny or future. This future determines, constitutes, or defines the essence and meaning of things in the present, as well as the essence and meaning of things as they will be. Thus, a zinnia, a plant of the sunflower tribe within the daisy family, is a zinnia as a cutting and remains one during the entire process of its growth up to its blossoming. Yet, the flower received its name based upon its blossom. It is throughout its growth what it reveals itself to be at the end. It possesses essence through anticipation of its end, even though only the of the process will reveal its essence. The end of the process reveals it was a zinnia all along.[172] In the context of eschatology, creation and the secret history of the covenant in Jesus Christ as the reconciling event of God will find their essence and meaning in the future event of redemption. We may well be able to suggest signs of that end in world history, cultures, and human nature. However, we cannot read off the end or destiny of creation from our experience. Only the event of revelation in Jesus Christ allows us to gain a feeble vision of our destiny and therefore the destiny of creation. The future coming of the rule of God determines the meaning, identity, and essence of the space-time moments on the way to that end. The future retroactively determines, constitutes, and defines the present and past. The future has a face in Jesus Christ, a future that reveals the essence of the

---

[170] (Hitchcock 2013), Chapter 4.
[171] (Hitchcock 2013), Chapter 5.
[172] Wolfhart Pannenberg, "Concept and Anticipation," in *Metaphysics and the Idea of God* (Grand Rapids: Eerdmans, 1990), p. 105.

present. Looked upon from the present, this means the present is full of meaning and purpose because our present anticipates its end or destiny in Jesus Christ. Thus, we are not yet what we shall be, but this hardly means our present is empty. Our present anticipates our end because we participate in it. We already are our destiny, but we are not yet our destiny as well. Further, we can see this form of eschatology operative in the basic gospel witness. The life and death of Jesus were ambiguous in that even the disciples had lost hope. Only when the risen Lord came to them, stressing that they were not looking for him, did they re-read the life of Jesus and Jewish Scripture to view Jesus of Nazareth as the promised Jewish Messiah and therefore the Savior of the world. The event of resurrection, and with it the ascension and glorification of Jesus to the Father, defines the future of Jesus and therefore reveals and constitutes the essence and meaning of his life and death. The resurrection of Jesus retroactively reveals the meaning and essence of his life and death. The course of the life and death of Jesus anticipates its end in resurrection and glorification to the Father through the life-giving event of the Spirit. Jesus of Nazareth becomes a prolepsis or representation of the future coming of the rule of God as if it were already present. The resurrection of Jesus has provided a foretaste of the meaning and nature of the past and present, which awaits its full consummation at the eschaton.[173]

Barth discusses the positive goal of in the existence of the church as the transition from faith to sight, from reconciliation to redemption, and from temporal to eternal life. Even Israel will find its fulfillment by its full participation in the grace of God. Israel participates in the faith and salvation of the church that will coincide with the revelation of the eschatological character of the Messianic present. Israel participates in the time that follows the resurrection of Christ. In that day, when all Israel gathers in faith in Jesus as its Messiah, God will reveal hidden things. The glory promised in the riches of reconciliation in Christ is a foretaste of the future even for the church. In that day, God will reveal Jesus Christ as the one who overcomes. The church waits for that day, which coincides with the fullness of Israel. God promises and fulfills the union of church and synagogue. Redemption is the revelation of the end of all things. Barth will write of the possibility of final redemption of all things. Paul will write of the lost humanity and of the omnipotence of God. We see this omnipotence in the resurrection of Christ and in what God will finally unveil in the second coming. The thought of the future of this man and of the omnipotence is a thought of faith and hope that neither over-estimates

---

[173] http://trinityhaus.org/blog/back-from-the-future-wolfhart-pannenbergs-retroactive-ontological-eschatology/

humanity nor infringes upon the freedom of God. He stresses the impossibility of expecting too much from God, to fail to recognize the supremacy of this God, and therefore the promise resting upon this human being despite human unbelief. We can never believe in unbelief. Rather, he encourages believing only in the future faith of those who at present do not believe. He views this as the concrete Christian thought of hope.[174]

Again, I stress that the basis of Christian hope is in the event of the grace of God in Jesus Christ for us as rebellious sinners. In that context, Barth discusses the resurrection of the dead. The new presence of Jesus Christ is the content of Christian hope. Since human beings are persons only in the unity of body and soul, redemption must mean more than the immortality of the soul. It must include resurrection of the body. Embodiment is the end of the way of God. God must transform this body. God must renew this world. In redemption, however, humans remain creatures. In the resurrection, human beings become true subjects of all the predicates which on this side of the Parousia one can attribute without qualification only to Jesus Christ.[175]

I want to suggest that for Barth, eschatology means the disclosure of the secret God has hidden in the world through the calling of Israel, the sending of Jesus of Nazareth disclosed in the resurrection, and the creation of the people of God through the outpouring of the Spirit.

I have wrestled much with the notion of time. Theology and philosophy reflect upon the topic in a way that often confuses me. However, eschatology naturally raises the question.

Revelation meets us and fulfills our time. The course of things is held up in face of the end of our time. Our end is not yet accomplished. Revelation is not redemption. The event of redemption means Christ has come in the glory of the Father. Redemption means the new time of God fully comes. Redemption means that the announcement of the end of all things in revelation becomes the completed end of all things. Until this fulfillment of time, in which time becomes the time of God, we still have our time, the time of revelation. This means human time is finite.[176]

In a discussion of the time of revelation as the time of recollection, Barth stresses that due to what we have in the event of revelation of God in Christ, which is behind us, we also have the event of revelation in front of us. We know what has happened to us in Christ, and therefore we know what will happen in the future. Our future is determinate. Our future is the

---

[174] CD II.2, 34.4.
[175] (K. Barth, The Gottingen Dogmatics: Instruction in the Christian Religion 1990, 1991, based on lectures delivered in 1924-5), Section 37.
[176] CD I.2, 14.1.

result of our estimation or capacity. In Christ, we are what is to happen to us. We see that God has not left our future to chance. The New Testament becomes an eschatological message in direction and intention in terms of its relation to the Old Testament. God becomes the coming God. As faith accepted justification offered in 30 AD, it also expects justification at the judgment of God. Christ reveals what we shall be in the final future of our existence (I John 3:2). In the event of the revelation of Christ to come, that coming will reveal our being. Confessing the resurrection of Christ means we must confess our future resurrection. He who came is also He that will come. The New Testament is a witness to hope and completely eschatological in intention. It clarifies and sharpens the expectation in which Israel already lived. Everything depends upon understanding the eschatological trend of New Testament faith. The New Testament faith has Christ as it hopes in Christ.[177]

The future of Christ is only a matter of unveiling. The coming again of Christ is the revelation as viewed in the New Testament. God will reveal Christ to everyone as the Person He is. In full clarity and publicity, the "it is finished" will occur. What is the future bringing? It will no longer be a turning point in history. Rather, it will be the revelation of that which is. This future will be a future the church remembers. The primary event has already taken place. The Alpha and the Omega are the same thing.[178]

Barth discusses the meaning of scriptural references to humanity in the cosmos. He thinks of it as an eschatological pointing. The eschaton towards which they move is identical with that which from which they come. They refer to divine revelation, the covenant of grace, and Jesus Christ as Lord. Such biblical witnesses point the statement in Revelation 11:15, in which the kingdoms of this world become the kingdoms of our Lord.[179]

The Book of Revelation opens with the statement in 1:4 that the source of the message of the book is "him who is and who was and who is to come." Further, in 1:8, "I am the Alpha and the Omega,' says the Lord God, who is and who was and who is to come, the Almighty." This passage opens the door for reflection on the notion of time. In particular, I want to reflect upon the relationship between God and time. Of course, I am doing so with Karl Barth.

If one can translate Exodus 3:13-14 as "I shall be that I shall be" or "I shall exist as I shall exist," it will suggest a emphasis on the relation of present and future. This passage may interpret what Exodus says. It declares

---

[177] CD II.2, 14.3.
[178] (Moltmann, Theology of Hope 1965, 1967), 228.
[179] CD II.1, 26.1.

that now, after the fulfilled time, recollection adds to expectation as a category not yet belonging to the Old Testament or at least not yet customary.[180] The verse shows that divine eternity means readiness for time. We have good reason to give clear emphasis to this truth. The Christian message of creation, reconciliation, and redemption as the revelation of human existence as consummated by God, which also means the revelation of the meaning of creation by God, is the word of truth and not a myth of the pious self-consciousness. The eternity of God has temporality. The content of the message depends on the fact that God was, is, and is to be, our existence stands under the sign of a divine past, present, and future. Without the complete temporality of God, the content of the Christian message has no shape. Everything depends on whether the temporality of God is the simple truth that has its basis in God. Barth develops the notion of the three forms of eternity as pre-temporal (the decision of God in eternity), supra-temporal (time), and post-temporal (eschatology). These terms suggest the readiness of God for time. In post-temporality, God is already in the time-full eternity that remains in the future for the rest of creation. The event of the revelation of God in Jesus Christ, who is the self-disclosure of God, we stand before the goal and end of time. In fact, these three forms of eternity are his guidance to theology and church through the complexity involved in the Bible regarding time. Time has beginning and end. Of course, God is equally in all three forms of eternity. Therefore, time has meaning and fullness, as God embraces and is present and active in each of the forms of eternity. He even suggests that we use perichoresis as a way of thinking about the relationship of the three forms of eternity to each other. He wants to avoid competition between the three forms of eternity, and clearly sees precise theological expression as holding them together. In a letter to Jürgen Moltmann, Barth clearly thought the young theologian had placed too much emphasis upon post-temporality.[181]

    The key point here is that Barth is moving away from his view of eternity as timelessness which he held in his commentary on *Romans* to a notion of eternity that gives fullness to time. Every moment we stand on the frontier of time and therefore in time-full eternity. Moving in the direction of a positive view of eternity, he discusses it under the theme of the perfections of divine freedom. The temporal limits on creation do not apply to God. Distinctions remain in eternity, but now a peaceful relation of origin, movement, and goal.[182] The result of his reflection is eminently biblical. The result is also a way of making eternity temporal. Time and

---

[180] CD I.2, 14.1.
[181] CD II.1 [31.3].
[182] (McMullen 1988), 6-8.

history are as real for God as they are for creation.[183]

When the passage in Revelation speaks of the being of Jesus in time, it implies much more than that time has a beginning, duration, and end. The use of "alpha and omega" does not speak of timelessness. The risen Lord ascribes to himself a being in time, just as the letters alpha and omega in the Greek alphabet are part of the alphabet. Further, the introduction stresses that the life of Christ embraces a present, past, and future. Here is a strictly temporal being, though it differs from all other temporal being. Again, note the connection to Exodus 3:14, "I am that I am." The passage speaks of a being in time, but the reference is to the divine coming. It means something like, "I am all this simultaneously. I, the same, am; I was as the same; and I will come again as the same."

First, the today of Jesus does not cancel his yesterday. The presence of Jesus impels toward His future. He who comes again in glory is identical with the one proclaimed by the history of yesterday and the one present today. The thorough-going eschatology for which the interim between now and one day necessarily seems to be a time of emptiness, futility, and lack only an "unspiritual" community could tolerate such a view. The fact that Jesus will be includes the fact that He is. The fact that He is does not exclude that He is not yet. When this verse says, "I am he that is," the present in which there is real recollection of the man Jesus and the particular and preliminary revelation accomplished in Christ, and real expectation of this man and the final and general revelation of God with Him, this present "between the times" is His own time, the time of the man Jesus.

Second, Jesus not only is. He has also been. The passage directs our gaze backward from the present. What do we see? Of course, we see the pre-crucifixion time of Jesus, but we also "see" the Easter Jesus and the apostolic presentation of him. His "yesterday" includes the prophetic time and history of the people of Israel. As we find in this passage, we can sum it up as "I am – which was."

Third, the being of Jesus in time is a being in the future, a coming being. From the standpoint of the apostles and their communities, we must also say, and with no less reality and truth, that He comes. Christians live in expectation, as well as in recollection and presence. The message of the church is eschatological as well as soteriological and pneumatological. The message involves proclamation of his future and the approaching end of time than of the past in which time has found its beginning and center, or of the present in which we move from that beginning and center to the end of time. If all that we had was past and present, we could look forward to a

---

[183] (McMullen 1988), 10-14.

progressive immanent development of the new life opened by the resurrection. Entire periods of history have had this view of the church. Such a notion is utopian fabrication. Yet, the New Testament does not contain evidence to support this view. Such a view can do without Jesus. The last time, the event of the consummation, is the time of Jesus, the time of His being. The New Testament is the coming of the Lord in a definitive and general revelation. The Christian community gathers in this hope. He who comes is the same as He who was and who is. The consciousness of time is inherent in the phrase "I am ... which is to come." The future to which we look forward from the past of the man Jesus, is, like this present itself, and the past that lies behind it, His time, the time of the man Jesus.[184]

In a discussion of Jesus as the Lord of time, Barth discusses the event of Easter. Its truth does not depend on our acceptance or rejection. Easter is hardly an appendix to its thought, but rather, is the starting point of the gospel story. These observations lead to a discussion of the demythologizing program of Bultmann. He interpreted the event of Easter as the rise of faith in the risen Lord, and this faith led to apostolic preaching. Barth says this will not do. Faith in the risen Lord springs from his historical manifestation. Bultmann admits that the New Testament witness is different from his presentation. He agrees with Kummel that the rule of God is present in Jesus and is yet to come. He agrees with Cullmann that New Testament authors start with a memory, time, and history of Jesus, and developed a conception of time of that specific history. Bultmann also viewed the resurrection as the revelation of the meaning of the cross. He makes it clear that the meaning of the cross is beyond time as an eschatological event. Eschatological events include the death of Jesus, rise of Easter faith, their preaching, the church, the sacraments, and Christian life. One cannot accept the resurrection as an event in time and space. The Easter event in the sense of Bultmann is a matter of objectifying primitive Christian Easter faith in terms of the mythical worldview of the time. As such, it has no validity on the believer in our time. Easter faith becomes the first chapter in the history of faith. The apostles drew too heavily on their mythical worldview. Barth maintains the opposite. Jesus did rise and appear. This simple statement is the content of Easter history. It forms the basis of the existence of the church and its sacraments. The resurrection is the act of God in which God appeared objectively in the glory of the Incarnate Word. They were not alone with their faith. Their faith awakened in this objective encounter. We do violence to the texts of the New Testament if we take the line of Bultmann. Although Bultmann comes across as an exegete, his writings are full of

---

[184] CD (III.1, [47.1].

dogmatic presuppositions. Barth disagrees that a theological statement is valid only when one can prove it as a genuine element in the understanding of human existence. Bultmann is forcing theology into an anthropological straitjacket. Yet, Barth would also challenge the modern worldview that Bultmann so readily accepts. Bultmann wants to limit the resurrection to a nature-miracle to discredit it. Yet, the manifestation of God the Creator occurred in the resurrection. The mystery before which the apostolic community could only respond with adoration was in fact to include nature. Barth agrees that the resurrection is not a "historical" event like any other. He thinks it highly superstitious, in fact, to suppose that only things that are open to historical verification can have happened in time. Barth questions whether things that we might accurately describe as saga or legend are simply blind acceptance of myth. Bultmann says such an act is a work. Barth questions whether modern science and the modern world-picture is of a stature that one should use it as a basis for rejecting the biblical message. Barth finally gets to the whole notion of the Christian and worldviews. Christians are to be eclectic in their relation to worldviews. Thus, the fact that something was compatible with the mythical worldview is not enough to reject it. His conclusion is that despite Bultmann, we must still accept the resurrection of Jesus and his appearances as genuine history in its time. He will later stress that the presence of Jesus in the Spirit is a pledge or first installment of what awaits the community and the universe, namely, the return of Christ in glory. The one who comes again in glory, this future Jesus, is identical with the one proclaimed yesterday who is present today. He rejects a thorough-going eschatology for which the interim between now and one day necessarily seems to be a time of emptiness of futility, of lack and disillusionment. Such eschatology is not that of New Testament Christianity. The man Jesus will include the fact that He is. The fact that He is suggests that He is "not yet." Later, he also says that the being of Jesus in time is a coming being. The proclamation of the church is eschatological in that sense, in that it proclaims the future of Christ and the approaching end of time. The New Testament thinks and speaks eschatologically, but always also Christologically. We understand the being of Jesus yesterday and today only in the light of the resurrection and his coming as judge, consummator, and new creator. If we do not know of this "tomorrow" of Christ, we rightly question whether we know yesterday or today. The New Testament looks forward to a future that sets an end to processes of time. This future is a new order that contains an immediate hope. This future is not the result of a historical process. This future is the coming of the Lord, a definitive and general revelation of the justification and redemption of individuals, for the end and new beginning of the cosmos, and for the final rule of God. Christian hope cannot ignore this dimension of the being of Jesus in time. Later, Barth refers to this interim time as fulfilled time. The unity of his glory and our glorification already achieved in the resurrection of Jesus has again become the future of Christ for us. The resurrection is the anticipation of the Parousia and the Parousia is the completion and fulfillment of the resurrection. The community hopes for Jesus, who will be the rule of God, restoration, salvation, perfection, and joy. He refers to the immanence of the coming rule of God. This rule could not be remote. Would Christ be the one who has come and is present if he is not also the who comes? We live with an immanent sense of his coming and an imminent hope for it that renews us daily from disappointment, frustration, and skepticism. Later, Barth will refer to the Christian consciousness of time in its forward direction and eschatological orientation. He refers to John as emphasizing the event of Easter and that of Parousia as under the present power of the Holy Spirit. He again rejects thoroughgoing eschatology as superfluous once one realizes the truth of John. We do not suppose the delay disillusioned either Jesus or the early church. He sees an eschatological outlook behind and above the Gospel writers. Jesus is both present and not present. Jesus waits, looking forward to things to come and thus to his own future. The New Testament has an immanent expectation. The community of the last time has the resurrection as the driving force behind it and the consummation as a drawing force before it. This reality determines the logic and ethic of the community of the end. The Christ who comes in glory is as close to this community as is the Christ of the resurrection. The Christ of the resurrection is never merely history, while the Christ of the Parousia is never an empty future. He wants to avoid the error of underestimating the origin of the community in the resurrection or the consolation of the Holy Spirit in the present. A failure of this kind does not take account of the Holy Spirit as the driving and drawing force behind the community in the time between the resurrection and the Parousia. Through the Spirit, the lordship of Jesus is never merely past or future. He is always present, but in such a way that we must expect this imminent coming and wait with patience. The assumption of anxiety within the New Testament over the delay is a pseudo-problem. He also warns of an exaggerated sense of the present of the community, where it will tend to look at its present as absolute. This view would remove eschatology vigorously. Both mistakes amount to the absence of the fullness of Christ.[185]

    For us, the past is the time that we live and are in no longer. The future is the time that we do not yet have but will have if we are fortunate. The real nature of our being in time is most obscure of all at the very point

---

[185] CD III.2, 47.1.

where it ought to be clear, namely, at the moment that we regard as our present. Here, where midway between the vanished past, and which we have forgotten or only dimly remember, and the unknown future that awaits us, or perhaps does not await us we think we can take our ease and enjoy in impregnable security our being and having, and our identity with ourselves, we find that we are insecure. This is our "being in time."[186]

It can be difficult to discern where Barth stands in relation to some of the typical themes of eschatology. One such theme is eternal destiny. Barth can make the brief statement, "In eternity when we see God face to face, either we will be those who love, or we will not be."[187] Such a statement at least moves in the direction of the annihilation of some. However, Barth moves in a universalist direction, as discussed in his doctrine of election. Barth will not engage in speculation about what he thinks is unknowable in the specific condition of the afterlife. He will not ground his thinking on nonbiblical anthropology. He will affirm human destiny as life with God in Christ.[188]

Barth has a significant discussion of humanity in its time. He concludes that God has allotted to humanity its time. This means it has a beginning. It also means that the last grim fact is that we shall die. Finite life has its anxiety and care. Life desires life. As such, it demands a future. He considers the possibility that our lives are a flight from non-being. Yet, it may well be that we cannot escape non-being. As much as death is a reality, how is the reality compatible with God? How could the futility of our flight from non-being be a good creation? We must conclude that the finitude of our time in death is an evil that God has suspended over us. Death is a return to non-being and thus to the same God who called us out of non-being at the beginning of our time. Between our emergence from God and our final confrontation with God is the guilt we have incurred from the beginning. Guilt means retrogression. Retrogression consists in failure to use our freedom in relation to God and our fellow human beings. This guilt will confront us at the end of our time. In our transgression, death shall translate us from being to non-being and bring us face-to-face with our creator. We shall meet God and be dependent upon God in that moment. Thus, death can mean nothing but the approach and execution of the judgment of God upon us. Such judgment will mean our rejection. Such judgment will mean our destruction. As we approach our end, we approach God. We live our lives under the shadow of this end of our guilt and divine

---

[186] CD (III.2, 47.2)
[187] CD 1.2, 372, first becoming aware of this at
https://derevth.blogspot.com/2015/08/karl-barth-annihilationist-recent.html
[188] (McMullen 1988), p. 24.

judgment. Death is a sign of divine judgment. Yet, the New Testament holds out the possibility of God sparing us such a death because Another has suffered it in his death for us. Still, we must admit that the fact that God has allotted time at all, that it begins and ends, is a sign of judgment. The threat of death overshadows and dominates our whole life. Death as it meets us is a sign of divine judgment. Death meets us as sinful and guilty people. From our side, God can only regret having made us. Humanity has failed. Humanity has not used the freedom God gave it for the purpose God intended. Humanity has squandered the opportunity God has given humanity. Humanity lives in fear of this end. One who fears death is nearer the truth than one who tries to put a better face on it. Death is not our friend or deliverer. We resist our end, even though we know it is futile to do so. In this sense, death is not the natural end to the good creation of God. Rather, death is an alien intrusion into the good creation of God. Death is an enemy with its own destructive purpose and power in virtue of the right of God against us. Death is the threat on the frontier. Yet, when death confronts us, God confronts us as well. Yes, the God against whom we have done wrong will meet us. Death reveals our nothingness before God. Fear of death expresses the deeper reality of our fear of God. The deeper reality is that in death, God awaits us. We ought not fear death, but God. God is angry with us and judges us in our death. Death serves the purpose of God. It also belongs to chaos, and thus stands under the No of God. Death exists only as God denies it. It acquires form and power in the conflict between God and humanity, but it still stands under the power of God. Death is our last enemy. God can dismiss it, disarm it, and take away its power. The Lord of death is present as judge and avenger. In death, we fall into the hands of the living God. What would happen if God does not will to shield us from death and help us find happiness in it? If so, it will be from God that we receive the eternal pains of death. Even in Hell, we shall be in the hands of God. We shall not be alone in death. We shall be with God, who is the Lord of death. Yet, Christian theology is clear that the God who awaits us in death is the gracious God who is for humanity. If the fire of wrath scorches us, it will be wrathful love and wrathful hate. Those whom God loves God also chastens. Death strips us of everything so that God is all in all. God will convict us of our most secret sin and guilt. We shall look quite foolish as we stand naked before God. We shall not press even the slightest claim upon God. Even in our death, however, God will find a way to be the gracious God who is for us. We can hold fast this notion only because the Son has died for us. God has elected us to be with God in the Son. Yes, we fear this God, but how can we fear the gracious God without also finding comfort in God? God is our Helper and Deliverer amid death. We are not only in death, bot already out of its clutches and victorious over it in God. Even in death, we are not lost to God. When we cease to be, God will be for us. Our future non-being will not be our negation. As death does its work under the direction of God, we remain objects of divine love. Yes, we are mortal and transitory. God is unchangeable, not subject to decay, and not transitory. God dismisses, disarms, and removes the power of death. Death is our frontier. However, God is at the frontier of our death. God is our hope. Thus, even in death, we are already out of its clutches and victorious. As we suffer death, death is already behind and beneath us. Death imprisons us, but we are already free. As those who must die, we shall nevertheless live. Death is not omnipotent tyrant. In the end, what can death do? It cannot destroy us. It cannot make God cease to be God as our Helper and Deliverer and therefore our hope. The light of our lives shines despite the darkness of death. The sadness of funeral rites is not the last word about the end of human being in time. Can we not already hear the joy of resurrection over the funeral as we proclaim the Word of God? New Testament revelation and perception offers a positive answer given by God regarding our ending time. The positive answer comes in the union of God with the man, Jesus of Nazareth. In Christ, God is our gracious God. He became sinner and debtor to release us from the penalty and debt. In Christ, God has dethroned death. Death is no longer our condemnation. We have nothing to fear from death now that God has suffered and overcome it for us. God has given us the promise of eternal life in Christ. We must look to Christ, for in Christ we have God as our gracious God, our hope, our Helper and Deliverer. Christ is our hope, future, victory, resurrection, and life. We rightly gather around Christ to receive such consolation. We must look nowhere else. We rightly see death as a sign of divine judgment. We live under that sign and shadow. Yet, Christ has suffered divine judgment in his death so that we do not suffer it. Christ relativizes the divine judgment of which death is the sign. Humanity as such has no beyond. God, who is creator, covenant partner, judge, and savior, is the beyond of humanity. Humanity belongs to this world. Humanity is finite and mortal. The divinely given promise, hope, and confidence, in confrontation with God, is that humanity will share the eternal life of God. The beginning and end of a human life occurs before the eyes of the gracious God. God will reveal its merited shame. God will also reveal its unmerited glory in eternal life from God. Humanity hopes for the revelation of its redemption completed in Jesus Christ, and thus the redemption of this finite and mortal existence.[189]

   Barth stresses that the biblical message concerns itself with the eternal life of humanity. One enters this new life through the resurrection

---

[189] CD (III.2, 47.5)

of the dead, which gives eternal life an eschatological aspect, the limitation of this life by the eternal. This does not devalue present time. Yet, even eternal life is a matter of this present temporal life, for God will not bring humanity to this time to live it in vain. The life of a human being belongs to God. God has granted life as a loan. God has determined the individual for eternal life, leading the individual through this life and to another. Later, he discusses the notion of joy as provisional fulfillment of life received with gratitude. Joy here and now is a provisional fulfillment. We have anticipatory joy. The whole of life is provisional, of course. We live our lives in time in expectation of eternal life. We live in expectation of the revelation of our lives in union with the eternal life of God. Every sense of fulfillment in this life is provisional. This life has its limits, fragmentation, and frailty. In that sense, all ethics is provisional and interim. Hope sustains faith as it clings to the future in every present. God is from and to all eternity and therefore in time her and now. In fact, here and now is the great prelude to what God will one day reveal and constitute the goal.[190]

Barth will offer some hints of the direction he is heading in Volume 5 in IV.3, 69.

Christ will speak the definitively last Word in with his concluding return in glory. This Word belongs to his work of redemption.[191] The basis for thinking about redemption is the Easter event. Christians think and speak in terms of the Easter revelation. We know Christ as reconciler based upon the knowledge of its revelation and declaration in the event of resurrection. It becomes truth and reality for the world. Easter tells us that we can think of the coming of Christ in three ways. He came as the light of life and the victor of the battle against evil and darkness. The outpouring of the Spirit empowers Christians and the church to participate in the reconciling work of God in Christ. Christian theology thinks of these first two comings of Christ considering eschatology, the final return of Jesus Christ. These first two comings of Christ have an eschatological character. Even now, as the church lives in the outpouring of the Spirit, it has an eschatological character. In this final form, the coming of Christ is an eschatological event having to do with the manifestation and effective presence of Jesus Christ in its definitive form. His revelation is the goal of the last time in which we now live. The goal of this last time is the coming of Christ again. Our last time will reach the end that is already set for it in the death of Christ as revealed in his resurrection. Thus, throughout the three forms of the coming of Christ we have eschatology. Eschatology is present in the Easter event and in the outpouring of the Spirit. The Easter

---

[190] CD III.4, 55.1
[191] CD (IV.3, 69, 261)

event is only the first form of the new coming of Jesus Christ. Its second form is the impartation of the Holy Spirit. The final appearance of Jesus Christ is for the resurrection of the dead, the last judgment, and the creation of a new heaven and new earth. The resurrection of Jesus is the definitive determination given to the world and humanity. It holds good not merely for the beginning, in the Easter event, but also for the end and all that we find between. His coming in the resurrection is a new coming of the one who came as Jesus of Nazareth. He also comes from the frontier of all creaturely life as the one resurrected from the dead. God alone can be the future of the life of a creature after death. It has life from God and for God. God alone is above death and after it. Even the resurrection of Jesus can only refer us to the presence of the God who alone is immortal and transcendent. Only God can be the future of this-worldly existence terminable by death. The glory of God is here present in the personal, real, visible, audible, and tangible coming again of Christ at Easter. Barth wants to preserve the mysterious character of Easter. Once we recognize the newness of the structure of the Easter event, in the appearance of the man Jesus in the glory of God we also have seen the future, goal, and end of the world as reconciled to God and its future salvation. Thus, the world is no longer a lost world. Its reconciliation with God in Christ carries with it a call to advance toward a corresponding future redemption from its downward movement. The Easter event reveals its future of salvation as redemption from the shadow of death and the antithesis that pursues it. Its future is salvation as its completion by the creation of its new form of peace and being in the glory of God. Easter already signified the end of the being of the world and humanity in its form of death and the beginning of their being in the new and eternal form of life given them in God. The news of the presence of this future, of the dawn of the redemption and consummation of the world, is the Easter message. Easter plants the seed for the future redemption of the world. Easter reveals the future of the world reconciled to God in Christ. Our future is already present in Easter. The doctrine of redemption reminds us that the work of Christ as reconciler is not finished. Christ has not yet reached His goal. He is still moving toward the goal of redemption. The new and future redeemed and perfected world is already present. Christ has reached the goal. The world and humanity have not yet reached the goal. It has commenced in Easter. Easter is anticipation of the redemption that awaits the world. God has already actualized the presence of the future of salvation in Christ. Our present is provisional. Redemption is a question of harvesting the time given humanity to participate in the reconciling work of God. God gives us time to invoke and proclaim as witness to the work of God. This suggests that the reconciling work of God is not yet complete. The reconciled world awaits the revelation of its redemption and consummation. We still move toward the time when God will destroy sin and death. We shall live in righteousness and true holiness.[192]

The resurrection of Jesus is the commencement of the return of Christ, with the work of Christ in the temporal and historical sphere finding its full revelation in the completion of the return of Christ as the consummating work of God for the redemption of creation. Our time moves towards the consummation of the glory of God and the salvation of humanity.[193]

Even the Sabbath day is eschatological. It points us to the ultimate consummation of the history of the covenant to the omnipotent grace of God that rules time. It moves toward a special history and time that will become the last history and time. The concluding judgment of the world is also the grace of God. It brings the establishment of the new age in which everything that has been will be as it was in eternity. Eschatology is the grace of revelation in the light of which everything that is now dark will be bright. Its future power is secretly present already. The particularity of the last day is the mystery toward which every day is hastening toward. The particularity of the holy day interrupts and places limits on our working day. As such, it has inner connection with the particularity of the last day. It corresponds to each individual human life in the day of death, the particularity of which we do not need to elaborate. The goal, set by God, is toward the being of all creatures established in creation. This means the inexorable end of the form of their present existence.[194]

The condemnation of humanity hangs over humanity like a sword. Falsehood has brought humanity into the danger of damnation. This condemnation is a threat and menace. Human falsehood would make such condemnation the future of humanity. God will nail humanity to its falsehood, and in that moment, humanity will receive damnation and become lost. The time before the end means that the sword has not yet fallen, that condemnation has not yet taken place. This threat and danger have had significance throughout time and history. Falsehood has carried humanity into the shadow of that threat. The human choice of falsehood means that the future condemnation determines the present in which humanity is moving toward condemnation and perdition. Embracing falsehood, humanity implicates itself in a lost and false situation that leads to condemnation. Humanity lives in the untrue situation of misery and of lostness. Humanity lives in the distorted image that falsehood presents.

---

[192] CD (IV.3, 69.4)
[193] CD IV.3, 391-2.
[194] CD III.4, 56

Seeing things in this way, leads to a defaced form of a human life. Humanity lives in a subjective reality alien to and contradicting the reality of human life as we discover it in Christ. This misery is an anticipation of the coming condemnation of humanity. If humanity truly lives under the threat of damnation, it means an eternity in which God rejects us and therefore we are lost. Condemnation is to have what we wished throughout the course of time and history, for we live in untruth. The sword will have fallen. The worst thing would have taken place. It was bad enough, of course, for human history to persist under the threat of such damnation. Human life is the warning sign. Can we count upon it that God will not execute this threat or have the sword fall? Only the unexpected work of grace and its revelation would stop such condemnation. We can only hope for such an undeserved work of God. Further, in the reality of God and humanity in Jesus Christ we may find contained far more than we might expect I the unexpected withdrawal of that final threat. In the truth of the reality of humanity in Christ we might find contained the super-abundant promise of the final deliverance of all humanity. We have good reason to be open to this possibility. We cannot count on this as if we have claim upon it. We can hope and pray for it. We can pray that the compassion of God will not fail, for divine mercy is new every morning and will not cast us off forever (Lamentation 3:22-3, 31).[195]

---

[195] CD (IV.3, 70.3)

CHAPTER XXI

The Command of God the Redeemer

Chapter XXI would have dealt with the command of God the redeemer. After presenting the truth of the Christian hope for the event of redemption, completing the work of the intra-trinitarian work of God in dealing with temporal and finite creation, he would have presented its implication for the obedient response of one who places their faith in this truth. As with the writing pattern of Paul, Barth followed his doctrinal discussion with an invitation to consider its implication for a transformed, faithful, and obedient life. Regardless of our intellectual grasp of the truth of revelation of the Word of God in Jesus Christ, it would be an abstraction if it did not lead to a consideration of how we live. Although such considerations fall within moral and ethical writings, Barth is clear that the Christian way of life will not neatly fit into such philosophical concerns. Rather, a faithful life will arise out of giving prayerful precedence to the written word of God.

Barth says he first learned of the ethical implications of eschatology from the Blumhardts.[196] His eschatological ethics is the enacted prayer corresponding to the promise it seeks. We will see the promise of truly evangelical, liberative, and Christ-centered ethic. It invests our present discipleship with urgent possibility. It delivers us from the presumption

---

[196] (K. Barth, Church Dogmatics 2004, 1932-67), II.1, 633, 636.

inherent in glorifying human action on the one hand and the despair to which the inevitable human failure can lead. It challenges us with the ultimate revolt of a people who pray for the rule of God to come.[197]

The eschatological gift of the Holy Spirit empowers the Christian to correspond enthusiastically and joyfully to the promised final victory of Jesus Christ. We are to live through all our penultimate responsibilities a gleeful prayer of petition and praise, zealously seeking that the will of God done on earth as in heaven. The Christian life is one of a venture of responsibility in the presence of the Giver and the fellow receives of the gift of the past, present, and future. A Christian makes use of this freedom to pray and to live in the hope of the end that will be the revelation of the beginning. Such an ethics of redemption presents us with a thoroughly evangelical alternative to the tired political theologies of many current mainline protestant denominations. Such an ethics seeks correspondence on earth with our guaranteed destiny in Jesus Christ. Such an ethics brings us beyond merely baptizing a version of current political pre-occupations. It confronts us with a full personal communion with the time-full Jesus Christ in all his original, transformative, and redemptive power. Time and history have their secret meaning in the three-fold coming of Jesus Christ, especially as the promise of the Spirit. Even if secret outside of faith, this meaning has external, moral, social, and political dimensions.[198]

In one essay, Barth says that Christian ethics has a history between God and humanity that has taken place, still takes place, and will take place in the future.[199] To that future, we now turn. The point here is that only in this eschatological context can theological ethics attain its goal. Theological ethics is the claim made upon humanity by the command of God because according to the promise we are heirs, expectant of eternal life in the reign of God. By this command of God, it holds out the consummation, ascribes it and even appropriates it, because the command of God inevitably summons us to live before the Word and advance towards a genuine, qualitatively, and better future. Yet, this command reveals human resistance to redemption. It reveals our controversy with God as our redeemer.[200] The command of God is one, even if his considerations consider in order God the creator, reconciler, and redeemer.[201] Barth notes that the lives of individuals have their limitations that give them urgency and we might aptly describe it as eschatological. Ethics has an eschatological tone and

---

[197] (McMullen 1988), p 75.
[198] (McMullen 1988), p. 67-8.
[199] (K. Barth, God Here and Now 1964, 2003), Chapter 6, 1947.
[200] CD I.2, 24.2.
[201] CD III.4, 52.2

character, for individual life occurs within limited time, which hastens from its beginning to its end. We have a call and a warning. Yet, this does not involve simply human finitude, the approach to the frontier of life and beyond, or of a dark future. Rather, the creator and Lord has wisely willed and created human life. The call, admonition, and warning of the command of God comes urgently and with the demand for obedience. We do not talk about the command but fulfill it. Later, he asks about the New Testament consciousness of time. He discovers that time has a limit defined by its beginning and by the coming of Christ as its goal, and so it belongs to Christ in its progression. Christ rules and limits time, the time is short, and its duration is unknown to those who live in it. Thus, we need to orient our lives to the reality that time expires quickly. The eschatological character of the command of God arises out of the unknown nature of its end. The command is one powerful summons to take seriously the existence of this human being in the limited time he or she has as this opportunity. The power of this summons is that it understands the time of a person as a moment within the interval of time that begins and ends with Jesus Christ. The summons is urgent. God is the limit of this time.[202]

The knowledge of God as Redeemer and humanity as the child of God and future heir is the theme of the command of God the redeemer (*The Christian Life*, 7). The one command of God of the one God is gracious to humanity in Jesus Christ has an eschatological form and human action requires an examination in this distinct way as well (*The Christian Life*, 9). Barth cannot refer to the command of God the Reconciler without also referring to God as Redeemer. The advent of the rule of God has begun. Redemption is the completion of that rule. We are between the times in an ambiguous mixture of light and darkness. We have seen the reconciling grace of God, but we depend upon the final revelation of a grace yet to come. We hasten toward the consummation of the rule of God. Of course, again, we do not have the power to actualize that rule. We cannot identify our activity straightforwardly as the activity of God. We can aim toward our action as analogy of that rule or corresponding to that rule, but never identical. Our engagement in the service of the rule of God is subject to radical eschatological qualification. We hasten toward a future that is the gift of God rather than the result of our achievement. We are decidedly NOT the future for which we have been waiting. Our hastening is one of prayerful waiting upon the gracious initiative of God.[203]

The coming revelation of Jesus Christ, in which Christians rejoice,

---

[202] CD III.4, 56.1.
[203] (Cambridge Companion to Karl Barth 2000), Nigel Biggar, "Barth's Trinitarian Ethic," 218-20.

is the new heaven and the new earth. That event will be the glorification of the cosmos in the new form the reconciliation to God has given to it. That event is the fulfillment of the will of God that all people should receive salvation and come to a knowledge of the truth. This all-embracing glorification includes that of the church and of every individual Christian. The world suffers because of its love of darkness. Thus, it sighs for the fulfillment of the promise that God has given to the church and to Christians. The promise concerns its radical renewal.[204]

Again, the basis of Christian hope is in the event of the grace of God in Jesus Christ for us as rebellious sinners. In this context, Barth discusses the glory of God. Barth wants to avoid all narrow otherworldliness in eschatology, or as he calls it, every hot-air balloon flight of eschatological speculation, which he thinks is a constant danger in this field. Hope has a communal and personal dimension. The hoped-for community is not reducible to the marital relationship, the family, or the nation. The church is the community anticipated by Christian hope. He declares that there is an eternal damnation as well as an eternal salvation. God is merciful and righteous. In whom will God demonstrate the one and in whom the other? Each of us hears the question addressed personally. The end of the mighty acts of God is the glory of God. Even in its final word, Christian doctrine reminds us that God remains the Lord and subject of Christian proclamation. God is the subject, and creation, reconciliation, and redemption are for the glory of God. Redemption does not occur solely or primarily for the sake of humanity. The glory of God alone can constitute the satisfying conclusion of Christian dogmatics. If not, it becomes just another worldview. Yet, the glory of God is not antithetical to the glorification of the people of God. The glory of God includes the salvation of humanity. God comes to glory in the realization of a people who see God as God is in the vision of God and who love God as God wants to be loved.[205]

Christians pray for the coming of the rule of God. It will be the full manifestation of Jesus Christ. The faith of the people of God in time will become sight. This sight remains a hope in the appearance of Christ. The people of God cannot expect such sight during world history. The community has the privilege of knowing the end as seen in Christ. It has this knowledge through faith in Christ. The knowledge of a new heaven and a new earth comes through Christ. The vision of this end compels the community to see world history in an unusual way. Its knowledge of the

---

[204] CD IV.4 (Fragment on Baptism, 199).
[205] (K. Barth, The Gottingen Dogmatics: Instruction in the Christian Religion 1990, 1991, based on lectures delivered in 1924-5), Section 38.

end allows the community to be part of world history in a unique way than it would be if it did not have that knowledge. Its faith in Jesus Christ gives knowledge of what has taken place on behalf of the rest of creation through Christ. It anticipates the appearance of that which it sees by faith. The community, through faith, lives with new knowledge and a special form of obedience. It awaits the transformation of world history in the definitive revelation of Jesus Christ. Thus, such faith and anticipation are not idle speculation. It calls for resolute being and action. The community witnesses to this coming reality. It looks forward to the coming rule of God in its direct and universal visibility. The people of God participate in the world with the knowledge that it is passing away. God has already judged it in Christ. It takes the present world seriously, but not with ultimate seriousness. The secret presence of the rule of God in Jesus Christ gives the community the insight that it must not treat this moment of world history with final seriousness. All attempts to improve this world have a provisional quality that the community can take seriously but not treat with ultimate seriousness. It does not fear or have anxiety because of the secret presence of the rule of God and toward which we pray for its full manifestation. It cannot hate. It can only love. God has decided in Christ to be for humanity, and the community shares that position. It cannot be against individuals. The nothingness that assaults humanity in time is what God will set aside in the full manifestation of divine rule. God has decided in Christ in favor of a new humanity living at peace with God and honoring the goodness of creation. The old form of the world can only disappear. The community cannot accomplish this. It can only attest to the coming rule of God. It will look forward to the future, perfect manifestation of the victory of God, of the Yes and No spoken in Christ. The people of God can only hope that its resolute participation in world-occurrence will erect a modest sign of the coming rule of God. To fail here would be surrender to a cheap notion of grace. Its resoluteness comes from the fact that it looks forward to the goal appointed and thus to the revelation of the new reality of history. It lives with quiet confidence in what it sees as the destiny of humanity in Jesus Christ. It has resolute confidence in relation to the future, to the goal of the totality of world history. Since it has hope in Jesus Christ it has hope for the world. The form of world-occurrence that confronts the people of God today is not its final form. It waits for Jesus Christ. The new reality will appear in which the world lives reconciled to God, a fulfilled covenant, and the order reconstituted by Christ. Christ will emerge from concealment in our present time and show Himself to people of every age and place as the one who is its Lord. The community waits for Christ and rejoices in His manifestation. It sees His coming as the goal and end of world history. It has the very best hope for the world precisely because of its hope in Christ.

It looks for the coming of Jesus Christ in His glory.[206]

    Jesus Christ causes the Christian to become a person who may stride toward the future in personal hope in Christ. The basis of Christian hope is the revelation of the hallowing of the name of God, the prayer for the coming of the rule of God and the doing of the will of God that Christ has already accomplished, and therefore the revelation of humanity as justified and sanctified in Christ. This basis is moving towards its fulfillment and thus toward its radical alteration. Christ will speak a final, universal, and immediate word in such a way that all, Christian and non-Christian, living and dead, must receive it. When spoken, humanity will have no option but to live under Christ in the rule of God and to serve Christ in eternal righteousness, innocence, and blessedness. This final coming of Christ arises out of his coming in the resurrection and in his coming in the outpouring of the Spirit. It will complete the three-fold coming of Christ. This Not Yet determines the time in which Christians now live out their vocation and sending. The prophetic witness of Christ continues in the witness of the community. This prophetic work has not reached its goal. Even Christians may learn they have become liars against the truth and do not serve righteousness. The removal of this limit will occur only at the complete revelation of Christ. Christians are still on the way into a future unwritten, impenetrable sea of mist that is the coming of Christ in his third form. Christ has not yet brought to its end this last time in which we live. Christians live in the provisional form of the coming of Christ in resurrection and in the outpouring of the Spirit. The completion of the prophetic work of Christ belongs to Christ and not to the witness of the Christian. Since Christ has not yet spoken the last Word, the Christian lives with doubt and in a vulnerable situation. How are Christians to understand the future toward which they march? The revelation of Jesus Christ is not complete. From one perspective, of course, the future of the Christ is not open, neutral, or divided. The future arises out of coming of Christ in the resurrection and is present the power of the Spirit. By faith, Christians do not live in twilight, but in light, good, and salvation. They live in confidence. Christian hope is an uninterrupted and unequivocally positive expectation of the future. Christians also live with the confidence that the Already revealed in the coming of Christ in resurrection and in the outpouring of the Spirit are part of the one form of the coming of Christ as Not Yet. The commencement of the coming of Christ on Easter Day, the continuing of the coming of Christ in Pentecost, is of one piece with the future coming of Christ in the fullness of the consummation. The commencement and continuing of the coming of Christ anticipate the One

---

[206] CD IV.3, 72.1, 715-21

Day of the future coming of Christ. Christians believe in the one who came in resurrection, loves the one who comes in the present, and hopes in the one who is to come. Christian hope has the power of a positive and certain expectation of the future. It derives this power from the One in whom Christians hope. God in Christ is the future of the Christian and thus creates this expectation. Christians can wait for the last Word because they have taken to heart the first and second words. The first and second forms of the coming of Christ point like an arrow to the third form of the coming of Christ. Christ has preceded Christians, accompanies Christians in time, and comes to meet Christians from the end and goal. Even though Christians live with the dark and empty time before them, including the hour of death, hope gives Christians the possibility of being and witness as Christians. Christ gives clarity of this future. Such hope sustains faith and gives wings to love. Christians live in this type of freedom, knowing God will take away the veil. This can happen only when the future becomes present. The consummation of revelation has taken place. The glory of God will fill creation. The glory of God is the redemption that will take place in the consummation of the revelation of Christ, bringing the last Word of Christ. Christians can offer praise in anticipation of the last day. In that moment, the consummation of the revelation of Jesus Christ and its redemptive work will take place. The One in whom Christians hope will become manifest to all. Christian hope will have its confirmation in its essential and unalterable character. What is true in itself will become true. The possibility and reality of Christian existence will work itself out in that day as salvation in life and death. Christ will speak His last Word that will end all conflict. Even with the decline of Christendom in Europe and the West, Christians may still hope for this positive end of world history. Christians have their faithful witness and obedience to offer the world. Christians face conflicts in the weakness of their witness, and yet, they have the freedom to hope in the coming of Jesus for the consummation of His revelation, bringing clarity to world history. Christian hope means the clarity of the light of the last day will bring, which is the first day of redemption. It fulfills the promise of reconciliation. Finally, Christians will receive judgment for their works even as the rest of the world will receive judgment. Thus, the future of the Christian has a distinctive and disturbing edge. What remains in the future of Christians is their end. Christians will participate in the transition to participation in the glory that will come to the creaturely world with the coming of Jesus Christ. Christians look toward the end of this time and humanity in Christ, but an end that will also be their true beginning in reconstitution. The end will be death for most of humanity, but for those alive in the third coming of Christ, death will not be their end. Christians must also face the fact that their time has ended.

They have no more time. The end toward which Christians move is the consummating revelation and judgment of Jesus Christ. Christians may think of this end as coming too soon and await it with terror. Yet, coming from Christ, the end becomes a welcome and gracious event. Christ takes us out of the darkness of the not yet and brings us into the light of the consummating revelation of Jesus Christ. Passing through the fires of judgment, what remains will be ripe fruit because of the atoning work of Christ. The end will contain strict justice but will be the justice of divine grace. Looked upon theologically, death is the calling of God out of this temporal existence, transformed by receiving the clothing of true, incorruptible, and immortal being. They experience full restoration. This end has been the goal and therefore a new beginning. The end of this temporal existence is the beginning of the exaltation of this temporality into eternal life. With this expectation, one can move into one's future, which at some point will become the future of one's end. Such an expectation provides the freedom to fear the end, but rather, to rejoice in the end, for one's final parting brings an encounter with the Lord and the fullness of personal life in the eternal light of eternal life. One can move toward this end only in hope. What the end brings me can only be the fulfillment of the promise in the preceding light. Even if the end comes at the earliest stages of our path as pilgrims, we believe, witness, cry, and live well or badly in the service of Christ so long as God gives us time.[207]

Thus, we can see that the future toward which Christians can have confidence in the clarity Christian hope brings as to the content of that future. The future toward which we look is the event of the coming of Jesus Christ in His third and final form, completing His prophetic work in a way that consists in His consummating manifestation. Barth now wants to consider how this general Christian hope affects what the Christian can hope for oneself.

First, Barth makes it clear that Christian existence is not primarily about oneself. We do not act for private ends. Of course, Christian existence is a matter of profound and supreme personal participation and commitment. Faith, love, and hope, as Barth has discussed them in Volume IV, are profoundly personal and existential. Yet, the individual is not the true or central object of Christian life and thought. Faith, hope, and love direct our attention away from self and its concentration of attention on personal glory, reward, or advantage that it might secure. Christian hope focuses on the coming of Jesus Christ in glory, the consummating revelation of Jesus Christ that has remained hidden during world history. It focuses on the event that will bring the doing of the will of God on earth as

---

[207] CD IV.3, 73.1

it is in heaven. The Christian can hope for glory, reward, and gain in this event. It means pardon. It means departing this time and being with Christ. It means translation from this darkness into the coming light. It means transformation into a new being, restoration, and the beginning of eternal life. Yet, the focus of this final event of the coming of Christ is not the individual. The focus is the final redeeming act of God that involves the manifestation of the reconciliation of the world accomplished in Jesus Christ. It means the conclusion of peace between God and world. It means the establishment of the rule of God. It means the alteration of human and cosmic reality effected in Christ. Thus, this event of revelation focuses on the universal, but embraces the individual on the periphery. The focus is not the individual, but the community of every age and place, known and unknown members, and indeed, it embraces humanity. This event will overthrow the contradictions of this present life. Every knee will confess Christ as Lord. Thus, Christians must not turn Christian hope into a private event. Throughout IV.3, Barth has reminded us that witness is not a private enterprise. Rather, the calling of the Christ is toward public ministry, service, and witness to the Word of God directed toward all people. Christ is Savior and Prophet who speaks to the world. The calling of the Christian is personal participation in the ministry of the community sent into the world. Christian hope moves one forward in parent participation within the world to the future fulfillment of the divine Word and the consummating revelation of the future of the world. Having received the promise of redemption, the Christian can hope for others as well. The Word of God applies to them as well; its fulfillment is before them as well, even if they are strangers to the previous revelation of Jesus Christ. Christian hope stands as witness that humanity may have hope. The Christian, standing between Christ and an unbelieving world, seeks to show by word and deed that Christ is for them as well. The focus is not on personal glory, reward, or advantage, but hope for the world. Christian hope means the Christian represents humanity in the form of looking forward to the morning and the rising of the Sun of righteousness, and thus toward the end and goal of all things, and therefore to the promised new beginning. Yet, Christians are also representative of the slumber of humanity that will need the awakening of the final trumpet. To put it another way, Christian hope is the seed of eternity already sown in the present.

    Second, Christian life in hope is expectation of the coming of Jesus Christ to judgment, expectation of the end, and expectation of the dawn of eternal light. This event is a step out of the present and into a future event of the revelation that remains on the horizon. The goal of Christian hope looks and moves toward this horizon. The horizon is the redemption of the created world. Such redemption will include one's personal life. It will mean liberation from bondage, healing of what was sick, correcting what one had perverted. It will mean the hallowing of the name of God, the coming of the rule of God, and the doing of the will of God in Christ. One moves toward such a goal in hope. The veil will lift. The coming of light will illuminate the created world. The created world will receive the gift of redemption. Yet, such hope can lead to a form of resignation and even hopelessness in the present. It could lead to a rigid turning away from the visible and a concentration only on the one final thing. Living in expectation of this one final event is just as dangerous to discipleship as viewing the event for only personal gain. The danger is closing one's eyes to the needs of the present. Such a focus would forget the importance of personal participation in faith, love, and hope in the present witness of the individual and of the community. Discipleship avoids such a pious illusion. Christian hope must not lead us to warm love for the eternal and cool contempt for the temporal. Our hope for the fullness of the future must not lead us to view the present as empty. Christian hope leads to serve the Lord in this time. We need to remember this time will receive its new clothing, and therefore, this time is worthy of our attention even as we move toward the future event of the coming of Christ. Christians look for signs of this future event. The hope for the ultimate future gives provisional hope in our time. The hope for the dawn of the great light gives hope for little lights along the way. Hope for the Last Day gives hope for the next day and the next year. Such ultimate hope gives the Christian the freedom to embrace the optimistic and pessimistic dimensions of every time. Such ultimate hope empowers the Christian for service. Such ultimate hope keeps the focus off the individual.

    Third, such life in hope is life that derives from God. As such, its reality brings orientation, peace and movement to Christian life. It has solidity due to its origin, theme, and content. God frees humanity to live in this hope through the mighty activity of the Holy Spirit, who awakens individuals to be Christians who hope in God, offer serve to God in and for the world, and have ultimate hope. As Spirit, God awakens humanity to freedom. Yet, God treats humanity as a free subject. God sees humanity has a partner. God wants humanity to stand and walk on its own feet, choosing faith, love, and hope. We come to ourselves with the help of the Spirit.[208]

    In his *Ethics,* Barth will offer his early reflections on the command of God the redeemer.

    Barth begins with reflections on the command of the promise.[209] Being a child of God, I am an heir of eternal life, and therefore the

---

[208] CD IV.3, 73.2
[209] (K. Barth, Ethics 1928-9, 1973, 1978, 1981) (15)

command of God applies to me. God promises me the presence of God as redeemer, first from the provisional state in which I am a creature of God and second from the contradiction in which I am a Christ. God bids me wait for this divine future and hasten toward it.

To the extent that, in this chapter, we speak about the goal of humanity, the proper course here is formally to lay down our arms and accept the inadequacy of the most eloquent theological endeavor in relation to this theme, to the eschatological character of this theme, which we cannot truly ignore in ethics either. Inevitably, our breath runs out when we venture to speak about the last things. If we try to say a lot, we do not know what we ought to say. Yet, the little that we have to say cannot just as well become something we leave unsaid. Far too many works of theological ethics suffer because their authors seem not to have remembered that dogmatics has an independent eschatological standpoint that inalienably has a place with all the others, even though differing from them. How can we seriously present what God wants *of* us without recalling what God finally wants to be *with* us? We can sum up our understanding of the command of God thus far in the formula: Be what you are, a creature of God, in such a way appropriate to one reconciled to God. Yet, this formula leaves something out, consisting in the future. We are beings claimed by the God who not merely wanted something with me in creating me, and not merely wanted something with me in the presence of the conflict between divine grace and human sin, but also wants something with me as the goal and purpose of what God wants Creator and Reconciler. We should note the great presupposition of the invocation in the Lord's Prayer, namely, that we may and should really address "Our Father." We should also note the Pauline statement: "For all who are led by the Spirit of God are children of God (Romans 8:14). We should also note John's saying: See what love the Father has given us, that we should be called children of God (I John 3:1). Too many treat these verses as minor change by those who ought to know better, as well as by those who know no better. Eschatological refers to the final, conclusive, definitive, and unsurpassable. "Final" is only one aspect of eschatological. The other is that eschatological truth is truth as the future in the present, as the truth the Word of reconciliation that comes to us. In the twofold sense of being final and of coming, then, it is an eschatological truth that we are the children of God. I say that the Word of God requires of us the obedience of children.

Because obedience, considered in this light, has the character of an orientation, within the great 'Be what you are," we must briefly consider the goal of this orientation. As God is not only our Creator, but also speaks to us as such, giving us the Word of God by means of which God reveals Himself as our Redeemer. As Redeemer, God stands above the provisional state of this world, wills to give us a share in this freedom from death, a share through the Word of God, and a share in the promise. We are the children of God. Our citizenship is in heaven (Philippians 3:20), in the Jerusalem that is above (Galatians 4:26). Such statements express a truth as sure as the fact that we must die. In fact, it replaces that truth. Where we see death coming, the Lord comes, the rule of God comes, that which is perfect comes (I Cor. 13:10). We are responsible to this future of ours. Whether our conduct can stand when measured by the standard that we are the children of God and on the way to this goal is the ethical question from this final standpoint. Theological ethics requires of us that we should walk and act as those who have the promise, who are heirs of God and joint heirs with Christ (Romans 8:17).

We overlook a whole sphere of ethical problems if, in understanding the claim under which we stand, we do not consider as supremely relevant the eschatological determination of humanity. Ethicists who find a place only for a command of life or law when they come to speak of this not concealed tendency in human life, and especially in the Christian life, usually reject it with an unkindly glance. They tend to speak about mysticism, illusionism, enthusiasm, and the like. Ethics should speak only about the order of creation and the law of the neighbor, usually trying to reduce the two to the same thing. Anything beyond that is an approach we must suspect as a humanistic and idealistic failure to take seriously the true human situation. We have a heavenly calling that we cannot reduce to what we said about calling in the previous chapters. We have more than life and more than law. We also have promise, the promise of redemption, of the perfect that is coming. In addition to life and the neighbor, does not our being as children of God form a third point of orientation without which we do not really see the other two even though this is itself a will-o-the-wisp if we have not first sought the other two? Some would go to the extremes of enthusiasm, while others, such as Ritschl, suggest that only sobriety is worthy of Christian life.

We will have to deal with the possibility of prayer. Prayer, as talking with God, in which we can count on an answer as well as a hearing, is what we can understand only if we humans are more than the creatures of God and more than sinners saved by grace. Prayer is the actualization of our eschatological reality that is possible here and now. Christian prayer must say finally, "Not my will but they will be done," in Luke 22:42. The purpose in prayer is to talk with God and to be heard and answered by God. All that we need to say about our claiming by God from this third standpoint we may best understand if people will see it in the light of prayer.

Barth next takes up the issue of conscience.[210] Mentioning this term now makes one realize the small role conscience has played in the finished portion of *Church Dogmatics*. However, the fact that Barth includes the discussion of conscience under the work of the Holy Spirit as redeemer in this early volume suggests that he intended to discuss it here.[211] He says the command of God strikes me as my co-knowledge of the necessity of what I should do or not do in its relation to the coming eternal reign of God. In the concrete fellowship of mine with God the redeemer, it claims me, and I must listen. To have a conscience is to know what is in God, to know divine judgment upon our conduct. To have a conscience is to look and reach beyond the limits of our creatureliness and our reconciliation, as we do in prayer. Conscience is the living and present message of the coming rule of God. Busy waiting for the Lord at its core was also the concern of Pietism. "Hastening," means that we hear a summons. It means that God summons us in the present, but for our future. Conscience is our future self as a child of God addressing us in the present as sinners.[212]

Barth then considers in his *Ethics* the theme of gratitude.[213] The command of God means the liberation of my action. It wins me for orderliness (creation) and humility (reconciliation) but also for the God to whom I owe my existence. Gratitude is the appropriate response. What *shall* we do? When we look particularly at this meaning of our standing before God in the previous sense, our encounter with God is an encounter with God the Redeemer. As our attention focuses upon the promise, we receive the command of God. The content of the promise is that we belong to God, that no one and nothing can pluck us out of the hand of God, as in John 10:28-29, and that in our creatureliness as the righteous sinners that we find ourselves in the present we are one with God as children are with their father. We live by this. Here and now, and not just in the future, we live by the fact that God has promised it to us in all the hiddenness of future truth. In Redemption, God wills to win me for God as the new and future human being. We are to live in gratitude. We live by the fact that we are children of God, already standing at the side of God, triumphing over the contradiction and the limits of our existence. We need to accept the fact that God gives us this gift. As I Corinthians 15:28 tells us, God will be "all in all." Redemption is the fulfillment of the promise. What comes into our present with the command, however, is not the fulfillment and redemption itself. Redemption is the promise. In the present, we are still sick and frail.

---

[210] (K. Barth, Ethics 1928-9, 1973, 1978, 1981) (16)
[211] (McMullen 1988), p. 73.
[212] (McMullen 1988), p. 74.
[213] (K. Barth, Ethics 1928-9, 1973, 1978, 1981) (17)

We still experience imprisonment, bondage, and confinement. We find this view in Romans 7 and 8. Paul fully confesses the sighing of creation and the yearning expectation of divine sonship. Nevertheless, there is a release and relaxation even in this sighing, even in the despair that often enough does overpower the comfort. At this point, where we understand the required character of our action to be gratitude, it is in place to consider the bold thesis that our conduct bears the mark of good, of what is pleasing to God, when it is not done in earnest but in play. This is in truth a thesis that we can understand correctly only from an eternal standpoint, which we cannot advance except in this context. In the last resort, our life is truly only a game. Asserted too hastily and casually, this thesis can very easily mean that we overlook our being claimed by the command of God, the validity of the command, and the seriousness of our situation as those who refuse to obey it. We despise the riches of the mercy of God by which God upholds us in all our opposition to the command, and finally the miracle that God calls us the children of God. It would be more profitable for us, instead of rejoicing in the character of our existence as a game, to wake up finally out of sleep and see what it really means to be before the face of God, moving each moment into the judgment of God. What this thesis demands of us is that our action should be play. Our reference here is to the release of which we have just spoken and of which we have said that it is both a task and a gift, and that its presupposition is the Holy Spirit.

Having said this, we should not fail to say that as the children of God, God releases us from the seriousness of life and allows us to play before God. A question that this view puts to our conduct is whether it has also the character of play or whether it is only serious, in which case it cannot really be good. For three reasons, the term play is in truth appropriate for good conduct, the conduct the command of God requires of us, when we consider this in the present context. 1) God commands us to find the concept of our essential relationship to God in the promise that we are the children of God in the sense of the little children of God. Even in our most serious roles in life, we are the little children of God at play. One can walk before God in full seriousness only when one realizes that God alone is fully serious. 2) Our participation in the promises characterizes our action as provisional, as preceding our true action as those who live eternally in the kingdom of God. We can understand our eternal life and conduct only from the perspective that God promises it to us. Thus, we cannot allot final seriousness to what we do here and now. We do it under the divine patience that gives us time. We can regard our action only as play. Children play before growing up. Even the greatest people still must grow up. We are children and will be so until the end. 3) We have described gratitude as an action in which we act gladly, voluntarily, and cheerfully. It encourages us to be present to ourselves and fully open. In conclusion, the insight that, from the eternal standpoint, the good action required of us has the character of play brings to light two special possibilities of life that theological ethics can only now consider. Barth has in mind art on the one side and humor on the other. We must consider art and humor in an eschatological context because one does them gladly, voluntarily, and cheerfully, something we can do only considering our eschatological reality. Art and humor play with reality. They focus upon future possibilities, refusing to take reality as it is. Art does not take reality with final seriousness, or even that reality does not have the final word. We experience liberated laughter and artistic expression.

Barth lastly considers in his *Ethics* the theme of hope.[214] This theme seems like a fitting way to conclude our reflections on redemption. I fulfill the commandment of God. My work is good, my work is obedience to the command of promise, and is conscientious and grateful work, as done in unity with the will of the Redeemer. The Holy Spirit is the one who communicates this will and is the reality of hope. Thus, reflection on the creator led to the human response of faith, and reflection on the reconciler let to the human response of love. Here, reflection on the redeemer leads to reflection on the response of hope.

We begin by asking what it must mean that my conduct as a child of God is good at this moment, that it is now a fulfillment of the command of promise, that I am now obedient to my conscience, and that I am now profoundly grateful in what I do. We have reason to consider that what we might mean is nothing other than what the Lord's Prayer calls the doing of the will of God on earth as it is done in heaven, so that the limit and distinction that this petition denotes cannot be removed. Hope gives us to the possibility of a good will, a human will unite to the will of God. In hope, we are citizens of the future world amid the present. The voice of conscience has its basis in hope. In hope, we must be grateful. Of course, hope could be folly.

When we pray, confessing that we have no control of our own over this future of ours, but that we must seek it, not just anywhere or in any way, but with God, then hope becomes wisdom. Christian hope is this prayerful seeking with God for our won future and for the goodness of our conduct therein enclosed. Like faith and love, hope bridges the gap between God and humanity without removing it, but in such a way as to affirm it and thus to give the glory to God and not to humanity. To repeat, the person who hopes looks gladly, willingly, and joyfully beyond the present and away from self. Why? Because such a person has been born again to a

---

[214] (K. Barth, Ethics 1928-9, 1973, 1978, 1981) (18)

living hope (I Peter 1:3), because such a person practices his or her own new existence as one who hopes. Paul does not focus upon the person who hopes, but upon the God in whom we can hope. Like faith and love, hope rests in the Word that God speaks to us. Here, because the subject of hope is our own future, we are to understand the Word specifically as the Word of the Holy Spirit. As such, the Word is the pledge that God has given to us, as the Paraclete in a presence in which we may be certain of the coming Lord as such. In this Word that God speaks to us we are the children of God, and we have the divine hope in the light of which alone there can be human hope.

A BRIEF AFTERWARD

Toward the end of his life, Karl Barth humbly reflected upon his astounding impact on twentieth-century theology by recounting a dream he often had. In his dream Barth was now in heaven toting his many volumes of the *Church Dogmatics* in a wagon behind him. Instead of standing in awe, the angels begin to laugh and mock Barth saying, "Look here he comes now with his little pushcart full of works of the Dogmatics." Barth knew that his work, great as it was, was only a shadow of a full understanding of the deep mysteries of God.[215]

On the biographical side of matters, I have a few reflections on how Barth ended his life on a personal note.

Emil Brunner would die on April 6, 1966 in Zurich. Barth got a message to him. Barth had famously said "No" to Brunner on the theme of natural theology. However, now, at the end of their lives, Peter Vogelsanger delivered a message from Barth to Brunner.

> 'If he is still alive and it is possible, tell him again,
> "Commended to our God," even by me. And tell him,
> Yes, that the time when I thought that I had to say "No"
> to him is now long past, since we all live only by virtue of
> the fact that a great and merciful God says his gracious Yes
> to all of us.'

---

[215] Quoted in George Casalis, Portrait of Karl Barth (New York: Doubleday, 1963), 3.

These words were the last that Brunner heard in his life.

Charlotte von Kirschbaum would leave the Barth home in 1964 for a nursing home. Charlotte felt gripped by a sense of the greatness of Barth's contribution, an excitement that she once described simply with the words, "This is it!" During one of Barth's last visits to her in the nursing home, she said, "We had some good times together, didn't we?"

Barth died on 10 December 1968, at his home in Basel, Switzerland. The evening before his death, he had encouraged his lifelong friend Eduard Thurneysen that he should not be downhearted, "For things are ruled, not just in Moscow or in Washington or in Peking, but things are ruled – even here on earth—entirely from above, from heaven above."

Charlotte would die in 1975, with her burial next to Karl Barth.

I have not mentioned much about Nelly, the wife of Barth. Nelly never ceased to believe in her husband and his work. We know that the two of them experienced reconciliation after Charlotte departed the household, that she and Karl both visited her at the nursing home on Sundays. Nelly continued those visits after Karl died in 1968. Nelly honored Karl's wishes by having Charlotte buried in the Barth family grave. Nelly herself died in 1976. Visitors to the Basel Hörnli cemetery today can see the names of all three together engraved one by one on the same stone.

Bibliography

Barth, Karl. 2004, 1932-67. *Church Dogmatics.* New York: T & T Clark.

—. 1947, 1949. *Dogmatics in Outline.* London: SCM Press.

—. 1918, 1921, 1933. *Epistle to the Romans.*

—. 1928-9, 1973, 1978, 1981. *Ethics.* Edited by Dietrich Braun. Translated by Geoffrey W. Bromiley. New York: The Seabury Press.

—. 1979, 1963. *Evangelical Theology: An Introduction.* Grand Rapids, MI: William B. Eerdmans.

—. 1964, 2003. *God Here and Now.* Translated by Paul M. van Buren. New York: Routledge & Kegan.

—. 2018; 1952; 1932-3 Lectures on Exercises in Sermon Preparation and 1947-9 Lectures on Prayer. *Prayer and Preaching.* Translated by Sarah Frantz Terrien. Kraus House.

—. 2002. *Prayer: 50th Anniversary Edition.* Edited by Don E. Saliers. Translated by Sarah F. Terrien. Louisville, KY: Westminister John Knox Press.

—. 1981. *The Christian Life: Church Dogmatics Lecture Fragments.* Translated by Geoffrey W. Bromiley. Grand Rapids, MI: William B. Eerdmans Publishing Co.

—. 1990, 1991, based on lectures delivered in 1924-5. *The Gottingen Dogmatics: Instruction in the Christian Religion.* Edited by Hannelotte Reiffen. Translated by Geoffrey W. Bromiley. Grand Rapids, MI: William B. Eerdmans.

—. 1960. *The Humanity of God.* John Knox Press.

Barth, Markus. 1969, 1971. *Justification:Pauline Texts Interpreted in the Light of the Old and New Testaments.* Translated by A. M. Woodruff III. Grand Rapids, MI: William B. Eerdmans Publishing CO.

—. 1988, based on lectures in 1986-7. *Rediscovering the Lord's Supper: Communion with Israel, with Christ, and Among the Guests.* Eugene, Oregon: Wipf & Stock Publishers.

Bodley-Dangelo, Faye. 2016. "Veiled and Unvelied Others: Revisiting Karl Barth's Gender Trouble."

2000. *Cambridge Companion to Karl Barth.* Cambridge, UK: Cambridge University Press.

Campbell, Douglas A. 2020. *Pauline Dogmatics: The Triumph of God's Love.* Grand Rapids, MI: William B. Eerdmans Publishing Co.

Congdon, David W. 2016. *The God Who Saves: Dogmatic Sketch.* Eugene, OR: Wipf and Stock Publishers.

—. 2015. *The Mission of Demythologizing: Rudolf Bultmann's Dialectical Theology.* Minneapolis, MN: Fortress Press.

Ellul, Jacques. 1976. *The Ethics of Freedom*. Edited by Geoffrey W. Bromiley. Translated by Geoffrey W. Bromiley. Grand Rapids, MI: William B. Eerdmans Publishing Co.

Griswold, Daniel M. 2015. *Triune Eternality: God's Rela;tionship to Time in the Theology of Karl Barth*. Minneapolis, MN: Fortress Press.

Hitchcock, Nathan. 2013. *Karl Barth and the Resurrection of the Flesh*. Eugene, Oregon: Pickwick Publications.

Hohne, David A. 2019. *The Last Things*. Downer's Grove, IL: InterVarsity Press.

Jenson, Robert W. 1997. *Systematic Theology*. New York: Oxfort University Press.

Jungel, Eberhard. 1976, 2001. *God's Being Is in Becoming: The Trinitarian Being of God in the Theology of Karl Barth - A Paraphrase* .

Karkkainen, Veli-Matti. 2013. *Christ and Reconciliation: A Constructive Christian Theology for the Pluralistic World*. Grand Rapids, MI: Wm B Eerdmans.

—. 2015. *Creation and Humanity: A constructive Christian theology for the pluralistic world*. Vol. Volume 3. Grand Rapids, MI: William B. Eerdmans Publishing Company.

—. 2016. *Spirit and Salvation: A Constructive Christian Theology for the Pluralistic World, Volume 4*. Grand Rapids, MI: William B. Eerdmans Publishing Company.

—. 2014. *Trinity and Revelation, Volume 2 of A Constructive Christian Theology for the Pluralistic World*. Grand Rapids, MI: William B. Eerdmans Publishing Company.

Karkkhainen, Veli-Matti. 2017. *Hope and Community: A Constructive Christian Theology for the Pluralistic kWorld*. Grand Rapids, MI: Wiliam B. Eerdmans Publishing Co.

McMullen, Christopher W. 1988. "Eschatology and Ethics in the Theology of Karl Barth." June.

Moltmann, Jurgen. 1985. *God in Creation*. London: SCM Press.

—. 1973, 1974. *The Crucified God*. New York: Harper & Row.

—. 1980, 1981. *The Trinity and the Kingdom: The Doctrine of God*. New York: Harper & Row.

—. 1965, 1967. *Theology of Hope*. New York: Harper & Row.

Pannenberg, Wolfhart. 1985. *Anthropology in Theological Perspective*. Edinburg: T & T Clark.

—. 1967, 1971. *Basic Questions in Theology (2 Volumes)*. Philadelphia: Fortress Press.

—. 1964, 1968. *Jesus -- God and Man*. Translated by Lewis L. Wilkins and Duane A. Priebe. London: SCM Press.

———. 1998, 1991. *Systematic Theology.* Grand Rapids, MI: Wm. B. Eerdmans Publishing Co.
———. 1973, 1976. *Theology and the Philosophy of Science.* Philadelphia, PA: The Westminster Press.
———. 1993. *Toward a Theology of Nature: Essays on Science and Faith.* Louisville, Ky: Westminster.
Peacocke, A. R., ed. 1981. *The Sciences and Theology in the Twentieth Century.* Notre Dame, IN: University of Notre Dame Press.
Richardson, Kurt A. 2004. *Reading Karl Barth: New Directions for North American Theology.* Grand Rapids, MI: Baker Academic.
Sonderegger, Katherine. 2015. *Systematic Theology.* Vols. Volume 1, The Doctrine of God. Minneapolis, MN: Fortress Press.
Tanner, Kathryn. 1988. *God and Creation in Christian Theology: Tyranny or Empowerment?* Minneapolis, MN: Fortress Press.
Taylor, Charles. 2007. *A Secular Age.* Cambridge, MA: The Belknap Press of Harvard University Press.
Tillich, Paul. 1951. *Systematic Theology.* Chicago: The University of Chicago Press.
von Balthasar, Hans Urs. 1951, 1961, 1992. *The Theology of Karl Barth.* Translated by S. J. Edward T. Oakes. San Francisco, California: Ignatius Press.
Webster, John. 1995. *Barth's Ethics of Reconciliation.* New York: Press Synbdicate of the University of Cambridge.
Zahrnt, Heinz. 1966, 1969. *The Question of God: Protestant Theology in the Twentieth Century.* Translated by R. A. Wilson. New York: Harcourt Brace Jovanovich, Inc.

ABOUT THE AUTHOR

Rev. Dr. George M. Plasterer spent much of his early years in Austin, MN, graduating from High School in 1970. He graduated from Marion College, now Indiana Wesleyan, in 1974, and from Asbury Theological Seminary in 1979. He received ordination through the South Indiana Annual Conference, later the Indiana Annual Conference, in 1983. He received his Doctor of Ministry from McCormick Theological Seminary in 1987. He especially found the spiritual formation focus meaningful in his spiritual journey. He had an early involvement in the growth of the Walk to Emmaus movement in Indiana. He has taken the teaching role of pastor seriously throughout his ministry, pursuing biblical, theological, and philosophical studies throughout. These studies prepared the way for what would become more than a decade of working with the massive work of Karl Barth, *Church Dogmatics*. Among the gifts in retirement was to hear Jurgen Moltmann speak at an event honoring him on his 90th birthday in Lakeland, Florida at Florida Southern College.

He is the father of two boys, Michael and David, and husband to Suzanne. He served several churches in Indiana. His bishop appointed him to retirement in July 2017. He still enjoys occasional tennis, keeping physically fit, walk or run along the beach, and the beautiful setting of Clearwater, FL.

If you would like further discussion with him, please contact him at https://karlbarthchurchdogmatics.blogspot.com or email him at george.plasterer@icloud.com.

Made in the USA
Columbia, SC
24 September 2022